Cooking with

CARRIER

Cooking with
CARRIER

by Robert Carrier

A&W Publishers, Inc.
New York

Published in the United States of America in 1981 by
A&W Publishers, Inc.
95 Madison Ave.
New York, NY 10016

Published in 1980 by Sidgwick and Jackson Limited

Designed by Gillian Allan and Ray Hyden

Library of Congress Catalog Card Number: 81-66192

ISBN: 0-89479-059-5

Printed in the United States of America

To my favorite ladies Eileen Dickson, Ailsa Garland,
Psyche Pirie and Doris Shaw—who over the years have
shared so much with me—my grateful thanks.

Contents

The Story of a Garden

Once you grow your own tomatoes, the chances are you will never again buy the tough-skinned bullets passed off under that name at the local supermarket. But at least you can get tomatoes there; the same cannot always be said for salsify, sorrel, fresh new potatoes and peas, or fresh herbs.

That is why growing vegetables in the eighteenth-century manner—in small plots decoratively edged with colorful herb and flower borders—is the great new craze for all cooks with a back garden to play with.

And this sort of gardening is easy, too. Only four years ago, my eighteenth-century kitchen garden at Hintlesham Hall was the grim setting for the best nettle and boulder crop in East Anglia. Today, after a year of preparation—clearing the area of rocks, roots and shrubs, activating and feeding the soil and even irrigating the sub-strata with folded-up cardboard boxes to facilitate drainage—the garden is the pleasure-ground that you see now.

The crop and border in each bed have been specially chosen for the most exciting combinations of colors and shapes; dark green wild strawberry plants with a border of silver grey cotton lavender; cool green curly lettuces edged with serried rows of blue-green chives; and cascading "wigwams" of green beans teamed with bright-orange-flowered nasturtiums.

Guests who lunch or dine at Hintlesham come and walk through this garden, and are allowed to pick any amount of herbs. One favorite is French tarragon, which grows wonderfully in the garden both as a main crop and as a border plant. I use this pungent herb in salads, chicken and veal recipes, and for fish sauces.

Another favorite herb is *roquette,* which Queen Elizabeth I called "sweet rocket." It has a dark-green, spiky leaf with a peppery flavor that is almost meaty. I like to put whole sprigs of it in salad with tarragon, green and purple basil, flat-leafed Italian parsley, feathery fennel and lemon-scented *pourprier. Pourprier,* or purslane as it was called in old herbals, has a fat succulent leaf, giving great body and interest to "sallet" in the old English way.

Above *Once a grim setting for the best nettle and boulder crop in East Anglia, the eighteenth-century kitchen garden is a pleasure-ground of ordered* parterres *separated by herb-bordered walks that make gardening simple for lazy gardeners like me.*

Plants are seeded in nearby greenhouses in small batches before being transferred to the kitchen garden. We sow a row or two of each variety, then wait a week and sow again. The seedlings are then transplanted at intervals, providing a succession of tasty young crops throughout the summer.

Far left *Head gardeners George Trinder and Mark Nunn are responsible for the day-to-day running of the greenhouses, gardens and grounds.*

Near left *Terrine de Saumon Persillé is a fresh-tasting terrine of salmon and chopped smoked salmon and hard-boiled eggs, and herbs from the garden. (Recipe, page 4)*

Cooking with herbs

Fresh herbs from the garden add much to good cooking: rosemary goes wonderfully well with roast lamb when combined with a little finely chopped garlic and crumbled bay leaf. Sage is marvellous with pork in the Provençal manner. Just cut slits in the deep fat of the roast and tuck a little sliver of garlic, a leaf or two of sage and a tiny sprig of rosemary in each incision.

I recently visited the Troigros brothers' famous restaurant in Royanne. There I had the most marvellous sole dish that I've ever tasted: the sole had been sautéed in butter, covered in fresh breadcrumbs and baked until the crumbs were golden; the fish was served in a sauce of thick *crème fraîche* liberally spiked with freshly chopped chives.

Les Farcies aux Herbes

Ingredients

Butter
2 tablespoons all-purpose flour
⅔ cup milk
¾ cup freshly grated Gruyère cheese
Salt and freshly ground black pepper
Freshly grated nutmeg
1 cup button mushrooms
1 tablespoon lemon juice
1 teaspoon chopped fresh tarragon leaves
½ teaspoon dried oregano
4 small brioches, or rolls

1 Make a thick white sauce with 1 tablespoon butter, flour and milk. Beat in cheese smoothly over a low heat and season to taste with salt and freshly ground black pepper, and freshly grated nutmeg.

2 Trim mushroom stems but leave them intact. Wash and wipe mushrooms clean and slice very thinly lengthwise. Brush a few of the most attractive mushroom slices with a little lemon juice to prevent discoloration and put them aside for garnish.

3 Sauté remaining sliced mushrooms gently in 1 tablespoon butter for 3–4 minutes, sprinkling them with remaining lemon juice. Add to sauce, together with fresh tarragon and dried oregano, and season to taste.

4 Preheat oven to moderate (350°F).

5 Remove tops from brioches or rolls, and scoop out centers to leave firm cases about ¼ inch thick.

6 Fill brioches, or rolls, with mushroom sauce and arrange them in an ovenproof dish. Garnish each brioche, or roll, with reserved mushroom slices; replace top and brush with a little melted butter. Heat through in preheated oven for 10–15 minutes, or until very hot. Serve immediately.

Serves 4

Terrine de Saumon Persillé *(Illustration, page 2)*

Ingredients

6 11-inch strips lightly poached salmon
8 teaspoons powdered gelatin
5 cups well-flavored fish stock
Salt and freshly ground black pepper
Diced whites of 4 hard-boiled eggs
¼-¾ cup diced smoked salmon
1 bunch parsley, chopped

1 To make aspic: dissolve gelatin in 8 tablespoons hot water and add to fish stock. Season with salt and freshly ground black pepper, to taste. Blend in diced egg white, diced smoked salmon and chopped parsley and allow aspic to set until it is syrupy, stirring from time to time.

2 To assemble terrine: cover bottom of rectangular terrine (11¾ × 3¼ inches) with a thin layer of aspic; allow to set in refrigerator; arrange 2 strips of poached salmon on top of aspic, leaving space between strips; cover salmon with aspic; return to refrigerator to set as above; place another 2 strips of poached salmon on top of aspic; cover with aspic; allow to set; place remaining 2 strips of fresh salmon on top. Fill terrine with remaining aspic.

3 Place terrine in refrigerator and chill overnight or until set. Serve with cucumber cream (see page 49).

Note: keep aspic syrupy while aspic-filled terrine sets in refrigerator by immersing bowl containing aspic in a larger bowl of warm water.

Fifine's Tomato Salad

1 Wash tomatoes and cut in half horizontally. Arrange tomato halves, cut side up, on a serving dish and season generously with salt and freshly ground black pepper.

2 Sprinkle each tomato half with finely chopped onion or scallions. Mix fresh herbs together and sprinkle each tomato half with a thick green layer of chopped herbs.

3 Make a well-seasoned Fresh dressing (3 parts olive oil to 1 part wine vinegar, Dijon mustard and salt and freshly ground black pepper, to taste). Dribble 2–3 tablespoons dressing over each tomato half.

Serves 4

Ingredients
4 large tomatoes
Salt and freshly ground
   black pepper
8 tablespoons finely
   chopped onion or
   scallions
4 tablespoons finely
   chopped tarragon leaves
4 tablespoons finely
   chopped basil leaves
4 tablespoons finely
   chopped parsley
Olive oil
Wine vinegar
Dijon mustard

Italian Herb Pancakes

1 To make crêpes: sift flour and salt into a mixing bowl. Beat egg and add to dry ingredients. Mix in milk and melted butter or oil gradually to avoid lumps. Strain through a fine sieve; add finely chopped basil and leave batter to stand for at least 2 hours before cooking the crêpes. Batter should be as thin as light cream. Add a little water if too thick.

2 For each crêpe, spoon about 2 tablespoons batter into heated pan, swirling pan to allow batter to cover entire surface thinly. Brush a piece of butter on or around edge of hot pan with the point of a knife and cook over a medium heat until just golden, but not brown (about 1 minute each side). Repeat until all crêpes are cooked, stacking them on a plate as they are ready. The mixture makes 8–12 golden crêpes.

3 To make filling: wash watercress and lettuce. Drain. Remove stalks and yellowed leaves from watercress. Remove outer leaves from lettuce. Chop rest of lettuce coarsely. Combine chopped watercress and lettuce with chopped fresh herbs and sauté in 2 tablespoons butter. Season with salt and freshly ground black pepper, to taste. Press dry and then add ricotta, or cottage cheese, together with beaten eggs, freshly grated Parmesan cheese, cream and nutmeg to taste.

4 Spread each crêpe generously with filling. Roll pancakes and put them in a well-buttered rectangular baking dish. Chill until 1 hour before using.

5 When ready to serve: brush each pancake with melted butter; sprinkle with freshly grated Parmesan cheese and bake for 20 minutes in a moderate oven (350°F). Serve with a well-seasoned tomato sauce.

Serves 4–6

Ingredients

CRÊPES
3 tablespoons flour
1/4 teaspoon salt
1 egg
1 cup, scant, milk
1 tablespoon melted butter,
   or oil
6 tablespoons finely
   chopped fresh basil
Butter or oil, for cooking

FILLING
1 bunch watercress
1 head lettuce
2 tablespoons chopped
   tarragon
2 tablespoons chopped
   chives
Butter
Salt and freshly ground
   black pepper
1 cup ricotta cheese, or
   cottage cheese
3 eggs, lightly beaten
3/4 cup freshly grated
   Parmesan cheese
6 tablespoons heavy cream
Freshly grated nutmeg
1 1/4 cups well-seasoned
   tomato sauce

Cooking with spices

Four thousand years before the birth of Christ, in the Valley of the Indus, the people of what is now known as Pakistan were grinding mustard seeds with fennel and cumin seeds to flavor sophisticated stews of meats and poultry. They knew how to grind their grain into flour; made use of ovens to bake their breads and meats; and cultivated melons and dates, coconuts and bananas, pomegranates and, perhaps, even lemons and limes. Sheep, goats, buffalo, pigs, elephants and camels were all common species, and the Indian jungle fowl—later to become the world's chicken—was already domesticated.

It was this same remarkable people who first invented the mortar and pestle to grind spices and blend them into exciting flavoring compounds that changed culinary history. And it was they who first collected the little green berries, dried them in the sun, and ground them to produce pepper, the aromatic spice that one day would be deemed as valuable as gold.

Whenever I see the beautiful, sharp acid yellow of mustard fields growing alongside the roads in East Anglia, I think back to the twin cities of Harappa and Mohenjodaro, which have influenced so greatly what we eat today.

Mustard seed—either ground or whole—was later used by the ancient Greeks and Romans, who sprinkled it onto cooked dishes much as we now use salt and pepper to season our foods. Indeed, the Roman legions liked this pungent herb so much that they carried mustard seeds with them wherever they went. It is thanks to them that mustard is such an important culinary crop in Britain today.

There are recipes calling for the use of mustard in the earliest recorded cookbooks from ancient Greece and Rome. But it was not until centuries later that mustard became the prime agent in preparations of honey and vinegar, or *verjuice*, as we call it now. In France particularly, mustard mixing became such a fad in the eighteenth century that the crushed seeds were blended with a common variety of foods, including capers, rose water, honey and anchovies.

English mustard—a plain dry powder—is mixed with cold water (not hot water

Mustard seeds—either ground or whole—were used by the ancient Greeks and Romans, who sprinkled them on to cooked dishes much as we use salt and pepper. The Roman legions liked this pungent herb so much that they carried mustard seeds with them wherever they went. It is thanks to them that mustard is such an important culinary crop in France and England today.

Opposite page *A field of mustard in France.*

Above *Antique mustard-pots in a mustard shop in Dijon.*

Left *Seventeenth-century mustard-jar from Dijon.*

or vinegar, which tend to make mustard less flavorful and bitter) and left for 10 minutes to develop its typical flavor. It is a clean and pungent seasoning, the perfect accompaniment to roast beef, grilled beef steaks, pork chops and hot or cold boiled ham.

Dry mustard is wonderful with baked ham. Just add 1 teaspoon to glaze. Combine with olive oil to spread over steak before grilling. Add to coating mixture for croquettes or fried chicken. Add to baked macaroni and cheese. It is very good in casseroles of ham, turkey and seafood, croquettes and baked beans.

Add dry mustard to a French dressing, you'll find it helps the emulsifying process. It is also a necessity for mayonnaise (for the same reason). Add to tuna, crab, lobster and salmon salads, to macaroni and ham salads and to potato salads.

Dry mustard is excellent to spark up cream sauces and cheese sauces. Mix with butter and lemon juice, to taste, to dress cooked cabbage, broccoli and Brussels sprouts.

Add a tablespoon of whole mustard seeds to poaching liquid for spiced shrimp or spiced meats. Mustard seeds are an essential ingredient of cucumber pickles, vegetable relishes, chutney, pickled onions and pickled lemons.

Add 1 teaspoon mustard seeds to cole slaw. Add to mixed vegetable salads and potato salads. They also provide good flavor change for French dressing.

Arabian Kefta

Ingredients

1½ lb. lamb, from leg
½ lb. lamb fat,
1 medium onion, finely chopped
6–8 mint leaves, finely chopped
6–8 sprigs parsley, finely chopped
½ teaspoon dried marjoram
Salt and fresh black pepper
¼ teaspoon each powdered cumin, cayenne pepper and paprika
1 generous pinch of two or more of the following: powdered nutmeg, cinnamon, cloves, ginger and cardamom
Butter

KEFTA SAUCE

1 lb. tomatoes, peeled, seeded and chopped
1 medium onion, finely chopped
2 tablespoons finely chopped parsley
1 clove garlic, finely chopped
4 tablespoons olive oil
1¼ cups water
Paprika
Cayenne pepper
Salt

1 To made *kefta* sauce: combine ingredients (sauce should be very highly flavored) and simmer for 1 hour, uncovered.

2 Put lamb, lamb fat and finely chopped onion through the finest blade of your grinder 3 times.

3 Combine mixture in a large mixing bowl with finely chopped mint leaves and parsley, marjoram and salt and freshly ground black pepper and spices, to taste. Mix well. The *kefta* mixture should be very highly flavored.

4 Form *kefta* mixture into little balls the size of a marble and poach gently in water for 10 minutes. Then sauté gently in butter until lightly browned.

5 Finally, simmer in *kefta* sauce for at least 10 minutes before serving. Serve *kefta* in sauce or on a bed of rice with sauce apart.

Serves 6–8

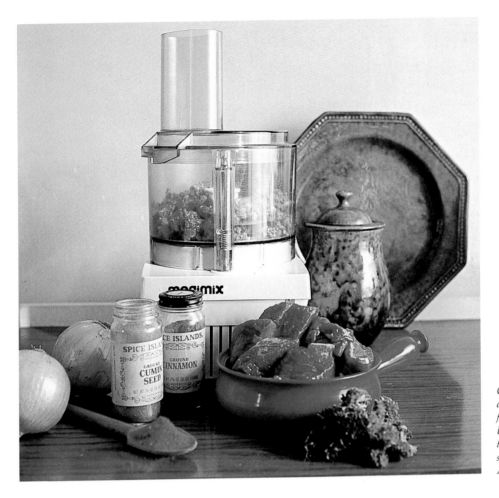

Cumin seed, ginger, cinnamon, cayenne pepper and paprika are the five magical spices of Arabian cooking. Use them to add interest to stews, terrines and mixed vegetables and to spike Spiced Grilled Hamburgers and Arabian Kefta.

Spiced Grilled Hamburgers

1 Combine ground rump steak, chopped beef marrow, finely chopped onion and parsley, spices and salt and freshly ground black pepper, to taste. Form mixture into 8 patties.

2 Brush patties with melted butter and broil under pre-heated broiler for 4 to 5 minutes on each side.

Serves 4

Ingredients

- 2 lb. rump steak, ground
- 6 tablespoons chopped beef marrow
- 4 tablespoons finely chopped onion
- 4 tablespoons finely chopped parsley
- $\frac{1}{2}$ teaspoon powdered cumin
- $\frac{1}{4}$ teaspoon powdered paprika
- $\frac{1}{4}$ teaspoon powdered cayenne pepper
- Salt and freshly ground black pepper
- 4 tablespoons melted butter

Madras Chicken Curry

Ingredients

4 tablespoons ghee or clarified butter
1 chicken (about 3 lb.)
2 large onions, chopped
2 cloves garlic, chopped
2 tart green apples, peeled, cored and coarsely chopped
2 bananas, peeled and sliced
2 tablespoons Special Curry Blend (see below)
4 tablespoons raisins
2 tablespoons mango chutney, chopped
2 cups chicken stock
Salt and freshly ground black pepper
Ground ginger
Cayenne pepper
Juice of ½ lemon

1 Cut chicken into 8 serving pieces and sauté pieces in *ghee* or clarified butter in a large, thick-bottomed frying pan until golden. Transfer to an ovenproof casserole.

2 Sauté the chopped onions, garlic and apples in the remaining fats until onions begin to turn color. Stir in sliced bananas and sauté for a few minutes more. Add ingredients with a slotted spoon to the chicken pieces in the ovenproof casserole.

3 Stir the Special Curry Blend into the fat remaining in the pan, adding a little more *ghee* or clarified butter if necessary, and cook for 5 minutes, stirring from time to time, being careful not to let it burn.

4 Stir in raisins, mango chutney and chicken stock. Pour this mixture over chicken pieces. Chicken stock should just cover chicken. Add more, if necessary.

5 Cook, covered, for ½ hour, then taste sauce—adding salt and freshly ground black pepper, ginger and cayenne pepper, to taste. Continue to simmer curry, uncovered, until the chicken is tender and the sauce is thick. Stir in lemon juice just before serving.

Serves 4–6

Special Curry Blend

Ingredients

4 tablespoons coriander seed
3 tablespoons cumin seed
2 teaspoons mustard seed
2 teaspoons fenugreek seed
2 tablespoons ground cinnamon
3 tablespoons ground black peppercorns
2 teaspoons ground nutmeg
1 teaspoon ground cloves
1 teaspoon ground cardamom seeds
1 tablespoon ground turmeric seeds
1 tablespoon ground ginger
1 tablespoon cayenne pepper

1 Put the coriander, cumin, mustard and fenugreek seeds into a thick iron-bottomed frying pan and toast over a medium flame until the mustard seeds pop. Do not allow spices to burn.

2 Cool spices and then grind them and combine with the remaining ingredients.

3 Put through a fine sieve and store in an air-tight jar until ready for use.

Indian Rice

Indian rice is always carefully rinsed and drained, and cooked in a large container with boiling salted water in the proportions three of water to one of rice. The rice is then drained, seasoned with carefully ground spices—a mixture of equal parts of ground cinnamon, cardamom and mace—and tossed with *ghee* (Indian clarified butter). Or try the following variations:

Finely chop 1 medium onion and sauté it, stirring constantly in 4 tablespoons of butter or *ghee* until the onion is transparent. Remove the onion with a slotted spoon and reserve for later use. Add 6 tablespoons each of cashew nuts and raisins to the pan and sauté for a few minutes more. Then add ½ teaspoon each of fennel seeds, cumin seeds, mustard seeds and powdered turmeric to the pan. Stir in 2 tablespoons butter or *ghee* and sauté spices, stirring, for two minutes more. When ready to serve, combine sautéed onion, nuts, raisins and spice mixture and heat through. Then add drained rice and toss gently over a low heat until rice is hot. Serve immediately. In Southern India, freshly grated coconut is added to the nuts and raisins.

Jamaican Curry

1 Grind peppercorns, ginger root, coriander seeds, bay leaves, dried red peppers and cardamom seeds in a mortar. Add 1 tablespoon curry powder, freshly grated nutmeg and salt, to taste.

2 Cut lamb into 1–1½ inch cubes, or chicken into serving pieces, and rub ground spices well into each piece. Leave for at least 4 hours.

3 Sauté prepared lamb or chicken pieces in olive oil and butter in an ovenproof casserole until golden; remove lamb or chicken. Sauté chopped onion and garlic in remaining fat until transparent; add diced green pepper and chopped tomato and continue cooking until vegetables are soft.

4 Return lamb or chicken pieces to casserole; add any ground spices that remain with the cinnamon stick, lemon peel and lemon juice, thyme and chicken stock; stir well and simmer gently, covered, for 1 hour. Add remaining curry powder and continue to cook for 10 to 15 minutes, or until lamb or chicken is tender.

Serves 4

Ingredients

1 shoulder of lamb (3–4 lb.) or 1 roasting chicken (about 3 lb.)
Black peppercorns
1 small piece ginger root (or ¼ teaspoon ground ginger)
½ teaspoon coriander seeds
2 bay leaves
2 dried hot red peppers
4 cardamom seeds
3 tablespoons curry powder
⅛ teaspoon freshly grated nutmeg
Salt
2 tablespoons olive oil
2 tablespoons butter
1 large onion, finely chopped
1 large clove garlic, finely chopped
1 small green pepper, diced
2–4 tomatoes, chopped
1 stick cinnamon
Grated peel of 1 lemon
Juice of ½ lemon
1 sprig thyme (or ¼ teaspoon dried thyme)
2 cups chicken stock

Spicy Rice Casserole

I often serve Jamaican Chicken Curry at outdoor parties on the lawn. It is an expansive dish, that doubles or triples easily for large parties. With it, I usually serve a delicious Spicy Rice Casserole. To make Spicy Rice: sauté 1 medium onion, thinly sliced, in 6 tablespoons butter in a large heatproof casserole until the onion is transparent and soft. Add 1¾ cups washed and drained rice to the casserole and stir until rice begins to turn golden. Then stir in 2 bay leaves, 4 cloves, 6 cardamom seeds and all 6 allspice berries (all lightly crushed), 1-inch stick of cinnamon and ½ teaspoon powdered turmeric. Add 2½ cups chicken stock; stir once to dislodge any grains stuck to the bottom of the casserole; cover casserole and simmer until rice is tender.

Roast Sliced Sirloin with Aromatic Mayonnaise

1 Sear beef on all sides in hot melted bacon fat or butter, or a combination of the two.

2 Transfer meat to a roasting pan, fat side up; sprinkle generously with salt and freshly ground black pepper and crumbled rosemary and roast in a preheated hot oven (450°F) for about 25 minutes for rare beef, longer if you prefer it more thoroughly cooked, adding 4 tablespoons warm water or red wine to the pan after the first 15 minutes.

3 Remove beef from oven and allow to cool; then cover meat loosely and chill overnight in refrigerator.

4 Slice beef thinly and arrange slices on a serving dish. Delicious served with chilled aromatic mayonnaise (made by combining mayonnaise with freshly grated horseradish and cayenne pepper, to taste).

Ingredients

1½ lb. trimmed sirloin steak, in 1 piece
4 tablespoons hot melted bacon fat, or butter
Salt and fresh black pepper
Crumbled rosemary
4 tablespoons warm water, or red wine
Mayonnaise (see page 49)
1–2 tablespoons freshly grated horseradish
Cayenne pepper

Cooking with Wine

You will find that cooking with wine is as easy as opening the bottle and taking a sip. If, like some of my friends, you are a little inhibited in your use of this magic cook's aid, think of it as just another ingredient like butter, olive oil, fresh herbs or cream.

"Take 2–3 lb. of an inexpensive cut of meat. Cut into 1½–1¾ inch slices; dust the pieces generously with flour, salt and freshly ground black pepper and sauté in equal quantities of olive oil and butter until the meat is browned on all sides. Simmer some coarsely chopped onion and garlic in the same combination of fats; combine vegetables and meat; add strips of orange peel which you have dried in the oven, 2 cloves, 2 bay leaves and a reduction of red wine. Cover the casserole and simmer gently over the lowest of heats, until the meat is meltingly tender and the vegetables and wine dissolve into a smooth, richly flavoured sauce."

This easy casserole recipe probably originated centuries ago on the sun-washed hillsides of southern France, when the natives of the region were learning how to cultivate the local grapes to make wine. The casserole was undoubtedly cooked in the ashes. Today the task is easier, but all the magic "constants" remain.

Slow, even cooking

All casseroles—vegetables as well as meats, poultry, fish and game—respond wonderfully well to "low heat" cookery. Over the many years that I have been experimenting with heat I have gradually lowered the temperature at which I like to cook stews, daubes, ragoûts and casseroles to 225°F or 275°F, and when cooking this type of dish on top of the stove I always use an asbestos or wire mat to help keep the cooking down to a very faint, barely perceptible simmer. It is a good idea, the first few times you follow this method of cooking, to check up on your casserole frequently. Thermostats vary, and you may find you have to adjust the setting slightly to keep the casserole at this low "barely simmering" point. And always make sure that you bring the ingredients up to a bubble on top of the stove before you put the casserole in the oven.

Reduction

Wine "reduced" to a quarter of the original quantity by a fast boil over a high heat is one of the best ways of adding flavor to a casserole. Professional cooks often use this method of seasoning to intensify the depth of flavor of their wine dishes.

Opposite page *Red Wine Marinade for fish and meats. (Recipe, page 15)*

Below *Raw ingredients for a classic Boeuf à la Bourguignonne. (Recipe, page 17)*

I like to reduce stock in the same manner, adding a combination of two separate reductions to the dish at the last minute to give hidden depth and interest to a ragoût of meat, poultry or game. Try combining separate reductions of fish stock and dry white wine to add excitement to a fish soup, casserole or fish-based cream or velouté sauce.

Small quantities of wine can make a great difference to your cooking

1 Add 2 tablespoons dry white wine to your usual salad dressing; add a little finely chopped spring onion, onion or garlic and mix with sliced, boiled new potatoes for a delicious potato salad. Always remember to toss the potato slices with the dressing when potatoes are still warm.

2 Combine 6 tablespoons each olive oil and dry white wine with 2 crumbled bay leaves, a little finely chopped onion and parsley, and salt and freshly ground black pepper, to taste. Use to marinate brochettes of lamb, chicken or fish before grilling.

3 Combine 1 glass red wine with 2 cloves crushed garlic, ¼ teaspoon dried marjoram or thyme (or a combination of the two), ¼ chicken stock cube and freshly ground black pepper, to taste. Reduce these ingredients over a high heat to half the original quantity and use this aromatic sauce with a little butter swirled in to baste lamb, veal or chicken.

4 Always add 2 or more tablespoons red wine just before serving a casserole of meat or game which you have marinated or simmered in red wine. You will find it helps the flavor of the finished dish.

5 Try adding a tablespoon or two of dry sherry or Madeira and a tablespoon of Worcestershire sauce to your deep-dish meat pies just before serving.

You will find recipes for wine-simmered dishes on the following pages, and then again, on pages 117–123.

White Wine Fish Stock (*Fumet de Poisson*)

Ingredients

2 lb. fish heads and bones
1 large onion, sliced
4 carrots, sliced
2 stalks celery, sliced
4 tablespoons olive oil
3¾ cups dry white wine
Dash of dried fennel
4 parsley sprigs
2 bay leaves
Salt and freshly ground
   black pepper

1 Chop fish heads and bones into pieces about 3 inches long. Combine chopped bones and sliced vegetables in a large ovenproof casserole and sauté in olive oil, stirring constantly, until vegetables begin to take on color. Add dry white wine and 3¾ cups water and bring to the boil.

2 Skim surface of stock. Add fennel, parsley and bay leaves. Simmer for 2 hours.

3 Strain stock through a fine sieve lined with muslin. Season with salt and freshly ground black pepper, to taste.

White Wine Cooked Marinade

(For fish or chicken)

Ingredients

3¾ cups dry white wine
3¾ cups water
1 large onion, sliced
4 carrots, sliced
2 stalks celery, sliced
Dash of dried fennel
4 parsley sprigs
1 bay leaf
Salt and freshly ground black pepper

Combine marinade ingredients in a large casserole. Bring gently to the boil; skim impurities from surface; lower heat and simmer for 20 minutes. Cool.

Red Wine Marinade

(For fish, poultry or meat)

Ingredients

1 bottle full-bodied red wine
2 large onions, thinly sliced
2 large carrots, thinly sliced
2 stalks celery, thinly sliced
1 clove garlic, peeled
2 sprigs parsley
1 sprig thyme
1 bay leaf
2 tablespoons olive oil

Combine marinade ingredients in a large bowl and mix well. Cover bowl tightly with foil and leave overnight in a cool place.

Poached Fillets of Sole in White Wine

1 Season sole fillets with salt and freshly ground black pepper and place in an ovenproof, shallow casserole or *gratin* dish.

2 Mix dry white wine and vermouth with 6 tablespoons melted butter and tomato purée and pour over fish. Add finely chopped onion; bring to the boil; reduce heat to a simmer and cook fish gently for 5 minutes or until fish is just tender.

3 While fish is cooking, sauté mushrooms in 2 tablespoons melted butter and a little lemon juice over a low heat for 10 minutes.

4 Remove sole fillets from casserole with a perforated spoon and place on a heated serving dish. Cover and keep hot.

5 Strain sauce into a clean saucepan; add mushrooms and their juices to sauce and heat through.

6 Beat cream and egg yolks together in a small bowl; add to contents of pan. Reheat gently, stirring constantly, until sauce has thickened slightly. Do not allow sauce to reach boiling point or it may curdle. Season to taste with salt and freshly ground black pepper and a little more lemon juice or vermouth, if desired.

7 Pour sauce over sole fillets; sprinkle with finely chopped parsley and serve hot, garnished with lemon slices.

Serves 4

Ingredients

2 sole, weighing about 1½ lb. each, filleted
Salt and freshly ground black pepper
6 tablespoons dry white wine
2 tablespoons dry vermouth
Butter
2 teaspoons tomato purée
1 medium onion, finely chopped
20 small button mushrooms
Lemon juice
⅔ cup thick cream
2 egg yolks
Finely chopped parsley
Thin lemon slices

SOLE AU CHABLIS

Ingredients

2 sole (about 1 lb. each)
Salt and freshly ground
  black pepper
1 bouquet garni (bay leaf,
  thyme and 4 sprigs
  parsley)
Butter
2 shallots, or small white
  onions, finely chopped
⅔ cup dry white Chablis (or
  other dry white
  Burgundy)

1 Have fish dealer fillet sole, but ask him for the bones, head and trimmings to make a fish *fumet* (or stock see page 14).

2 Preheat oven to moderate (375°F).

3 Simmer bones and trimmings for 15 minutes in ⅔ cup water seasoned to taste with salt and freshly ground black pepper and a bouquet garni. Strain and reserve liquid.

4 Place fillets of sole in a well-buttered ovenproof *gratin* dish, or shallow casserole. Sprinkle with finely chopped shallots, or onions, and add Chablis (or other dry white Burgundy), fish *fumet* and salt, to taste. Cover with buttered paper and bake in preheated oven for about 15 minutes.

5 Arrange poached fillets on a heated serving dish; put fish liquor into a small saucepan and reduce over a high heat to ½ the original quantity. Whisk in 2 to 4 tablespoons butter; correct seasoning and strain sauce over sole. Serve immediately.

Serves 4

Fillets of Trout in Lettuce Packets

Ingredients

4 fresh trout, skinned and
  filleted
8 large green lettuce leaves
Salt
Freshly ground black
  pepper
Butter
½ chicken stock cube
Dry white wine
2 tablespoons finely
  chopped onion
2 tablespoons finely
  chopped mushroom
  stalks

**HERBED
BREADCRUMB
STUFFING**

1 cup fresh breadcrumbs
  mixed with 1 tablespoon
  each finely chopped
  parsley, tarragon and
  chives

FISH VELOUTÉ SAUCE

1 tablespoon butter
1 tablespoon flour
Bones, heads and trimmings
  of trout
Salt and freshly ground
  black pepper
1 small onion, finely
  chopped
½ chicken stock cube
1 tablespoon tomato purée
⅔ cup heavy cream

1 Place lettuce leaves in a large saucepan of boiling salted water for a few seconds. Remove lettuce leaves and place in bowl of cold water until ready to use. When lettuce leaves are cool enough to handle spread them out on a kitchen towel to dry.

2 Preheat your oven to moderate (375°F).

3 Season trout fillets on both sides with salt and freshly ground black pepper and sauté in butter on both sides for about 1 minute each side or until they start to color. Remove from pan.

4 Cut a rectangle from each fillet about 2½–3 inches long, making 8 rectangles altogether. (Save remaining trout trimmings for sauce.) Place 1 trout segment on a lettuce leaf, spread with a quarter of herbed breadcrumb mixture; top with second trout segment, and make a packet with a second lettuce leaf, tucking in the ends, so that all holds together neatly. Make 3 other lettuce leaf packets in the same way.

5 To make fish velouté sauce: melt butter in the top of a double saucepan; add flour and cook for a few minutes to form pale roux. Add 2½ cups fish stock salt and freshly ground black pepper, and cook, stirring vigorously with a whisk until well blended. Add finely chopped onion, chicken stock cube and tomato purée; reduce heat and simmer gently, stirring and skimming from time to time, until the sauce is reduced to half the original quantity. Strain through a fine sieve. Stir in heavy cream; correct seasoning; keep warm.

6 To bake trout fillets: place the trout packets in a baking dish large enough to contain them side by side, without touching. Crumble ½ chicken stock cube into 1¼ cups dry white wine; pour over fillets and sprinkle them with finely chopped onion and mushroom stalks.

7 Set the pan in preheated oven and leave it for about 10 minutes, depending on the thickness of the fillets. Lift the packets onto 4 heated individual dishes and keep warm.

8 Add trout trimmings to juices in the baking pan; add a splash of dry white wine and boil the liquid over a high heat to reduce it until it is almost a glaze. Stir into sauce. Taste and adjust seasonings and heat to serving temperature. Pour sauce around each fish packet and serve immediately.

Serves 4

Turbot in Champagne

1 Melt half the butter in a large shallow saucepan with olive oil; sauté finely chopped shallots until transparent; add sliced mushrooms and continue cooking until tender. Remove.

2 Add remaining butter to pan and sauté turbot fillets until lightly colored. Add sautéed mushrooms and onions, fish stock and half the champagne, adding more if necessary barely to cover the turbot fillets. Season to taste with salt and white pepper and simmer very slowly for a few minutes until tender. Remove turbot fillets to a serving dish and keep warm.

3 Add cream to the liquid in the pan; let simmer without boiling until cream is warm.

4 Mix cornstarch with a small amount of water, add to sauce and cook, stirring constantly, over a very low heat, until sauce is smooth and rich.

5 When ready to serve, pour in remaining champagne, stir and mix with the sauce until warm. If you prefer a thicker sauce, use less champagne. Pour over turbot fillets and serve immediately.

Serves 4

Ingredients

4 turbot fillets, boned and skinned
½ cup butter
2 tablespoons olive oil
2 shallots, finely chopped
1¼ cups button mushrooms, sliced
6 tablespoons fish stock made from fish trimmings
½ quarter bottle of champagne
Salt and white pepper
⅔ cup heavy cream
1 tablespoon cornstarch

Boeuf à la Bourguignonne *(Illustration, page 13)*

1 Cut beef into large cubes; remove fat and roll cubes in flour. Heat 2 tablespoons olive oil and 2 tablespoons butter in a large frying pan and sauté diced salt pork until crisp and brown. Remove pork from pan and transfer to a large earthenware casserole. Brown meat well on all sides in remaining fat, season to taste with salt and pepper and moisten with warmed cognac. Ignite cognac; let the flame burn away and add meat to casserole.

2 Coarsely chop carrots, leek, shallots, onion and garlic, and cook vegetables in fat remaining in frying pan, stirring occasionally, until they are lightly browned, adding a little more butter and olive oil, if necessary.

3 Transfer vegetables to the casserole with the meat; add the calf's foot and bouquet garni. Pour over all but 4 tablespoons of the wine, and just enough hot water or good beef stock to cover contents of the casserole.

4 Cover and cook in a cool oven (225°F) for 1½ to 2 hours.

5 Remove fat from sauce; stir in, bit by bit, 1 tablespoon butter worked with 1 tablespoon flour; cover; continue to cook gently in the oven for about 2 hours or longer.

6 Brown onions in 1 tablespoon butter in a saucepan with a little sugar. Add 4 tablespoons red wine, cover and cook over a low flame until onions are almost tender. Keep warm. Sauté mushroom caps in remaining oil and 2 tablespoons butter and a little lemon juice. Keep warm.

7 When meat is tender, remove calf's foot and bouquet garni; correct seasoning; add onions and mushroom caps and sprinkle lavishly with finely-chopped parsley.

Serves 4–6

Note: like many wine-based dishes, *Boeuf à la Bourguignonne* is better when re-heated and served on the following day.

Ingredients

3 lb. round or rump of beef
Flour
4 tablespoons olive oil
Butter
¼ lb. diced salt pork
Salt
Freshly ground black pepper
4 tablespoons warmed cognac
2 carrots
1 leek
4 shallots
1 large onion
1 clove garlic
1 calf's foot, split (optional)
1 bouquet garni
½ bottle red Burgundy
Beef stock or water, to cover
18 button onions
Sugar
12 button mushrooms
Lemon juice
Finely chopped parsley

Below *Artichokes with Walnut Dressing, an appetizer star-turn, photographed among the artichokes at Hintlesham. (Recipe, page 24)*

Below right *Nasturtium Leaves and Sliced Cucumber makes a fresh-tasting summer appetizer when dressed with a well-seasoned vinaigrette. (Recipe, page 25)*

Appetizer Salads, Patés and Terrines

French "composition salads"—*salades composées*—make wonderful first course or luncheon salads for spring and summer meals. The procedure is simple: just toss the elements of your choice, raw or cooked, in a well-flavored vinaigrette dressing (1 part wine vinegar or lemon juice to 3 parts olive oil, ¼ teaspoon Dijon mustard and salt and freshly ground black pepper, to taste); add chopped fresh herbs or flavor with finely chopped onion, shallot, garlic or crumbled cooked bacon.

Salade Italienne
Lettuce leaves, crisp rings of fennel, sprigs of fresh fennel and stuffed green olives. Vinaigrette dressing.

Salade Mexicaine
Cos (romaine) lettuce leaves, canned corn kernels and red pepper strips. Vinaigrette dressing flavored with mustard and finely chopped parsley or chives.

Salade Japonaise
Lettuce leaves and sprigs of watercress, garnished with radishes cut into flower shapes. Vinaigrette dressing flavored with finely chopped garlic and soy sauce.

Salade Fermière

Lettuce leaves (Salad Bowl) and sprigs of watercress, garnished with tomato wedges and quartered hard-boiled eggs. Vinaigrette dressing flavored with mustard and chopped onion.

Salade Provençale

Lettuce leaves and barely cooked cauliflowerets, garnished with black olives and anchovy strips. Vinaigrette dressing flavored with mustard and finely chopped garlic.

Salade Gitane

Chick peas, lentils and cannellini beans (white kidney beans) soaked overnight and then cooked separately in water until just tender (you'll need three separate pans); each tossed, separately, while still warm, in a vinaigrette dressing flavored with chopped onion and anchovies. Garnish with tomato wedges and black olives.

Salade Tricolore

Lettuce leaves and thin strips of barely cooked carrot and celery tossed in a well-flavored vinaigrette dressing with strips of raw green and red cabbage.

Salade Paysanne

Lettuce leaves, sliced mushroom and diced Swiss cheese, tossed in a well-flavored vinaigrette dressing. Garnish with walnut halves and crumbled cooked bacon.

Salade Jardinière

Lettuce leaves (Salad Bowl), cooked green beans, carrot strips and raw cucumber strips. Vinaigrette dressing. Garnish, if desired, with nasturtiums.

Tomato and Egg Salad

Ingredients

4 ripe tomatoes
4 hard-boiled eggs
6–8 tablespoons olive oil
2–3 tablespoons wine vinegar
Salt and freshly ground black pepper
2 tablespoons finely chopped parsley
2 tablespoons finely chopped onion

1 Wipe tomatoes clean and slice crosswise into even slices.

2 Shell eggs and slice crosswise into even slices.

3 Place slices of egg and tomato in a large flat hors d'oeuvre dish; mix olive oil, wine vinegar and salt and freshly ground black pepper, to taste, and pour over salad.

4 Sprinkle egg slices with finely chopped parsley and tomato slices with finely chopped onion.

Serves 4

Green Beans Salad

Ingredients

1½ lb. young green beans
Salt
2–3 tablespoons wine vinegar
½ teaspoon Dijon mustard
6–8 tablespoons olive oil
Freshly ground black pepper
Lettuce leaves
2 tablespoons finely chopped onion
2 tablespoons finely chopped parsley

1 Trim off ends of green beans and cook them in boiling salted water until they are barely tender.

2 Drain and toss immediately while still warm in a French dressing made from wine vinegar, Dijon mustard, olive oil and salt and freshly ground black pepper, to taste. Chill.

3 When ready to serve, line a salad bowl or rectangular hors d'oeuvre dish with lettuce leaves; arrange green bean salad in the center of the dish and sprinkle with finely chopped onion and parsley.

Serves 4–6

Italian Pepper Salad

1 Heat broiler to maximum heat for 20 minutes.

2 Arrange peppers in broiler pan, reduce heat to moderate and broil peppers until their skins blacken and blister, turning them regularly so that they cook evenly. (Do not increase heat again: slow steady charring gives the peppers their delicious flavor.)

3 When peppers are thoroughly charred all over, place them under cold running water and rub off skins with your fingers. Pat peppers dry, cut them in half and discard seeds and stems. Slice peppers into thick strips.

4 Combine olive oil and wine vinegar with salt and freshly ground black pepper, to taste, in a cup or small bowl. Add thyme and ground fennel seeds, or celery salt, and beat vigorously with a fork until emulsified.

5 Arrange pepper strips in a shallow dish keeping colors separate if using a combination of peppers. Pour over dressing and toss lightly. Cover dish with foil, then place in the refrigerator and leave peppers to marinate for 8 hours, or overnight.

6 Before serving, arrange peppers in 1 large serving dish or 3 separate dishes. Garnish with green olives and stuffed anchovy fillets, and sprinkle parsley on top.

Serves 8 to 10

Ingredients

6 large peppers, all green, or a combination of yellow, red and green
6–8 tablespoons olive oil
2 tablespoons wine vinegar
Salt and freshly ground black pepper
Pinch of thyme
$\frac{1}{4}$ teaspoon ground fennel seeds, or celery salt
1 cup green olives, pitted
4 oz. canned, rolled anchovy fillets, stuffed with capers
2 tablespoons finely chopped parsley

Saffron Rice Salad

1 Dissolve saffron, cumin and cayenne pepper in dry white wine and rich chicken stock, and combine in a large saucepan with rice, coarsely chopped onion, and salt, to taste.

2 Cover pan and simmer until all the liquid is absorbed and the rice is tender. Add some more liquid if necessary.

3 Drain well and toss with dressing. Stir in diced peppers, anchovy fillets and black olives. Allow to cool. Add more olive oil, wine vinegar or seasonings, if necessary.

Serves 4–6

Ingredients

$\frac{1}{2}$ teaspoon powdered saffron
$\frac{1}{4}$ teaspoon powdered cumin
$\frac{1}{4}$ teaspoon cayenne pepper
6 tablespoons dry white wine
$2\frac{1}{2}$ cups hot chicken stock
$1\frac{3}{4}$ cups Italian rice for risotto
1 large onion, coarsely chopped
Salt
$\frac{1}{2}$ green pepper, seeded and cut into squares
$\frac{1}{2}$ red pepper, seeded and cut into squares

DRESSING

6 black olives, pitted and coarsely chopped
3 anchovy fillets, cut into squares
2–3 tablespoons wine vinegar
$\frac{1}{2}$ teaspoon Dijon mustard
6–8 tablespoons olive oil
2 tablespoons finely chopped parsley
Salt and freshly ground black pepper

Tuna Waldorf Salad

Ingredients

Large can tuna fish, drained
4–6 celery stalks, sliced
½ cup walnuts, broken or
  chopped
1¼–1½ cups mayonnaise
  (see page 49)
Lemon juice
Salt and freshly ground
  black pepper
Pinch of cayenne pepper
3 tart dessert apples
Crisp lettuce leaves

1 Flake tuna into bite-sized pieces and combine with sliced celery and walnut pieces in a mixing bowl. Stir in enough mayonnaise to bind the ingredients lightly together. Season with lemon juice, salt and freshly ground black pepper, to taste, and a pinch of cayenne pepper.

2 Core, but do not peel apples; cut into ¼- to ½-inch cubes and toss in lemon juice to prevent discoloration. Stir the apple cubes into tuna mixture.

3 Arrange 2 to 3 lettuce leaves on each individual serving plate to form a "cup." Divide tuna and apple mixture equally among plates, piling it in the center of the lettuce.

Serves 6

Mexican Seviche Appetizer

Ingredients

1½ lb. fillets of sole or
  salmon tail
5 oz. fresh lime or lemon
  juice
Fresh coriander leaves, or
  parsley, coarsely chopped

DRESSING

6–8 tablespoons olive oil
½ medium onion, finely
  chopped
2 tablespoons finely
  chopped parsley
1 garlic clove, finely
  chopped
Salt and freshly ground
  black pepper
Dash of Tabasco, or
  Worcestershire sauce

1 Skin fillets of sole or salmon by working a knife between the skin and flesh at the tail end until there is a piece of skin large enough to grasp. Then pull the skin free from each fillet. Cut fish across grain into thin strips.

2 Place strips in a bowl, cover with lime or lemon juice and place in the refrigerator for 4 hours, turning them in the juice once to ensure that all the fish is marinated.

3 To make *seviche* dressing: combine olive oil and finely chopped onion, pars-ley and garlic. Season with salt and freshly ground black pepper, to taste, and a dash of Tabasco, or Worcester-shire sauce; chill.

4 Just before serving: drain fish strips. Toss them gently in *seviche* dressing and place in a serving dish. Garnish with coarsely chopped fresh coriander leaves, or parsley.

Serves 4

Sliced Avocado and Orange Salad

Ingredients

2 ripe avocados
Juice of 2 lemons
2–3 oranges
Lettuce leaves

DRESSING

2 tablespoons wine vinegar,
  or lemon juice
Coarse salt and freshly
  ground black pepper
Pinch of mustard powder
½ garlic clove, finely
  chopped
6–8 tablespoons olive oil

1 Cut avocados in half lengthwise and remove pits. Peel avocado halves care-fully, taking care not to damage flesh. Cut avocado halves across into ¼-inch slices and soak in lemon juice to keep their color.

2 Peel oranges, removing all traces of white pith. Using a sharp serrated knife cut out segments from between mem-branes.

3 To make the vinaigrette dressing: mix wine vinegar, or lemon juice, with a generous pinch of coarse salt and freshly ground black pepper. Add a pinch of mustard powder and finely chopped garlic. Beat in olive oil with a fork, until dressing thickens and emul-sifies.

4 Make a nest of crisp lettuce leaves on a serving plate, or on 4 individual plates. Arrange avocado slices and or-ange segments in each nest. Pour vinai-grette dressing over each portion before serving.

Serves 4

Cooked Lentil Salad

1 Soak lentils overnight in cold water to cover. Drain.

2 Heat 2 tablespoons olive oil in a saucepan and sauté finely chopped onion until transparent. Add garlic clove, bay leaf, 1 teaspoon salt, lentils and 6 cups water; bring to the boil and simmer for 30 to 60 minutes, or until just tender. Drain lentils into a mixing bowl and leave them to cool.

3 Remove garlic clove and bay leaf from lentils, and add remaining olive oil, wine vinegar and salt and freshly ground black pepper, to taste.

4 To prepare dressing: place finely chopped onion in a bowl with finely chopped parsley, Dijon mustard, and salt and freshly ground black pepper, to taste. Mix well, then pour in olive oil, little by little, beating mixture continuously, until it thickens. Flavor with lemon juice.

5 Pour dressing over lentils and mix thoroughly. Transfer to a serving platter and garnish with anchovy fillets, tomato wedges and black olives.

Serves 4 to 6

Ingredients
1⅓ cups dried lentils
4 tablespoons olive oil
1 large onion, finely chopped
1 garlic clove
1 bay leaf
1 tablespoon wine vinegar
Freshly ground black pepper

DRESSING
½ large onion, finely chopped
4 tablespoons finely chopped parsley
1 teaspoon Dijon mustard
Salt and freshly ground black pepper
6 tablespoons olive oil
Juice of ½ lemon

GARNISH
Anchovy fillets
Tomato wedges
Black olives

Raw Mushroom and Shrimp Salad

1 Wipe mushrooms and trim stalks.

2 To make dressing: beat olive oil, wine vinegar and mustard powder in a bowl with a fork until mixture emulsifies (or shake ingredients together in a screw-topped jar). Season with the chopped rosemary, or parsley, salt and freshly ground black pepper, to taste, and a pinch of sugar.

3 Slice mushrooms thinly and place in herb-seasoned vinaigrette dressing. Toss until each slice is thoroughly coated. Cover bowl and leave to marinate for 1 hour.

4 Meanwhile, place the shelled shrimp in a small bowl. Add lemon juice, salt and freshly ground black pepper, to taste, and a pinch of cayenne pepper, and stir to mix.

5 When ready to serve: line a shallow dish with lettuce leaves. Drain shrimp and add to mushrooms. Toss well and pile into middle of lettuce-lined dish. Serve immediately, sprinkled with finely chopped chives.

Serves 4

Note: if you are buying freshly boiled, unshelled shrimp for this dish, it is a good idea to reserve one or more unshelled for the garnish. You will need to buy ¾ lb.

Ingredients
1¾ cups button mushrooms
8 tablespoons olive oil
2 tablespoons wine vinegar
¼ teaspoon mustard powder
¼–½ teaspoon chopped fresh rosemary, or 2 tablespoons chopped parsley
Salt and freshly ground black pepper
Pinch of sugar
12 boiled, shelled shrimp
Juice of 1 lemon
Pinch of cayenne pepper
Lettuce leaves
Finely chopped chives

Roman Vegetables

Ingredients

4 small zucchini
2 stalks celery
¼ lb. green beans
4 small carrots, scraped and cut into eighths
12 button mushrooms
12 pearl onions
½ head cauliflower
1 green pepper
2 red peppers
1 small eggplant
⅔ cup olive oil
2 cloves garlic, quartered
2 bay leaves
Salt and freshly ground black pepper
4 tablespoons dry white wine
4 tablespoons wine vinegar
⅔ cup ketchup
2 tablespoons sugar
12 stuffed olives
Lemon juice (optional)
Lettuce leaves and finely chopped parsley, to garnish

1 Cut zucchini into ¼-inch slices. Cut celery, green beans and carrot sticks into 1-inch segments. Wash mushrooms and trim stems. Peel onions. Trim cauliflower and break into flowerets. Remove stems, pith and seeds from green and red peppers and cut them into thick chunks. Cut unpeeled eggplant into slices ¼-inch thick; then cut each slice into quarters.

2 Heat the olive oil in a large thick-bottomed casserole; add vegetables, quartered garlic and bay leaves, and season generously with salt and freshly ground black pepper. Cover casserole and simmer vegetables gently over a low heat until the vegetables are tender, but still quite crisp.

3 Combine dry white wine, wine vinegar, ketchup and sugar; stir into casserole; add stuffed olives and continue to cook gently for another 10 minutes.

4 Remove casserole from the heat and allow vegetables to come to room temperature. Mix well and chill until ready to serve. Correct seasoning, adding a little lemon juice and a little more salt and freshly ground black pepper, if desired.

5 To serve: place crisply cooked vegetables on lettuce leaves and sprinkle with finely chopped parsley.

Serves 4–6

Artichokes with Walnut Dressing

Ingredients

4 artichokes
Salt
Juice of ½ lemon
Freshly ground black pepper
Finely chopped fresh herbs

WALNUT DRESSING

⅔ cup heavy cream
Salt and freshly ground black pepper
Walnut oil
Lemon juice

1 Remove the tough outer leaves of artichokes and trim tops of inner leaves. Trim the base and stem of each artichoke with a sharp knife. Cook until tender (30–40 minutes) in a large quantity of boiling salted water, to which you have added the juice of ½ lemon. Artichokes are cooked when a leaf pulls out easily. Turn artichokes upside down to drain.

2 Remove inner leaves of cooked artichokes, leaving a decorative outer ring of 2 or 3 leaves to form a cup around the heart of each artichoke. Season with salt and freshly ground black pepper, and chill in the refrigerator.

3 To make walnut dressing: beat heavy cream until stiff; flavor with salt and freshly ground black pepper, walnut oil and lemon juice to taste.

4 Just before serving: pile artichoke hearts with whipped walnut cream filling and sprinkle with finely chopped herbs.

Serves 4

To Choose and Store Artichokes

When buying artichokes, look for ones that are fresh and heavy for their size, with supple, tightly closed leaves. Stiff, dry leaves and an "overblown" appearance generally indicate that the artichoke will be tough and woody.

The size of an artichoke is no indication to its quality, but small ones are better for pickling, medium-sized and large ones for serving whole as an appetizer, or in dishes where only the heart is called for.

Artichokes can be stored in the refrigerator, tightly covered to preserve their moisture.

Cucumber and Nasturtium Leaf Salad

(Illustration, page 18)

1 Peel and slice cucumber thinly. Wash nasturtium leaves; remove stems and drain.

2 Combine mustard and vinegar in a bowl and stir until well blended. Add olive oil, and salt and freshly ground black pepper, to taste. Blend well. Stir in tarragon.

3 When ready to serve, combine cucumber and nasturtium leaves in a salad bowl; add vinaigrette dressing and toss well. Garnish with nasturtium flowers, if desired.

Serves 4–6

Ingredients
1 cucumber
36 small nasturtium leaves
1 teaspoon Dijon mustard
2 tablespoons wine vinegar
6 tablespoons olive oil
Salt and freshly ground
    black pepper
2 tablespoons finely
    chopped fresh tarragon
6 nasturtium flowers
    (optional)

Tomato and Mozzarella Cheese Appetizer Salad

1 Place 2 lettuce leaves on each salad plate. Arrange 2 slices of mozzarella and 3 slices tomato on each plate. Garnish each serving with 2 black olives and 2 anchovy fillets.

2 Sprinkle cheese and tomatoes with a little freshly crushed coriander seeds and finely chopped fresh marjoram. Dribble over 2 to 3 tablespons vinaigrette dressing.

Serves 4

Ingredients
8 lettuce leaves
8 slices mozzarella cheese
12 slices ripe tomato
8 black olives
8 anchovy fillets
Freshly crushed coriander
    seeds
Finely chopped fresh
    marjoram
Well-seasoned vinaigrette
    dressing (see page 19)

Japanese Noodles

1 Place dried mushrooms in a small bowl and add 3¾ cups boiling water to cover. Let mushrooms steep in water until soft. Squeeze dry. Add 1 tablespoon each sesame oil and soy sauce. Mix well.

2 Bring 3¾ cups water to the boil. Add contents of 2 packages *Udon* noodles to water, together with the contents of small seasoning packets (found in each package of noodles). Stir until noodles are separated. Cook noodles for 2 minutes in all.

3 Drain noodles and transfer to a large bowl. Add marinated mushrooms and 1 tablespoon each sesame oil, soy sauce and vegetable oil. Stir well and allow noodles to cool.

4 Sprinkle chopped coriander or parsley over the Japanese noodles and serve cold in an hors d'oeuvre dish as one of a selection of cold hors d'oeuvres.

Serves 4–6

Ingredients
2 packages Japanese Udon
    noodles
1 package dried Chinese
    mushrooms
2 tablespoons sesame oil
2 tablespoons soy sauce
1 tablespoon vegetable oil
2 tablespoons chopped
    fresh coriander or parsley

Pâtés and Terrines

When I was very young, pâtés always meant the extremely rich *pâté de foie gras* that we often used to have as a special occasion feast at Christmas. These expensive pâtés—made in France from the livers of specially fattened geese, usually studded with truffles, and eaten with hot, crisp slices of toast and farmhouse butter—were a sensuous treat that the whole family used to look forward to from year to year.

Now that I have been cooking my own pâtés for years, a pâté can mean almost anything that contains a mixture of ground meats, or poultry or game; the mix is "softened" in flavor with a little ground pork and veal, and then studded with strips of ham, tongue, poultry or game.

One of my favorite pâtés is a delicious green herb pâté, studded for texture and color contrast with diced tongue, diced ham, diced bacon, a little diced pork fat and some diced chicken livers sautéed in butter.

I first made *pâté aux herbes* (see page 28) in St.-Tropez. I had visited a tiny restaurant in upper Provence, and enjoyed a very gutsy herb and ham pâté that I tasted there. Deciding to make it at home, I simmered some fresh leaves of spinach and *blette* in a little butter. I added a little finely chopped pork to the mix, with cream and egg yolks for extra richness. Then the problem was how to recreate the wonderfully herby flavor of the original. It was time to experiment. Did it have thyme in it? Yes, it did have thyme. A little more thyme, a little rosemary, and a little sage. Now perhaps the flavor was a little *too* rich, so I softened it with a little added cream. Cooking is really like painting . . . all the flavors and seasonings that we use in our daily cooking are like the colors on an artist's palette.

Pâté aux Herbes: a gutsy herb-flavored green pâté that I created by a lucky mistake. I was trying to recreate a green, pink and yellow marbled pâté that I had once tasted at a tiny restaurant in the hills behind St.-Tropez. My first version—not "marbled" at all, but absolutely delicious—has been a firm favorite of mine ever since. (Recipe, page 28)

1 Add diced bacon, pork fat, ham and tongue to green pâté mixture.

2 Line bottom and sides of an ovenproof terrine with thin strips of pounded pork fat to "moisturize," pâté as it cooks.

3 Fill terrine with pâté mixture; and fold over overlapping strips of pork fat to seal terrine.

Cold Parsleyed Ham *(Illustration, page 27)*

(A simpler version of the French classic Jambon Persillé de Bourgogne)

Ingredients

2 lb. cooked ham (cut in 1 piece)
2½ cups well-flavored chicken stock
⅔ cups dry white wine
Freshly ground black pepper
Nutmeg
Finely chopped fresh parsley
2 tablespoons powdered gelatin
1–2 tablespoons tarragon vinegar

1 Cut ham into cubes. Bring chicken stock and dry white wine gently to the boil; add ham cubes and freshly ground black pepper and nutmeg, to taste. (No salt. The ham is salty enough.) Lower heat and simmer ham in this stock very gently for 5 minutes.

2 Drain, reserving stock, and place ham cubes loosely in a wet glass bowl which you have dusted thickly with finely chopped parsley.

3 Soften gelatin in a little water. Stir into stock; add 6–8 tablespoons parsley and tarragon vinegar. Allow to cool until syrupy, then pour over diced ham. If there is not enough liquid to cover ham, add a little more dry white wine, to cover. Allow to set for 12 hours in the refrigerator before unmolding.

Serves 6–8

Pâté aux Herbes *(Illustrations, pages 26 and 27)*

Ingredients

1 lb. lean pork
Butter
1 large onion, finely chopped
1 lb. fresh or ¼ lb. frozen leaf spinach
¼ lb. cooked ham
¼ lb. unsmoked bacon
¼ lb. pork fat
¼ lb. cooked beef tongue
2 cloves garlic, finely chopped
2 tablespoons finely chopped basil
2 tablespoons finely chopped parsley
2 tablespoons finely chopped chervil
24 spikes rosemary, finely chopped
4 eggs, beaten
Salt and freshly ground black pepper
Cayenne pepper
Freshly grated nutmeg
6 oz. chicken livers
⅔ cup heavy cream
2 tablespoons powdered gelatin
Thin strips of pounded pork fat
Gherkins

1 Cut the pork into small cubes; place in blender or food processor and blend until minced. Melt 2 tablespoons butter in a large frying pan; add finely chopped onion and sauté, stirring constantly, until it is transparent. Add spinach and continue to cook, stirring, until spinach has wilted (if fresh). Remove onions and spinach and chop coarsely. Add onion and spinach mixture to pork and blend again. Transfer mixture to a large bowl.

2 Dice ham, bacon, pork fat and beef tongue and add to green pâté mixture. Then add finely chopped garlic and fresh herbs. (If you use dried herbs, use only half the quantities.)

3 Stir in the beaten eggs and add salt and freshly ground black pepper, cayenne pepper and nutmeg, to taste.

4 Cut chicken livers into dice and sauté in 2 tablespoons butter until golden.

5 Stir in cream and powdered gelatin, which you have dissolved in a little water, and mix well. Add to pâté mixture and mix well. The raw pâté will now be a nice, loose, spoonable mixture ready for cooking.

6 Line the bottom and sides of an ovenproof terrine with thin strips of pounded pork fat. (*Note:* you can ask your butcher to do this for you. But I warn you, don't ask him on a busy Saturday morning when the shop is crowded.) Spoon pâté mixture into terrine; cover with thin strips of pounded pork fat and cook in a preheated slow oven (325°F) for ½ hour. Lower heat to 300°F and cook for another 30–40 minutes.

7 Remove from oven to cool, pressing excess juices out of the terrine with a board, or the back of a spoon. Serve cold, cut into slices, with gherkins.

Note: to remove pâté from terrine, place terrine in a pan of hot water for a minute or two, then insert a sharp pointed knife all around pâté, loosening it from the sides of the terrine. Turn terrine upside down over serving plate, and the pâté will slide out easily.

Serves 8 to 10

Hedgehog Pâté *(Illustration, page 30)*

1 Combine cubed ham and ham fat in bowl of electric blender or food processor and blend until mixture is like a coarse pâté.

2 Add chopped onion and garlic, Dijon mustard, wine vinegar, anchovy paste, ground nutmeg and ground black pepper, ginger, ground cloves and dried thyme or oregano. Blend again until mixture is smooth. Taste and correct seasoning, adding a little more of any of the above seasonings and spices, if necessary.

3 Pack mixture into a large bowl; cover and refrigerate for 2 days to allow flavors to blend.

4 To form hedgehog: mound mixture on a flat serving dish and then, using a spatula, shape into a smooth oval, bringing the front of hedgehog into a shart point to represent the "head" (see photo). Brush hedgehog with liquid aspic to give it a translucent look; stud with toasted sliced almonds for "spikes," bits of black olive or truffle for "nose," and currants for "eyes."

5 Chill in refrigerator until ready to serve. Serve with hot toast and chilled butter.

Ingredients

1¼ lb. cooked ham, cut into cubes
¼ lb. firm fat from cooked ham, cut into cubes
1 medium onion, chopped
1 small clove garlic, chopped
2 teaspoons Dijon mustard
1 tablespoon wine vinegar
½ teaspoon anchovy paste
½ teaspoon ground nutmeg
¼ teaspoon each ground black pepper, ginger, ground cloves and dried thyme or oregano
⅔ cup liquid aspic, cooled until it is syrupy
Toasted sliced almonds
Bits of black olive or truffle
2 currants

Italian Veal Pâté with Tuna

1 Have your butcher bone and tie a piece of leg of veal.

2 Cut anchovy fillets into small pieces; pierce holes in surface of meat with a sharp knife or skewer and insert pieces of anchovy fillet and garlic into the holes. Top meat with bay leaves, inserting them under strings. Place rolled meat in a ovenproof casserole with sliced onions, carrots and celery, parsley, cloves and salt and freshly ground black pepper, to taste. Pour in dry white wine and add just enough water to cover meat (or use water only); bring slowly to the boil, turn down heat, cover casserole, and simmer veal for 1½–2 hours. When veal is tender, remove strings and/or skewers and allow it to cool in stock.

3 To make tuna fish sauce: pound tuna fish, anchovy fillets and capers with lemon juice and freshly ground black pepper until smooth. Combine with mayonnaise in electric blender and blend (adding a little veal stock if too

thick) until the sauce is smooth and creamy.

4 When meat is cold, remove it from stock (reserve stock); dice thickly and place in a bowl; pour over tuna fish sauce; cover bowl and let the meat marinate in the sauce overnight.

5 Blend veal and half the sauce in a blender or food processor to a smooth paste, adding a little reserved meat stock if mixture seems too dry. Soak 1 tablespoon gelatin in 6 tablespoons cold water, until soft, then heat to dissolve. Add to veal and tuna mixture and blend again. Correct seasoning and pour into individual soufflé molds to set.

6 To serve: turn individual veal pâtés out of molds. Arrange lattice work of thin strips of anchovy on each pâté and garnish with sliced stuffed olives. Brush each pâté with melted aspic two or three times. Serve with remaining tuna fish sauce.

Ingredients

1 piece of veal (2 lb. when boned and trimmed)
6 anchovy fillets
2 cloves garlic, slivered
Several bay leaves
2 large onions, sliced
4 carrots, sliced
2 stalks celery, sliced
2 sprigs parsley
2 cloves
Salt and fresh black pepper
1¼ cups dry white wine
1 tablespoon gelatin

TUNA FISH SAUCE

6 oz. tuna fish
6 anchovy fillets
1 teaspoon capers
2 tablespoons lemon juice
Freshly ground black pepper
⅔ cups well-seasoned mayonnaise (see page 49)

GARNISH

Anchovy fillets, cut into thin strips
Stuffed olives, sliced
Aspic, to glaze

Gravad Mackerel

1 Combine sugar, salt, coarsely ground black pepper and saltpeter (the latter is not essential, but if obtainable from a pharmacy should be used to improve color of dish) and rub mackerel pieces on all sides with this spice mixture.

2 Line the bottom of an earthenware or porcelain terrine or pâté dish with sprigs of fresh dill. Place 1 piece of mackerel on this, skin side down, and sprinkle generously with spice mixture; add more sprigs fresh dill; top with sec-ond piece of mackerel, skin side up. Place a board cut to fit terrine on top; weight it with a weight and refrigerate for 48 hours.

3 When ready to serve: slice *gravad* mackerel across the grain into very thin slices and serve as an unusual first course with black bread, unsalted butter and a wedge or two of lemon. The uncooked mackerel will have a fine flavor.

Ingredients

- **2 even-sized pieces fresh mackerel, bone removed (about 1 lb. each)**
- **8 tablespoons sugar**
- **10 tablespoons salt**
- **1 tablespoon coarsely ground black pepper**
- **½ teaspoon saltpeter**
- **Fresh dill**

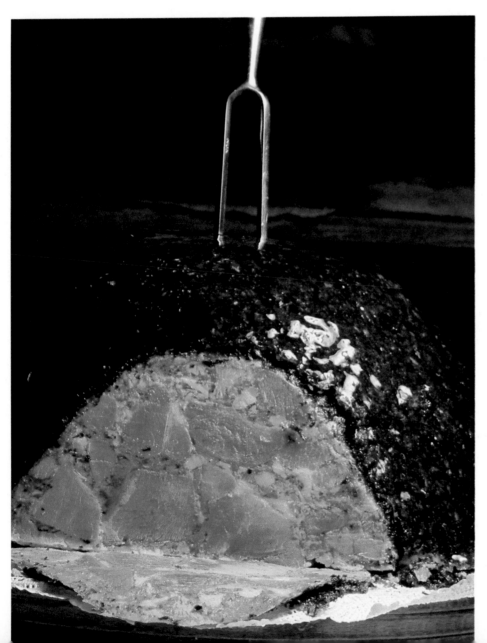

Opposite page *A truffle for a nose, two dried currants for eyes and carefully tailored almonds for a coat: this hedgehog is for eating. (Recipe for Hedgehog Pâté, page 29)*

Left *Cold Parsleyed Ham, a delicious combination of poached ham and finely chopped parsley in wine-flavored aspic. (Recipe, page 28)*

Smoked Trout Appetizer

Ingredients

3 smoked trout
6 slices white bread
6 tablespoons heavy cream
1–2 tablespoons grated horseradish
Finely chopped parsley
6 crisp lettuce leaves
6 slices firm tomato
6 large black olives, stoned and halved
6 lemon wedges

1 Skin and fillet smoked trout, and cut each fillet in two. Toast bread slices on both sides and remove crusts.

2 Beat heavy cream; add 1 to 2 tablespoons iced water and beat again until firm. Fold in grated horseradish, to taste, to make horseradish chantilly cream.

3 Spread each slice of toast with horseradish cream and arrange 2 pieces of trout diagonally on top. Sprinkle with a pinch of finely chopped parsley. Cut each slice of toast in half from corner to corner, so there is one fillet on each half.

4 Serve 2 toast triangles per person on individual plates garnished with lettuce leaves, tomato slices, black olives, and lemon wedges.

Serves 6

Cucumber Fish Mousse

Ingredients

2 cucumbers, peeled
½ lb. smoked trout or mackerel
2 egg yolks
Salt and white pepper
¼ cup heavy cream
1 egg white
2 teaspoons ketchup
1 tablespoon lemon juice
Cayenne pepper

LIGHT TOMATO SAUCE

1 lb. ripe tomatoes
1 small onion, finely chopped
1 whole clove garlic, unpeeled
4 tablespoons olive oil
¼ chicken stock cube, crumbled
⅔ cup water
2 tablespoons tomato puree
Salt and freshly ground black pepper
Cayenne pepper
Lemon juice
2 tablespoons chopped parsley

GARNISH

Raw carrot strips
Raw turnip strips
Salt
Cooked green beans
Vinaigrette dressing (see page 19)

1 Trim ends of each cucumber, and cut each cucumber in half. Using an apple corer, remove seeds from cucumber sections, and cut to within ¼-inch of outside of cucumber.

2 Place smoked fish in blender with egg yolks; process until smooth; add salt and white pepper, to taste; then add heavy cream and process again. Add egg white and process again until mixture is light and fluffy. Add ketchup, lemon juice, and cayenne pepper, to taste, and process until well mixed. Chill for 1 hour.

3 Place a cucumber section on a piece of foil; fill with chilled mousse, smoothing off ends of mousse even with cucumber. Wrap each cucumber section lightly in foil; simmer in water, to cover, for 30 minutes. Remove from pan and cool. Refrigerate until ready to use.

4 To make light tomato sauce: peel tomatoes by first dipping them in boiling water for 1 minute to loosen skins. Cut tomatoes in half and gently squeeze out seeds. Dice finely. Sauté finely chopped onion and unpeeled garlic clove in 2 tablespoons olive oil until onion is soft. Remove garlic clove. Add crumbled chicken stock cube and water, diced tomatoes and tomato puree, and simmer for 5 minutes. Add salt and freshly ground black pepper, cayenne pepper and lemon juice, to taste, and blend in electric blender, or food processor until smooth. Cool. Stir in chopped parsley and remaining olive oil.

5 Cook carrot and turnip strips in boiling salted water for 5 minutes, until vegetables are crunchy. Trim cooked green beans to carrot and turnip strip length. Marinate vegetables separately in well-seasoned vinaigrette dressing for at least 1 hour.

6 To serve: cut cucumber section into 3 rounds. Cover bottom of each chilled plate with 3 to 4 tablespoons light tomato sauce. Place 3 slices of stuffed cucumber in center of each plate, and garnish with colorful bands of marinated green beans and turnip and carrot strips.

Serves 4

Rillettes d'Anguilles aux Petits Légumes

1 Skin and fillet eel and trout.

2 Combine the trout and one-third of the eel in a blender or food processor; add cream and salt and freshly ground black pepper, to taste, and blend until smooth. Add lemon juice to taste.

3 Cut remaining eel into thin strips about the size of matchsticks and fold gently into eel and trout mixture.

4 To serve: shape *rillettes* mixture into 4–6 oval shapes using 2 tablespoons dipped in hot water (*Note:* shapes should resemble "eggs") and serve on individual plates. Garnish each plate with a ring of sliced radishes, diced beetroot, carrot rounds and sprigs of curly endive or corn salad. Dribble vinaigrette dressing over salad greens and vegetables. Sprinkle each *rillettes* "egg" with finely chopped fresh herbs.

Serves 4–6

Note: do not use frozen eel or trout because they produce too much moisture.

Ingredients

1 lb. fresh smoked eel, middle cut
1 fresh smoked trout
$\frac{2}{3}$ cup heavy cream
Salt and freshly ground black pepper
Lemon juice

GARNISH

4 small radishes, thinly sliced
2 slices cooked beetroot, diced
1 medium carrot, cooked until just firm, thinly sliced
Tiny sprigs curly endive or corn salad
Well-seasoned vinaigrette dressing (see page 19)
Finely chopped fresh herbs

Fondant de Volailles

1 Skin capon and remove meat from bones, leaving breasts whole.

2 Combine sherry, cognac, Noilly Prat, port, herbs, finely chopped shallots, carrots and onion with garlic and peppercorns in a large porcelain bowl. Add chicken pieces and marinate in this mixture for at least 12 hours.

3 Dice pork fat and loin of pork and combine with coarse salt and freshly ground black pepper, to taste. Leave in the refrigerator for 6 hours, so that meat does not change color during cooking. Pass through the finest blade of your grinder.

4 Place chicken pieces in a roasting pan with diced shoulder of pork and roast in a hot oven (450°F) for 4–5 minutes, or until meat has colored slightly. Then strain marinade juices over meat and continue to cook for 5 minutes more.

5 Remove chicken breasts and pass the remaining chicken pieces and pork shoulder, with juices, through the finest blade of your grinder, blending in *foie gras* at the same time. Combine ground pork and pork fat with chicken mixture; stir in pistachio nuts and place pâté mixture in refrigerator to "relax" for 2–3 hours.

6 When ready to cook pâté: line a large terrine or pâté mold with thin strips of pork fat; fill a quarter full with pâté mixture; scatter diced *foie gras* over this; cover with a layer of pâté mixture and place marinated chicken breasts on this. Repeat alternate layers of pâté mixture and diced *foie gras,* ending with pâté mixture. Top with thin strips of pork fat; cover terrine and seal edges with a dough made of flour, water and salt so that no moisture escapes. Place terrine in a pan of boiling water and bake in a preheated cool oven (225–250°F) for 1 hour. Keep pâté in refrigerator for 2 days before serving.

Ingredients

1 large capon (about $3\frac{1}{2}$ lb.)
$1\frac{1}{4}$ cups dry sherry
2 tablespoons cognac
6–8 tablespoons Noilly Prat
2 tablespoons port
4 sprigs thyme
1 bay leaf
4 sprigs parsley
4 shallots, finely chopped
2 carrots, finely chopped
$\frac{1}{2}$ large onion, finely chopped
2 cloves garlic
1 teaspoon peppercorns
$\frac{1}{2}$ lb. pork fat
$\frac{1}{2}$ lb. loin of pork
2 tablespoons coarse salt
Freshly ground black pepper
$\frac{1}{2}$ lb. shoulder of pork, diced
$\frac{1}{2}$ lb. foie gras
$\frac{1}{8}$ cup pistachio nuts
Thin strips pork fat
Diced foie gras
Dough (made of flour, water and salt)

Home-made stocks—chicken and beef—are the twin basics of good cooking. Keep strained stocks in stoppered jars in the refrigerator; every 5–7 days bring stocks to the boil, cool and return to refrigerator.

Magic with Stocks and Soups

In the world of good food, nothing offers greater variety for nourishing meals than soup. Fresh-tasting, clear soups are the new fashion in France today, piled high with slivers of chicken and beef and a mosaic of crisp vegetables, or with plump slices of gently poached seafood and a fine *julienne* of crisp vegetables for flavor and color contrast. I like, too, the great peasant soups of French and Italian country cooking—one-dish dinners in fact—made of lentils and pork or game; cannellini (white kidney beans), goose and garlic, or chick peas, chicken and Spanish sausage.

Today, many of us have gardens of our own once more, and through the summer months we have learned to enjoy delicious soups made from homegrown vegetables. The new trick is to handle such vegetables almost like seasonings, in a clear meat, poultry or fish-based broth, spiked with a little dry white wine and tomato and given a last-minute pinch of fresh herbs for extra savor. Or to purée them with a little well-flavored stock and heavy cream and blend them so skilfully that, while you don't taste any one vegetable individually, the result is a triumph of country flavors.

And remember: excellent soups and stocks can be made quite simply and economically from leftovers. Bones, scraps and carcasses, vegetable tops and leaves, even vegetable peelings and trimmings of meat, poultry or game, can find their way into the soup pot to add flavor and nourishment to a meal.

Basic stocks

Stock—the liquid into which the juice and flavor of various nutritive substances have been drawn by means of long, slow cooking—serves as a foundation for most soups, stews, gravies and sauces.

Stock can be made from various ingredients; and although meat and bones, cooked or uncooked, flavored with vegetables, are the usual basics, poultry, game or fish combined with vegetables, and even vegetables alone, may all be utilized for this purpose.

Stock—especially meat stock—should always be made the day before it is to be used, as best results can be obtained only by long, slow cooking. And it is only when the stock is cold that the fat can be easily skimmed off the surface.

35

Flavoring the stock

Do not let the flavor of the vegetables overpower the flavor of the meats used in a meat, poultry or game stock; one flavor must not predominate over another. Onions, shallots, carrots, turnips and celery are the vegetables generally used, but leeks, tomatoes, parsnips and mushrooms may also be used for the darker stocks.

Vegetables are usually diced or left whole for stocks. They must not be allowed to cook too long in the stock, for after a certain time they tend to absorb flavors instead of adding to them. If a large quantity of meat is used and the stock is likely to cook for many hours, the vegetables should not be put in at the beginning of the cooking time, or they should be lifted out before the stock has finished cooking. Stock vegetables may be served as a separate vegetable dish on their own, or made into a vegetable purée, with a little butter and cream added.

Different Kinds of Stock
Brown stock
Beef, beef bones and vegetables, with sometimes a little veal or some chicken or game bones added for extra flavor.
White stock
White meat such as veal, rabbit, chicken or lamb, and vegetables, with sometimes a calf's foot added for extra flavor.
Fish stock
Fish or fish trimmings with vegetables, and sometimes shellfish trimmings added for extra flavor (see page 62).
Game stock
Game, or game bones and trimmings, and vegetables.
Vegetable stock
This is made from vegetables alone, either dried or fresh or a mixture of the two. For vegetarian soups and dishes.
Glaze
A stock which is so much reduced in quantity that it forms an almost solid substance when cold. It is a means of preserving any surplus stock.

Different Kinds of Soups
Clear soups or consommés
are made from stocks as above, but clarified by adding beaten egg white and crushed egg shells to the stock and bringing it to the boil. The impurities in the soup adhere to the egg white and shell mass and can then be strained out through a double layer of cheesecloth.
Broths
differ from clear soups in that they are unclarified. The meat or poultry or game with which they are made is served either in the soup or after it as a separate course. A broth is usually garnished with rice or barley and diced vegetables.
Thickened soups
can be made of fish, meat or vegetables. They generally have some stock as their basis. The soups are thickened with flour, arrowroot, cornstarch, tapioca or sago. In some of the richer soups, a combination of eggs and cream is used.
Purées
are perhaps the simplest and most economical kind of soup. They can be made of almost any vegetable, either fresh or dried, and of meat, game and fish. They sometimes have farinaceous substances such as rice, barley or macaroni added. A small amount of diced butter is often added at the very last moment.

Rich Chicken Stock

1 Put the chicken in a large stockpot, with the veal knuckle for its extra gelatin content, and cover with 3 quarts cold water. Add salt, to taste, and peppercorns, and bring slowly to the boil. Skim any impurities from the top of the liquid, then reduce the heat and simmer, with the liquid barely bubbling, for at least 1 hour. You will notice that the stock will begin to get cloudy. These are the essences being released from the chicken. As these bubble gently to the surface, skim them off to remove all impurities from the stock. This is one of the most important parts of soupmaking, strange as it may seem, because it is so simple. Yet this is what makes the difference between a clear stock and a cloudy stock.

2 Add sliced leeks, carrots, onion, tomatoes and celery, bouquet garni, 1 mashed garlic clove and chicken stock cube, and continue to simmer very gently for 1½–2 hours longer, or until the chicken is cooked through.

3 Remove fat, correct seasoning and then strain the stock through a fine sieve, or a piece of cheesecloth in a colander. Cool the stock and store in the refrigerator for further use.

Makes 2 quarts

Ingredients

1 chicken (about 4–5 lb.) complete with neck, feet and giblets for added flavor
1 large veal knuckle
Salt
6–8 peppercorns
2 leeks, sliced
3 large carrots, sliced
1 large onion, sliced
2 tomatoes, seeded and sliced
4 stalks celery, sliced
1 bouquet garni (2 sprigs parsley, 2 sprigs thyme and 1 bay leaf)
1 clove garlic, mashed with the point of a knife
1 chicken stock cube

Rich Beef Stock

1 Ask your butcher to remove the meat from the shin (or neck) or beef and shin of veal, and to chop the bones up into large chunks.

2 Preheat oven to very hot (475°F).

3 Trim any excess fat from the meat.

4 Put beef and veal bones, and ham bone, if available, in a roasting pan. Add roughly chopped onions and carrots and thickly sliced leeks and celery, and dot with dripping.

5 Roast bones and vegetables in the oven for 40–45 minutes, turning occasionally, until richly browned.

6 Scrape contents of roasting pan into a large saucepan, casserole or stockpot. Add boned meat, ham (if used), mushroom stalks or trimmings and soft tomatoes.

7 Add 1¼ cups cold water to roasting pan; bring it to the boil, scraping bottom and sides of pan with a wooden spoon to dislodge all the crusty bits and sediment stuck there. Pour over vegetables, then add 3 quarts cold water.

8 Place pan over a low heat and bring to the boil. Allow foam to settle into a scum on the surface; skim it off with a slotted spoon, then add a little salt (not too much—remember stock will reduce), which will draw out more scum. Skim again.

9 When all the scum has been drawn out of the meat and bones, throw in herbs, bay leaf, clove and black peppercorns, and leave stock to simmer gently for 3 hours.

10 Strain stock through a fine sieve into a large bowl and allow to cool before skimming off fat. Store until ready to be used.

Makes 2 quarts

Note: meat can be eaten with coarse salt and freshly ground black pepper, or combined with fresh vegetables to make another, less rich, portion of stock.

Ingredients

3 lb. shin or neck of beef on the bone (see Step 1)
1 lb. shin of veal on the bone (see Step 1)
1 small ham bone (about ½ lb.) or ¼ lb. lean ham
2 large onions, roughly chopped
3 large carrots, roughly chopped
2 leeks, thickly sliced
3–4 stalks celery, thickly sliced
¼ cup beef dripping
A few mushroom stalks or trimmings
2–3 soft over-ripe tomatoes
Salt
3 sprigs parsley
1 sprig thyme or a pinch of dried thyme
1 bay leaf
1 clove
9 black peppercorns

Summer Tomato Soup. This uncooked tomato soup is garnished with diced cooked ham, raw cucumber and fresh herbs for flavor and texture appeal. (Recipe, page 41)

Cream of Spinach Soup

Ingredients

2 lb. fresh spinach or 1 lb. frozen chopped spinach
4 tablespoons butter
½ pint heavy cream
1¼–1¾ cups chicken stock (see page 37)
Juice of ½ lemon
Salt and freshly ground black pepper
Finely chopped hard-boiled egg, to garnish

1 If using fresh spinach, wash leaves in several changes of cold water, nipping off any tough stems and discarding yellowed leaves. Drain well in a colander, pressing out excess moisture, and chop roughly.

2 Melt butter in a heavy saucepan; add spinach, either fresh or still in a frozen block, and simmer gently, stirring occasionally, for 8–10 minutes, or until spinach is soft.

3 Purée spinach in an electric blender. Pour back into rinsed out pan.

4 Stir in cream and dilute to taste with chicken stock, using 1¼ cups of stock if you want a very thick, rich soup; 1¾ cups for a lighter consistency. Heat through over a moderate heat, stirring.

5 Season to taste with a little lemon juice and salt and freshly ground black pepper, and serve hot, each portion garnished with a sprinkling of chopped hard-boiled egg.

Serves 6

Chinese Seafood Soup

1 Make a light fish stock by cooking bones and trimmings of sole, sliced onion and carrot and chicken stock cube in 5 cups water until vegetables are tender. Strain, reserving liquid.

2 Slice each fillet of sole in half lengthwise; tie each strip loosely into a knot; poach knotted fish strips in enough fish stock to cover until just tender.

3 Sauté halved mushrooms in vegetable oil until just tender; add shrimp and stir for 1 minute. Add dry white wine and remove from heat.

4 Cook vermicelli or thin spaghetti in boiling salted water until tender but not mushy. Drain.

5 Add sole, mushrooms and shrimp to stock; bring to the boil; add curly endive or young spinach leaves and heat through.

6 To serve: place a coil of hot cooked vermicelli or spaghetti in the bottom of each small Chinese bowl, and then ladle soup, vegetables and seafood over. Top with bean sprouts, if desired, and serve with chopsticks and a Chinese porcelain spoon.

Serves 4

Ingredients

1 small sole, filleted
Bones and trimmings from sole
1 medium onion, sliced
4 slices of carrot
1 chicken stock cube
8 button mushrooms, halved
1 tablespoon vegetable oil
8 shrimp
1 glass dry white wine
Vermicelli (or thin spaghetti)
Salt
Curly endive or young spinach leaves
Bean sprouts (optional)

Seafood Saffron Soup

1 Combine sliced onions and potatoes with milk and chicken stock cube, and cook gently until potatoes are soft. Blend in electric blender and then strain through a fine sieve.

2 Poach fish in salted water until just tender. Drain; remove the bones from the pieces of fish and keep warm.

3 Place the strained mixture over a low heat; add cream and saffron (and a little turmeric for extra color, if desired), and bring to the boil. Simmer for 5 minutes; add the pieces of fish; correct seasoning and heat through.

4 Serve soup hot, with a piece of fish in each plate, and 2 *croutons* of fried bread.

Serves 4

Ingredients

1½ lb. halibut, flounder or sole
2 medium onions, sliced
2 medium potatoes, sliced
2 cups milk
1 chicken stock cube
Salt
2½ cups heavy cream
½ teaspoon saffron
Turmeric (optional)
Freshly ground black pepper
8 croutons

Seafood Saffron Soup.

Chinese Seafood Soup

Cream of Watercress Soup

Ingredients

4 tablespoons butter
2 tablespoons olive oil
1 large onion, finely chopped
1 clove garlic, finely chopped
1 large potato, peeled and thinly sliced
Salt and freshly ground black pepper
1½ bunches watercress
1¼ cups milk
1¼ cups chicken stock (see page 37)
⅔ cup light cream
2 egg yolks

1 Heat butter and olive oil until butter is melted in a large, heavy saucepan, and sauté finely chopped onion and garlic over a moderate heat until transparent but not colored.

2 Add sliced potatoes; sprinkle with salt and freshly ground black pepper and cover with 1¼ cups water. Bring to the boil; reduce heat and simmer until potatoes are almost tender, 5–7 minutes.

3 Wash watercress carefully. Separate stems from leaves. Put about a quarter of the best leaves aside for garnish. Chop stems coarsely and add them to the simmering pan, together with remaining leaves.

4 Stir in milk and chicken stock. Bring to the boil and simmer for 15–20 minutes, or until all the vegetables are very soft.

5 Rub soup through a fine wire sieve, or purée in an electric blender. Pour back into the rinsed out saucepan; correct seasoning if necessary and reheat gently.

6 Blend cream with egg yolks. Pour into the heating soup and continue to cook, stirring continuously, until soup thickens slightly. Do not allow soup to boil once the egg yolks have been added, or they will scramble and ruin its appearance.

7 Shred reserved watercress leaves, sprinkle them over the soup and serve immediately.

Serves 6

Vichyssoise

Ingredients

6 large leeks
4 tablespoons butter
4 medium potatoes
3¾ cups chicken stock (see page 37)
Salt and freshly ground black pepper
Finely grated nutmeg
1¼ cups heavy cream
Finely chopped chives

1 Cut the green tops from the leeks and cut the white parts into 1-inch lengths.

2 Sauté the white parts gently in butter until soft. Do not allow to brown.

3 Peel and slice potatoes and add to leeks, together with chicken stock and salt and freshly ground black pepper and finely grated nutmeg, to taste, and simmer until vegetables are cooked.

4 Force the vegetables and stock through a fine sieve, or blend in an electric blender until smooth. Chill.

5 Just before serving, add cream and serve sprinkled with chives.

Serves 4–6

Green Consommé

Ingredients

8 cups well-flavored beef stock (see page 37)
1 ripe avocado
Lemon juice
6 tablespoons diced cooked green beans
6 tablespoons frozen peas
Salt and white pepper
Tabasco

1 Peel, pit and dice avocado. Strain lemon juice over diced avocado and toss well in lemon juice to preserve color.

2 Add diced cooked green beans and frozen peas to avocado. Season vegetables with salt and white pepper and toss again so that flavors permeate vegetables.

3 Bring beef stock gently to the boil. Skim, if necessary, and season with a drop or two of Tabasco.

4 When ready to serve: add prepared vegetables and bring soup to the boil again.

Serves 6–8

Provençal Vegetable Soup with Pistou

1 Soak dried cannellini beans (white kidney beans) in water overnight. Drain.

2 Simmer beans in beef stock until tender. Drain.

3 To make soup: put green beans cut in ½-inch slices, sliced small zucchini, carrots, potatoes and leeks, into 2½ quarts boiling water. Season with salt and freshly ground black pepper and let them cook fairly quickly.

4 When vegetables are cooked, add prepared cannellini beans; add *pistou* sauce and cook gently for 5 minutes more. Serve this hearty soup with grated Parmesan cheese.

Serves 6–8

Ingredients

1 lb. dried cannellini beans (white kidney beans)
6 cups beef stock (see page 37)
1 lb. green beans
2 small zucchini, sliced
4 medium-sized carrots, sliced
2 potatoes, sliced
2 leeks, sliced
Salt and freshly ground black pepper
Grated Parmesan cheese

Pistou Sauce

1 Mash garlic cloves in a mortar; remove leaves from fresh basil and add to garlic. Mash with pestle until well blended.

2 Beat olive oil into this sauce very gradually; then add grated Parmesan cheese and pound until richly colored sauce is well-blended.

Note: this highly-flavored sauce is also delicious with hard-boiled eggs, poached fish, or to flavor mayonnaise or a fish salad.

Ingredients

8 large cloves garlic
12 sprigs fresh basil
6–8 tablespoons olive oil
8 tablespoons grated Parmesan cheese

Summer Tomato Soup *(Illustration, page 38)*

1 Quarter tomatoes and blend to a purée in an electric blender; put purée through a fine sieve.

2 Stir in lemon juice and rind, sugar, grated onion and salt, to taste. Chill.

3 Just before serving, add chilled heavy cream; mix well; pour into a bowl and garnish with diced ham, cucumber and finely chopped parsley.

Serves 4–6

Ingredients

6 large ripe tomatoes
Juice and finely grated rind of 1 lemon
4 teaspoons sugar
1–1½ tablespoons grated onion
Salt
1¼ cups heavy cream, chilled
½ lb. ham, cut into ¼-inch dice
½ lb. cucumber, peeled, seeded and cut into ¼-inch dice
4 tablespoons finely chopped parsley

Gazpacho—iced Spanish soup

According to Brillat-Savarin, a woman who can't make soup should not be allowed to marry. The Spanish solved this ticklish problem early in their history with *gazpacho,* a chilled summer soup that requires absolutely no cooking.

To make *gazpacho:* blend 6 tomatoes and 1 garlic clove in electric blender; add 1 to 2 tablespoons juice from a finely grated onion, and ½ cucumber, peeled, seeded and cut into cubes, to mixture and blend again. Strain into a large tureen or serving bowl and chill.

Just before serving, blend 6 tablespoons olive oil, 4 tablespoons lemon juice and 2 cups chilled tomato juice; add to puréed vegetables, mix well and season with salt and cayenne pepper, to taste.

Serve *gazpacho* with individual bowls of raw vegetables—diced tomatoes, onion, cucumber and green pepper—and fried garlic-flavored *croûtons*.

Try the basic recipe for *gazpacho* and then vary the ingredients by stirring in 2 to 4 tablespoons of fresh breadcrumbs, or a little well-flavored mayonnaise, finely ground almonds or the beaten yolk of an egg. Or add a little gelatin and serve it slightly jelled.

New Ways with Sauces

In French cooking, the word *sauce* means any liquid or semi-liquid that complements a dish—the lightly thickened gravy that inevitably accompanies the Sunday roast; the cream sauce for a steamed cauliflower; the melted butter and lemon dressing for a grilled or poached fish; and the many salad dressings with which we are all familiar—from a simple vinaigrette sauce to a mustard and lemon-flavored mayonnaise.

In other words, sauces—no matter how simple—are important in cooking.

But don't make the mistake of thinking that sauces should always be thick and rich. The modern thought in France is to use as little flour in cooking as possible—this makes the sauce more delicate in flavor, more suave in texture and more easily assimilated by the digestive system.

The heart of every sauce is its flavorsome stock, which is made by reducing home-made meat, poultry or fish broth to a concentrated essence, before adding it to the sauce. The liquid ingredient of the sauce—whether it is home-made beef stock, stock made from veal, fish or poultry, or more simply milk or cream—is most important to the final quality and flavor of your finished sauce.

In French cooking terminology, reduction is a magic word. Magic only because this terribly simple process (it just means cooking stocks over a high heat to reduce them to a third or quarter of their original quantity before adding them to the sauce) gives such intensity of flavor to the finished sauce.

It is no secret that French chefs use more liquid in their sauces—almost twice as much—and consequently cook them longer than do most other cooks; and, as a result of this concentration and blending of flavors, their sauces are more suave, more transparent, and consequently more delicious.

The secret of easy sauce-making, therefore, is the careful reduction of your sauce by slow simmering over a low heat, leaving the sauce thicker in consistency, smoother in texture and more concentrated in flavor.

Stuffed Fillets of Sole with Shrimp,
Sauce Hollandaise. (Recipe, page 67)

A flavorsome sauce trio. (Sauce recipes,
begin on page 45)

To strain sauce

Always strain all sauces before serving, except, of course, those which have chopped ingredients in them. A conical strainer is best, as it is easier to direct the flow of the liquid. For a finer sauce, line the strainer with a clean cloth to give a smooth, glossy appearance.

To add butter to a sauce

French chefs often incorporate finely diced butter into a sauce just before serving. The butter is usually whisked into the strained sauce with a wire whisk after the sauce has been taken off the heat. This makes the sauce thicker and more flavorsome. Do not return the sauce to the heat after the butter has been whisked into it, or it will separate and become fatty.

To keep sauces warm

When a sauce has to stand for some time before serving, place the saucepan containing it in a larger one with hot, not boiling, water, or in a bain-marie, and cover the saucepan to prevent a skin forming. With thicker sauces, a spoonful of liquid—water, stock or milk—or melted butter may be run over the top. Just before serving, whisk this protective covering into the sauce.

White sauces

Are you frightened of making sauces? Many of my friends tell me they are, and I don't really know why, for making a classic French sauce is very easy. Sauce Béchamel, for instance, the classic white sauce of French cooking, goes way back in culinary history to the time of Louis XIV of France. It is the Marquis de Béchamel, Louis' Maître d'Hôtel who ran the royal palace at Versailles, who has been given the credit for creating this sauce. At any rate, it was named after him because he was a famous gourmet. Cooks of the time were apt to name their dishes after their patron whether or not he himself actually created it.

In the days of the Marquis de Béchamel, the sauce was more complicated than it is now. The original sauce Béchamel combined a patridge, ham, chicken and perhaps a guinea fowl to flavor the rich, creamed sauce we know today.

Variations on the Béchamel theme

Add a touch of mustard and a tablespoon of capers and you have a mustard and caper sauce. Then add a little finely chopped fresh herbs and you have a terrific sauce for eggs, fish and even poached lamb.

Stir a little tomato purée, either fresh or canned, into the basic sauce to give it a pale blush, flavor it with a little Madeira or brandy and add a touch of cream to make it just that much richer. You'll find this a very subtle sauce for poached fish, boiled eggs and steamed vegetables.

Or, for another, more exotic variation, add a little lobster butter to the above sauce. Lobster butter is easily prepared from cooked lobster shells, pounded in a mortar and then simmered in $\frac{1}{2}$ cup butter with a bay leaf, 1 medium onion, a little bit of garlic, some tomato purée and some brandy. Chill the sauce in the refrigerator and then just skim off the top of your juices and you have lobster butter. So don't throw away those lobster shells. Keep them in the refrigerator to give a wonderful buttery richness to your sauces for poached fish.

Professional cooks use a spoonful of *glace de viande* (see page 48) to swirl into the pan juices of cooked meats to create a deliciously limpid sauce in a twinkling. This cook's aid keeps indefinitely in a stoppered jar in the refrigerator, and is well worth the trouble and expense involved. Use only a teaspoon or two with an equal quantity of lemon juice to create a delicious sauce from the pan juices of

---

To keep sauces

Velouté, brown and tomato sauces, like stocks, can be kept in covered jars in the refrigerator for 1 week. Seal jars by pouring a little melted fat over the sauce. If you want to keep your sauces longer, bring to the boil after 7 days and return to the refrigerator in a clean covered jar.

Sauces containing milk, cream or eggs should be stored in the refrigerator for only 1 or 2 days.

grilled or pan-fried steaks, chops, liver or kidneys. I like, too, to whisk a bit into melted butter with almonds or pine nuts before tossing this simple sauce with cooked noodles or rice as an accompaniment to meat, fish or poultry. And it is an invaluable "strengthener" for beef and game soups and consommés.

Butter always contains a little milk which, when brought to a high heat, is apt to make a sauce "gritty" or slightly discolored. I usually clarify butter before using it for the more delicate sauces by melting it in a small, thick-bottomed, enamelled saucepan over a very low heat. The butter foams, and the foam falls gently to the bottom of the saucepan, leaving the clarified butter as clear as oil. Be careful when you decant this transparent liquid not to disturb any of the sediment at the bottom. Use as directed.

Basic Sauce Béchamel

1 In a thick-bottomed saucepan, or in the top of a double boiler, melt 2 tablespoons butter and cook onion in it over a low heat until transparent. Stir in flour and cook for a few minutes, stirring constantly, until mixture cooks through but does not take on color.

2 Add hot milk and cook, stirring constantly, until the mixture is thick and smooth.

3 In another saucepan, simmer finely chopped lean veal or ham in 1 tablespoon butter over a very low heat. Season with thyme, bay leaf, white peppercorns and grated nutmeg, to taste. Cook for 5 minutes, stirring to keep veal or ham from over-browning.

4 Add meat to the sauce and cook over hot water for 45 minutes to 1 hour, stirring occasionally. When reduced to the proper consistency (two-thirds of the original quantity), strain sauce through a fine sieve into a bowl, pressing meat and onion well to extract all the liquid. Cover surface of sauce with tiny pieces of butter to keep film from forming.

Ingredients
Butter
1 medium onion, minced
2 tablespoons flour
2½ cups hot milk
2 tablespoons lean veal or ham, finely chopped
1 small sprig thyme
½ bay leaf
White peppercorns
Freshly grated nutmeg

Mornay Sauce

1 In a thick-bottomed saucepan, or in the top of a double boiler, melt 2 tablespoons butter and cook onion in it over a low heat until transparent. Stir in flour and cook for a few minutes, stirring constantly, until mixture cooks through but does not take on color.

2 Add hot milk and cook, stirring constantly, until the mixture is thick and smooth.

3 In another saucepan, simmer finely chopped lean veal or ham in 1 tablespoon butter over a very low heat. Season with thyme, bay leaf, white peppercorns and grated nutmeg, to taste. Cook for 5 minutes, stirring to keep veal from browning.

4 Add veal to the sauce and cook over hot water for 45 minutes to 1 hour, stirring occasionally. When reduced to the proper consistency (two-thirds of the original quantity), strain sauce through a fine sieve into a bowl, pressing meat and onion well to extract all the liquid.

5 Mix slightly beaten egg yolks with a little cream and combine with sauce. Cook, stirring constantly, until it just reaches boiling point; add 2 tablespoons butter and grated cheese. Cover surface of sauce with tiny pieces of butter to keep film from forming.

Ingredients
Butter
1 medium onion, minced
2 tablespoons flour
2½ cups hot milk
2 tablespoons lean veal or ham, finely chopped
1 small sprig thyme
½ bay leaf
White peppercorns
Freshly grated nutmeg
2 egg yolks, slightly beaten
Cream
2–3 tablespoons grated cheese (Parmesan cheese or Swiss cheese)

Celery Sauce

Ingredients
6 stalks celery, finely sliced
1¼ cups chicken stock (see page 37)
2 tablespoons butter
2 tablespoons flour
⅔ cup heavy cream
2 tablespoons finely chopped parsley
Celery salt
Freshly ground black pepper
Lemon juice

1 Combine finely sliced celery and chicken stock in a saucepan and cook until celery is soft. Keep warm.

2 In the top of a double boiler, melt butter. Add flour and cook gently over a low heat, stirring, until roux turns a pale golden color.

3 Add hot celery stock (including celery) and cook over simmering water, stirring occasionally and skimming surface from time to time, until sauce has reduced to two-thirds of the original quantity.

4 Stir in heavy cream; add finely chopped parsley; correct seasoning, adding a little celery salt, freshly ground black pepper and lemon juice, to taste.

Little Soufflés With Celery Sauce

Ingredients

LITTLE SOUFFLÉS

Butter
4 tablespoons flour
1¼ cups milk
¾ cup freshly grated Gruyère cheese
4 egg yolks
Salt and freshly ground black pepper
Pinch of grated nutmeg
8 egg whites

CELERY SAUCE

6 stalks celery
2½ cups chicken stock (see page 37)
2 tablespoons butter
2 tablespoons flour
⅔ cup heavy cream
2 tablespoons finely chopped parsley
celery salt
freshly ground black pepper
lemon juice

1 Melt 6 tablespoons butter in the top of a double boiler over direct heat. Blend in flour smoothly and cook over a low heat, stirring constantly, for about 3 minutes, or until flour is thoroughly blended into butter. Remove from heat and leave butter mixture to cool slightly.

2 Bring milk to the boil in a separate pan; gradually add hot milk to the butter *roux*, stirring vigorously with a wire whisk to prevent lumps forming. Bring to the boil and simmer over water for 3 minutes, stirring all the time. When soufflé mixture is smooth and well blended, stir in all but 3 tablespoons of grated Gruyère cheese, blend together and remove pan from heat. Cool mixture slightly and beat in egg yolks, 1 at a time. Season with salt and freshly ground black pepper, to taste, and a pinch of grated nutmeg; keep soufflé mixture warm.

3 Preheat oven to hot (450°F).

4 Make Celery Sauce (see page 46).

5 Put Celery Sauce into a large metal-handled chafing dish, or frying pan. Bring to the boil. Take off heat and keep warm.

6 Butter 6 individual oval pie dishes.

7 Select a bowl, make sure it is clean and dry. Put egg whites into it; add a pinch of salt and beat until stiff but not dry. Stir a large dollop (about 3 heaped tablespoons) of the beaten egg whites into the tepid soufflé mixture, then fold in remainder with a spatula, or a metal spoon, working as quickly and lightly as you can.

8 With a large spoon, spoon soufflé mixture into individual pie dishes and put into preheated oven for about 10 to 15 minutes, or until soufflés are well risen. Remove pie dishes from oven and turn soufflés gently upside down into large metal handled chafing dish, or frying pan, using a spoon to ease them out carefully, if necessary.

9 Sprinkle top of soufflés with remaining grated Gruyère cheese and put back into hot oven for a few more minutes, or until they are puffed and lightly golden colored. Serve immediately.

Serves 6

Ingredients for a classic sauce Béchamel. (Recipe, page 45)

Basic Sauce Espagnole

1 Heat butter in a thick-bottomed saucepan until it browns. Add thinly sliced onion and simmer, stirring constantly, until golden. Stir in flour and cook, stirring constantly, for a minute or two longer. The good color of your sauce depends upon the thorough browning of these ingredients without allowing them to burn.

2 Remove saucepan from the heat and pour in the stock; return to heat and stir until it comes to the boil. Allow to boil for 5 minutes, skimming all scum from the top with a perforated spoon.

3 Wash and slice carrot, turnip, celery, mushrooms and tomatoes or tomato purée, and add them with the bouquet garni, cloves, peppercorns, and salt, to taste. Simmer the sauce gently for at least ½ hour, stirring occasionally and skimming when necessary. Strain through a fine sieve; remove fat; reheat before serving.

Ingredients
2 tablespoons butter
1 small onion, thinly sliced
2 tablespoons flour
2¼ cups well-flavored brown stock
1 small carrot
1 small turnip
1 stalk celery or ¼ teaspoon celery seed
4 mushrooms
2–4 tomatoes or 1–2 tablespoons tomato purée
1 bouquet garni (3 sprigs parsley, 1 sprig thyme and 1 bay leaf)
2 cloves
12 black peppercorns
Salt

Madeira Sauce

1 Reduce sauce *espagnole* until it is half the original quantity.

2 Add Madeira. Heat the sauce well, but do not let it boil, or the flavor of the wine will be lost.

Ingredients
2½ cups sauce espagnole (see above)
6 tablespoons Madeira

47

Glace de Viande

Ingredients

8 lb. beef and veal bones
1 large onion, cut in half
1–2 chicken carcasses
2–3 carrots, cut in 2-inch segments
3–4 celery stalks and leaves, cut in 2-inch segments
4 medium onions, cut in quarters
6–8 tablespoons beef dripping
2 cups canned peeled tomatoes

Note: use half quantities of the above if you do not have a very large stockpot

1 Ask your butcher to supply you with 8 lb. beef and veal bones, with some meat on them, chopped into 4–6 inch segments. You'll have to give him warning.

2 Sear cut sides of onion in a large thick-bottomed frying pan, using no fat. Onion should be very dark on cut surface.

3 Brown the bones, together with 1 or 2 chicken carcasses, carrots, celery and onions, in beef dripping.

4 When bones and vegetables are well browned, transfer them to a very large stockpot or a large deep casserole. Fill the pot with unsalted water; add charred onion halves and peeled tomatoes and simmer bones and vegetables over the lowest of heats, or in the oven, for 18–24 hours.

5 Strain out the bones and vegetables; return stock to a clean stockpot and cook until it is reduced to half or less of the original quantity, skimming off fat and impurities as they rise to the surface of the stock.

6 Strain reduced stock into a clean saucepan through cheesecloth-lined sieve and cook again, stirring frequently, until it is very thick. Pour into jars, cool, and then store in the refrigerator until ready to use.

Glace de viande keeps for months in the refrigerator.

A Quick Meat Glaze

A good *glace de viande* or savory meat glaze is not difficult to make, but it is expensive and takes more time to prepare than most home cooks, however enthusiastic, are prepared to give.

To make A Quick Meat Glaze: take a 15-oz. can of the best quality canned consommé that you can find; add 1 large onion and 2 tomatoes, finely chopped, and boil it fast until reduced to half its original quantity. Strain the sauce into a clean pan and reduce to just 3 to 6 tablespoons of dark glaze.

Basic Sauce Béarnaise

Ingredients

3 sprigs tarragon, coarsely chopped
3 sprigs chervil, coarsely chopped
1 tablespoon chopped shallots
2 black peppercorns, crushed
2 tablespoons tarragon vinegar
⅔ cup dry white wine
3 egg yolks
1 cup butter, diced
Salt
Lemon juice
Cayenne pepper

Like its near cousin, Hollandaise sauce, the secret of successful Béarnaise is never to let the water in the bottom of the double boiler boil, or the sauce will not "take." Sauce Béarnaise is the perfect accompaniment to grilled steak; try it, too, with grilled, poached or fried fish.

1 Combine coarsely chopped herbs, chopped shallots, crushed black peppercorns, tarragon vinegar and dry white wine in the top of a double boiler. Bring to the boil and cook over a high heat until liquid is reduced to about 2 tablespoons in the bottom of the pan. Remove from heat.

2 Beat egg yolks with a tablespoon of water and combine with reduced liquid in the top of the double boiler. Stir briskly with a wire whisk over hot but not boiling water until light and fluffy.

3 Add pieces of butter to egg mixture one at a time, whisking briskly until completely incorporated. As sauce begins to thicken, increase the butter to several pieces at a time, whisking it in thoroughly as before until sauce is thick.

4 Season to taste with salt, lemon juice and cayenne pepper.

5 Strain sauce through a fine sieve and serve.

Hollandaise Sauce

1 Combine 1 teaspoon of lemon juice, 1 tablespoon cold water and salt and white pepper in the top of a double boiler or bainmarie.

2 Divide butter into four equal pieces.

3 Add the egg yolks and a quarter of the butter to the liquid in the saucepan, and stir the mixture rapidly and constantly with a wire whisk over hot, but not boiling, water until the butter is melted and the mixture begins to thicken. Add the second piece of butter and continue whisking. As the mixture thickens and the second piece of butter melts, add the third piece of butter, stirring from the bottom of the pan until it is melted. Be careful not to allow the water over which the sauce is cooking to boil at any time. Add rest of butter, beating until it melts and is incorporated in the sauce.

4 Remove top part of double boiler from heat and continue to beat for 2–3 minutes. Replace double boiler over hot, but not boiling, water for 2 minutes more, beating constantly. By this time the emulsion should have formed and your sauce will be rich and creamy. "Finish" sauce with a few drops of lemon juice. Strain and serve.

Note: if at any time in the operation the mixture should curdle, beat in 1 or 2 tablespoons cold water to rebind the emulsion.

Ingredients

Lemon juice
Salt and white pepper
1 cup softened butter
4 egg yolks
Lemon juice

Mayonnaise

1 Place egg yolks (make sure gelatinous thread of the egg is removed), salt and freshly ground black pepper and mustard in a bowl. Twist a cloth wrung out in very cold water round the bottom of the bowl to keep it steady and cool. Using a wire whisk, fork or wooden spoon, beat the yolks to a smooth paste.

2 Add a little lemon juice (the acid helps the emulsion), and beat in about a quarter of the olive oil, drop by drop. Add a little more lemon juice to the mixture and then, a little more quickly now, add more olive oil, beating all the while. Continue adding olive oil and beating until the sauce is of a good thick consistency. Correct seasoning (more salt, freshly ground black pepper and lemon juice) as desired. If you are making the mayonnaise a day before using it, stir in 1 tablespoon boiling water when it is of the desired consistency. This will keep it from turning or separating.

Notes: if the mayonnaise should curdle, break another egg yolk into a clean bowl and gradually beat the curdled mayonnaise into it. Your mayonnaise will begin to "take" immediately.

If mayonnaise is to be used for a salad, thin it down considerably with dry white wine, vinegar or lemon juice. If it is to be used for coating meat, poultry or fish, add a little liquid aspic to stiffen it.

If mayonnaise is to be kept for several hours before serving, cover the bowl with a cloth wrung out in very cold water to prevent a skin from forming.

Ingredients

2 egg yolks
Salt and freshly ground
    black pepper
½ teaspoon Dijon mustard
Lemon juice
1¼ cups olive oil

Cucumber Cream

1 Flavor whipped cream with salt and lemon juice, to taste.

2 Peel, seed and dice cucumber, fold into the cream and chill until ready to use.

Ingredients

⅔ cup heavy cream,
    whipped
Salt
Lemon juice
½ cucumber

Egg Dishes, Omelettes and Soufflés

The greatest virtue of the egg to most of us today is that it is always there, handy in the refrigerator, ready to lend its sophisticated magic to delicate little ramekins of eggs and cream, light and insubstantial soufflés and moistly golden omelettes whenever there are unexpected guests.

We depend on the egg—one of the great basics of all cookery—to enrich and flavor chicken soups and sauces; to bind croquettes, meat loaves, and stuffings for meat, poultry and game; to coat meat, fish and vegetables for deep-frying; to add substance to batters and richness to cakes and pastry, and to act as the foundation for sauces made from butter and oil—mayonnaise, sauce Hollandaise and sauce Béarnaise (see pages 48 and 49).

I like to use raw eggs to dress a salad, and to add color and quality to a spaghetti sauce. Even the shell can be used to clarify consommés and jellies.

Scrambled eggs

Most of us today think of scrambled eggs as a breakfast dish to be served with crisp slices of bacon or diminutive sausages sautéed until golden. But in France scrambled eggs can be a dish of creamy perfection, worthy of being served as a first course on its own at a luncheon party of distinction. I remember a remarkable luncheon at the elegant Plaza-Athénée in Paris, which started off with a delicious verson of scrambled eggs (3 eggs per person cooked in butter until soft and moist) mixed with diced truffles and asparagus, and piled into a golden *croustade* of flaky pastry surrounded by individual molds of ham mousse and asparagus tips. Elegant and different, and yet, except for the diced truffles and the ham mousses, not too extravagant or difficult to make.

Taking a leaf from the Plaza-Athénée's book, I have often served small, hot pastry shells filled just before serving with scrambled eggs lightly flavored with a little grated Parmesan cheese, and tossed with diced ham and mushrooms simmered in butter. Try this, too, with thin slivers of sliced smoked salmon or flaked smoked trout and sliced radishes.

The omelette

Brillat-Savarin, giving a recipe for an omelette made with blanched carp's roe, tuna, shallot, parsley, chives and lemon juice, recommends: "This dish should be reserved for breakfasts of refinement, for connoisseurs in gastronomic art—those who understand eating—and where all eat with judgment; but especially let it be washed down with some good old wine, and you will see wonders."

Omelette Ratatouille. (Recipe, page 56)

Facing page *Eggs—a beautiful still-life by John Stewart.*

The most important thing to remember in omelette-making—indeed in all preparations based on eggs—is that only strictly fresh eggs should be used, and that the butter must be of the best quality.

The first essential of successful omelette-making is a good pan. I keep a pan exclusively for eggs. It is a pan expressly designed for omelettes—one of good weight, with rounded sides so that the omelette can slide easily onto the plate when cooked. The best omelette pans are made of copper, steel or aluminum.

The size of the pan is important. It must not be too small or too large for the number of eggs used in the omelette. Unless it is well proportioned to the number of eggs generally used, the omelette will either be unmanageably thick or too thin. I find a pan 7 or 8 inches in diameter is just about right for a 4- to 5-egg omelette.

Never wash your omelette pan. Instead, just rub it clean after use with paper towels and a few drops of oil, then rub it dry with a clean cloth. If any egg adheres to the pan, it can be rubbed off with a little dry salt.

Once you have mastered the recipe for the basic omelette—*omelette nature,* the French call it—you are ready to try some of the many exciting variations on the omelette theme. Some of the most delicious are the easiest to make—but always remember to prepare the omelette filling before you make the omelette itself. In this way, your omelettes can come to the table crisply cased, with a wonderfully moist interior and filling. And always serve your omelette as soon as it is cooked, as the most successful omelette will spoil and toughen if kept waiting. It is far better to let your guests wait for the omelette than to let the omelette wait for the guests.

Soufflés
Soufflés, technically speaking, can be divided into three definite categories: the *soufflé de cuisine*—the famous savory soufflé of France—makes the perfect beginning to a meal, whether it is a simple cheese affair (try a combination of Gruyère cheese and Parmesan cheese), a concoction of fish or shellfish, or one made with a well-seasoned base of puréed vegetables (endive, onion, or mushroom and cheese). Savory soufflés can also make light-as-air entreés to dramatize a luncheon or supper party, for here you can let your imagination run riot. I remember one such superb duck soufflé, served to me in Rome, whose creamy interior was stuffed with olives stuffed in their turn with *pâté de foie gras.*

Why not experiment? What do you risk? The basic soufflé mixture of flour, butter, milk, eggs and grated cheese remains the same whether you add a cupful of diced kippers, chicken, lobster or sole.

Category number two in our soufflé line-up is the *soufflé d'entremets;* the choice is limitless. Chocolate, coffee, vanilla; *soufflé aux liqueurs;* or the whole gamut of sweet soufflés based on purées of fresh or cooked fruits (strawberries, raspberries, cherries, cranberries, or the sharp tang of lemon and orange, and the more muted note of mandarins).

Our third category, the *soufflé froid,* is not really a soufflé at all, but a molded mousse made with a base of whipped cream and gelatin, and served in round molds or soufflé dishes. Tie a strip of paper round the top of the dish to permit the mixture to be piled high above the edge, and *voilà,* when the paper is removed it gives the illusion of a real soufflé.

Soufflés are perfectly easy to make if you follow a few basic rules.

1 A rich, smooth sauce is the basis of all soufflés—a thick sauce Béchamel for a savory soufflé (see page 45), a *crème pâtissière* for a sweet soufflé (see page 160).

2 The egg yolks must be beaten one by one into the hot sauce after the saucepan is removed from the heat, or they will curdle.

3 The egg whites must be beaten until stiff but not dry. In separating eggs, be sure there is no speck of yolk left in the whites, or you will not be able to beat your whites stiff.

4 A slow to moderate oven (325–350°F) is an essential for a perfect soufflé. If your oven is too hot, the soufflé will be well cooked on the top and undercooked inside.

5 Sweet soufflés should be softer than entrée or vegetable soufflés.

6 A soufflé must never be too liquid before it goes into the oven. The addition of the beaten egg whites should just about double the volume of your mixture. Cooking will double it again.

7 Finally, a soufflé must be eaten immediately.

Eggs Lucullus—for Special Occasions

1 Peel eggs, then cut each egg in half lengthwise and arrange, cut side down, on a porcelain serving dish. Garnish each egg with a small leaf of lettuce and 2 tomato wedges.

2 Blend mayonnaise with sour cream and mask each half-egg completely with a tablespoon of mayonnaise, tapping the bottom of the dish if the mayonnaise does not flow smoothly over the egg of its own accord.

3 Dot top of each egg with a few grains of caviar and chill lightly until ready to serve.

Serves 4

Ingredients
4 hard-boiled eggs
4 small lettuce leaves
8 tomato wedges
8 tablespoons well-flavored mayonnaise
4 tablespoons sour cream
2 teaspoons black caviar, or, for simpler occasions, red caviar

Eggs in Aspic *(Illustration, page 57)*

1 Stir Madeira into liquid aspic jelly and pour a thin layer over base of each of 4 individual molds.

2 Pour boiling water over tarragon leaves; dry and arrange on aspic. Place 2–4 thin strips of ham across leaves, and dribble a little aspic over them to hold them in place.

3 Trim poached eggs with scissors and place in molds. Pour aspic over them to cover. Garnish, if desired, with cold cooked peas and diced cooked turnip and carrot. Cover with aspic. Chill. Unmold just before serving.

Serves 4

Ingredients
2 tablespoons Madeira
2½ cups liquid aspic jelly
8–10 fresh tarragon leaves
1 slice cooked ham, cut en julienne
4 poached eggs
2 teaspoons each cold cooked peas, diced cooked turnip and diced cooked carrot (optional)

Fried Eggs

1 Melt butter in a small frying pan.

2 Break 1 egg at a time into a cup; season with salt and freshly ground black pepper; slide eggs quickly into the sizzling butter and cook for 1–2 minutes, or until done as you like them. Lift out with a spatula or a perforated spoon; drain and serve immediately.

Serves 1

Ingredients
2 eggs
1 tablespoon butter
Salt and freshly ground black pepper

Oeufs sur le Plat

Ingredients

8 eggs
2 tablespooons butter
Salt and freshly black
 pepper

1 Lightly butter 4 flat ovenproof dishes and break the eggs into them without breaking the yolks. Season with salt and freshly ground black pepper, and place the remaining butter in small pieces on the top.

2 Bake in a preheated slow oven (325°F) for 4–5 minutes, or until the whites are set but not hard. Serve hot in the dishes in which the eggs were cooked.

Serves 4

Baked Eggs with Cream

Ingredients

⅔ cup heavy cream
2 tablespoons freshly
 grated Gruyère cheese
2 tablespoons lemon juice
2 tablespoons dry white
 wine
1–2 teaspoons prepared
 mustard
Salt and freshly black
 pepper
8 eggs
Butter
Buttered breadcrumbs

1 Mix together heavy cream, grated cheese, lemon juice and dry white wine; add mustard and salt and freshly ground black pepper, to taste.

2 Break eggs into individual buttered ramekins or casseroles, 2 eggs in each.

3 Cover the eggs with the sauce and sprinkle buttered breadcrumbs over the top. Place ramekins in a pan of hot water and bake in a preheated moderate oven (375°F) for about 15 minutes.

Serves 4

Spanish Tortilla, delicious served hot or cold. (Recipe, page 57)

Scrambled Eggs Provençal *(Illustration, page 56)*

1 Break the eggs into a mixing bowl; add salt and freshly ground black pepper, and cayenne pepper, to taste, and mix lightly with a fork.

2 Cut white bread into rounds about 4 inches in diameter and sauté lightly in a little butter and olive oil until just golden. Keep warm.

3 Scramble the eggs in butter and olive oil until they are just soft. Not too firm.

4 Spoon the scrambled eggs onto the fried toast rounds and garnish with a latticework of thin anchovy strips. Fill each lattice with half a black olive and sprinkle with finely chopped parsley.

Serves 6

Ingredients
9 eggs
Salt and freshly ground black pepper
Cayenne pepper
6 slices white bread
Butter
Olive oil
12 anchovy fillets, sliced in half lengthwise
Black olives, halved
3 tablespoons finely chopped parsley

Scrambled Eggs with Asparagus Tips and Ham

1 Break eggs into a bowl. Add salt and freshly ground black pepper, to taste, and stir well with a fork (don't beat) until yolks and whites are thoroughly mixed. Stir in heavy cream.

2 Melt 1 tablespoon butter in the pan in which you intend to scramble eggs. Add chopped asparagus tips and ham, and toss over a gentle heat for 1 or 2 minutes until thoroughly hot.

3 Pour in eggs all at once; set pan over a low heat and immediately start stirring with a large wooden spoon. Keep stirring, making sure the spoon reaches the corners of the pan and keeping the whole mass of liquid egg on the move, until eggs are creamy and almost ready.

4 Remove pan from the heat and stir for a few seconds longer until eggs are ready. Then fold in a few flakes of cold butter (½ teaspoon). Correct seasoning with a little more salt and freshly ground black pepper if necessary, and serve at once on a hot plate, or container of your choice.

Serves 1 generously

Ingredients
3 eggs
Salt and freshly ground black pepper
1 tablespoon heavy cream
Butter
3 canned asparagus tips, chopped
2 tablespoons finely chopped ham

Scrambled Eggs with Buttered Shrimp and Mushrooms

1 Wash or wipe mushrooms clean; trim stems and slice mushrooms. Sauté in 2 tablespoons butter for 5 minutes until softened. Stir in buttered shrimp and keep warm.

2 Beat eggs lightly in a bowl with cream, milk or water—just enough to mix them. (Water will make extremely fluffy eggs; cream gives a richer, smoother texture.)

3 Slip prebaked pastry shells into a moderate oven (350°F) to heat through.

4 Melt remaining butter in a large, heavy saucepan (about 8 inches in diameter). When butter is hot but not brown, pour in eggs and cook over low heat, stirring constantly with a wooden spoon, until eggs are just on the point of setting. Add sautéed mushrooms, shrimp and salt and freshly ground black pepper, to taste, at the halfway stage.

5 As soon as eggs are on the point of setting, remove pan from heat. Divide mixture among pastry shells and serve immediately.

Serves 6

Ingredients
6 oz. button mushrooms
½ cup butter
4–6 oz. buttered shrimp
12 eggs
6 tablespoons cream, milk or water
6 3-inch pastry shells, prebaked (see page 156)
Salt and freshly ground black pepper

Omelette Ratatouille *(Illustration, page 50)*

Ingredients

- 8 tablespoons olive oil
- 1 large onion, sliced
- 1 green pepper, diced
- 1 eggplant, diced
- 2 small zucchini, cut in thin slices
- 2–4 ripe tomatoes, peeled, seeded and chopped
- Salt and freshly ground black pepper
- 1 tablespoon chopped parsley
- Pinch of marjoram or oregano
- Pinch of basil
- 1 clove garlic, crushed
- 8 eggs
- 1–2 tablespoons melted butter

1 Heat half the olive oil in an oven-proof casserole; add onion slices and sauté until they are transparent. Add diced green pepper and eggplant and, 5 minutes later, zucchini and tomatoes. The vegetables should not be fried but simmered gently in a covered pan for about 30 minutes.

2 Add salt and freshly ground black pepper, to taste, chopped parsley, marjoram or oregano, basil and crushed garlic; then cook uncovered for about 10–15 minutes, or until ratatouille is well mixed.

3 Beat eggs lightly with a fork. Season to taste with salt and freshly ground black pepper.

4 Heat remaining oil in a large omelette pan; pour in eggs and stir over a moderate heat until they begin to thicken and have set underneath.

5 Spoon ratatouille mixture down center, reserving 2 or 3 tablespoons for garnish.

6 Continue to cook omelette until firm and golden brown on the underside but still creamy on top; then slide it up one side of the pan and fold it over on itself.

7 Slip folded omelette out carefully onto a heated serving dish. Brush with melted butter and garnish with remaining ratatouille mixture. Serve immediately.

Serves 2–3 generously

Poached Eggs Florentine. (Recipe, page 59)

Scrambled Eggs Provençal. (Recipe, page 55)

Spanish Tortilla *(Illustration, page 54)*

1 Heat 2 tablespoons olive oil in a medium-sized frying pan; add diced potatoes, coarsely chopped onion and pepper and cook, stirring constantly, until the vegetables are soft. Season generously with salt and freshly ground black pepper. Keep warm.

2 Season well-beaten eggs to taste with salt and freshly ground black pepper. Heat 2 tablespoons olive oil in a large frying pan; pour beaten eggs into the pan, lifting up edges of the eggs with a spatula to allow uncooked egg to run under. Add sautéed vegetables, and continue to cook, lifting up tortilla with a spatula, until omelette has a golden crust on the bottom. Then place a large plate on the omelette pan and invert pan so that omelette is on plate, crust side up.

3 Scrape free any crusty bits from pan; add a little more olive oil; return omelette to pan, moist side down, and continue to cook until omelette has browned on both sides. Cut in wedges and serve.

Serves 4–6

Ingredients
Olive oil
2 potatoes, peeled and diced
1 medium onion, coarsely chopped
½ green or red pepper, coarsely chopped
Salt and freshly ground black pepper
6–8 eggs, well beaten

Zucchini Frittata

1 Sauté finely chopped onion in 4 tablespoons olive oil in a large thick-bottomed frying pan until onion is soft and transparent. Remove onion from pan with a slotted spoon.

2 Add thinly sliced zucchini to pan and sauté, stirring constantly, until zucchini are cooked through.

3 Combine onion and zucchini in a bowl with beaten eggs. Add salt and freshly ground black pepper, to taste.

4 Melt 2 tablespoons butter in 2 tablespoons olive oil in a large frying pan. Pour in *frittata* mixture and cook *frittata*, proceeding as you would when making an omelette, slowly on one side until brown; add a little more butter before turning to cook other side.

5 Slip cooked *frittata* onto a heated serving dish and sprinkle with chopped fresh herbs.

Serves 4

Ingredients
1 large onion, finely chopped
Olive oil
2 zucchini, thinly sliced
6–8 eggs
Salt and freshly ground black pepper
Butter
1–2 tablespoons chopped fresh parsley or chives

Eggs in Aspic. (Recipe, page 53)

Souffléed Breakfast Egg. (Recipe, page 59)

Basic Cheese Soufflé

Ingredients

Butter
2 tablespoons flour
1¼ cups hot milk
5 egg yolks
1½–2¼ cups grated cheese
Salt and freshly ground
    black pepper
6 egg whites

1 Melt 2 tablespoons butter in the top of a double boiler; add flour gradually and mix to a smooth paste, stirring constantly. Add hot milk and cook until sauce is smooth and thick. Remove from heat and add egg yolks one by one, alternately with grated cheese. Mix well and return to heat. Cook until cheese melts. Add salt and freshly ground black pepper, to taste. Remove from heat and allow to cool slightly.

2 Beat egg whites until they are stiff but not dry, then gently fold into warm cheese mixture. Pile mixture in a buttered soufflé dish or casserole. Bake in a preheated moderate oven (350°F) for 35–40 minutes, or until soufflé is golden. Serve immediately.

Serves 4

Provençal Vegetable Soufflé

Ingredients

Butter
¾ cup zucchini, diced
¾ cup eggplant, diced
4 tablespoons olive oil
1 small tomato, peeled,
    seeded and diced
1¼ cups milk
½ chicken stock cube
4 tablespoons finely
    chopped onion
¾ cup freshly grated
    Gruyère cheese
½ cup freshly grated
    Parmesan cheese
1 tablespoon finely
    chopped parsley
¼ teaspoon dried oregano
5 egg yolks
Salt and freshly ground
    black pepper
Cayenne pepper
10 egg whites

1 Preheat oven to moderate (350°F). Butter a 5-cup metal ring mold, paying particular attention to the rim.

2 Toss diced zucchini and eggplants in olive oil until tender. Add diced tomatoes and cook for 1 minute more.

3 Combine milk and stock cube in a pan. Bring to boiling point, making sure cube has dissolved, and remove from heat.

4 In a heavy, medium-sized pan, melt 3 tablespoons butter. Add finely chopped onion and cook over a very low heat for 5 minutes.

5 Gradually add hot seasoned milk, beating vigorously to prevent lumps forming. Bring to the boil and simmer for 2 minutes, stirring. Add cooked vegetables, grated cheeses, parsley and oregano and simmer for 1 minute longer. Remove from heat.

6 Beat egg yolks lightly. Pour them into the hot sauce, stirring vigorously. Return pan to a low heat and cook gently for 1 minute longer, or until sauce has thickened, taking great care not to let it boil, or egg yolks may curdle.

7 Remove pan from heat and allow to cool to lukewarm, stirring occasionally to prevent a skin forming on top. Season generously with salt and freshly ground black pepper and cayenne pepper.

8 Beat egg whites until stiff but not dry. Using a large metal spoon or spatula, fold them gently but thoroughly into lukewarm sauce.

9 Spoon mixture carefully into prepared ring mold, and immediately transfer to a preheated oven.

10 Bake for 25 to 30 minutes, or until soufflé has risen well above the top of the mold and is golden and firm to the touch.

11 To serve: cover ring mold with a heated serving dish and invert the two quickly so that soufflé is not squashed.

Serves 6

Souffléd Breakfast Egg *(Illustration, page 57)*

1 Separate eggs.

2 Beat whites very stiff, and season generously with salt and white pepper.

3 Butter 4 individual ramekins or *cocottes,* and divide beaten egg whites equally. Use rather large dishes to allow egg whites to rise. Make a depression with the back of your spoon for each egg yolk. Place yolks in hollows (1 to each ramekin); cover each yolk with 1 tablespoon cream, and sprinkle with grated cheese. Bake in a hot oven (450°F) for 8–10 minutes.

Serves 4

Ingredients
4 eggs
Salt and white pepper
Butter
4 tablespoons heavy cream
4 tablespoons freshly grated Parmesan cheese

Croustade of Poached Eggs Benedict

1 Bake 4 individual pastry shells; remove from tins.

2 Place 1 round cooked ham in each shell; top with poached egg; season to taste with salt and freshly ground black pepper, and dot with butter; warm through for a few minutes in a moderate oven (375°F).

3 Top each egg with 2 tablespoons sauce Hollandaise; garnish with 2 tomato wedges and serve immediately.

Serves 4

Ingredients
4 individual pastry shells (see page 156)
4 slices cooked ham, cut to fit pastry shells
4 poached eggs
Salt and freshly ground black pepper
Butter
8 tablespoons sauce sauce Hollandaise (see page 49)
8 tomato wedges

Poached Eggs Florentine *(Illustration, page 56)*

1 To prepare spinach mixture: combine frozen spinach with butter in a heavy pan and allow to defrost over a gentle heat, stirring and mashing occasionally with a wooden spoon. Then simmer spinach for 5–7 minutes longer, stirring to rid it of excess moisture. Beat in grated Parmesan cheese and cream, and season to taste with a few drops of lemon juice, salt and freshly ground black pepper, and a pinch of freshly grated nutmeg.

2 Fill pastry shells with hot spinach mixture and top each one with a poached egg. Spoon hot Mornay sauce over the top and sprinkle with grated Parmesan cheese.

3 Slip pastry shells under a hot broiler for a few minutes until tops are bubbling and golden, and serve immediately.

Note: if you have no Mornay sauce or other rich cheese sauce available, simply sprinkle pastry shells more generously with grated Parmesan cheese and broil as above until cheese has melted.

Serves 6

Ingredients
6 prebaked individual fingertip pastry shells, 4 inches in diameter
6 eggs, poached and trimmed
6 tablespoons Mornay sauce
2 tablespoons freshly grated Parmesan cheese

SPINACH MIXTURE
1½ cups frozen spinach
4 tablespoons butter
4 tablespoons freshly grated Parmesan cheese
3–4 tablespoons light cream
Lemon juice
Salt and freshly ground black pepper
Freshly grated nutmeg

Aioli, a great one-dish luncheon from the South of France. (Recipe, page 63)

Cooking in Water

You can cook anything in water—from the ubiquitous poached chicken to the unusual *gigot à l'irlandaise* of French classic cookery (a tender leg of lamb, boned and stuffed with herbs, then rolled in a suet pastry, wrapped carefully in a sheet of muslin and simmered gently in water until deliciously tender).

Cooking in water does not, however, mean that you should not season it. Salt is, of course, used even when boiling a potato. But many cooks in France would never think of preparing their bouillon (the liquid in which anything is boiled) without adding a few peppercorns, a sprig of thyme or other herbs, a bay leaf, some onions, a little vinegar or equal quantities of wine and stock. I like to cook new potatoes, for instance, in a covered saucepan with just ½ inch water and 2–3 tablespoons butter or olive oil. Try this, too, with peas, spinach, carrots or sliced zucchini.

You will find it makes all the difference, whether you are cooking a fish in a delicately prepared court-bouillon; a fat, herb-stuffed chicken in a rich stock spiked with dry white wine; or fresh egg noodles in a light white stock flavored with a little olive oil and a touch of garlic.

Poaching
Other than when making tea or coffee, or when cooking the occasional new potato, green vegetable or hard-boiled egg, I prefer to think of boiling in terms of poaching (a boiling that does not quite boil), for the term "poaching" extends to all slow processes of cooking which involve the use of a liquid, not necessarily water, no matter how small the quantity. Thus the term "poach" applies equally to the cooking of a large fish—a turbot or a salmon—in an aromatic court-bouillon, as to fillets of sole simmered in a little fish *fumet,* or to eggs or vegetables cooked in stock or water.

Poached foods are usually served with a butter- or cream-based sauce or, more simply, with butter, olive oil or cream.

Cooking fish in water
Many cooks think that there is nothing in the world as difficult to cook really well as fish, for its delicate flavor is so easily lost, and its light, creamy flakiness so quickly destroyed. Yet if we follow the simple and elementary rules for its preparation, we can all cook fish to perfection.

To poach fish

Whole fish or thick pieces of fish such as salmon, halibut, cod, ling, hake or turbot are best for poaching. If small fish or thin slices, steaks, or fillets are to be cooked in liquid, they are better steamed, or "poached" in the oven (see below).

Always put all fish—except salt fish—into water that is very hot but not bubbling too hard, to which you have added 1 teaspoon salt and 1 or 2 tablespoons vinegar or lemon juice per 10 cups water.

A simple court-bouillon (quickly made stock) can be made to lend extra flavor by the addition of a bouquet garni (thyme, bay leaf and parsley), sliced carrots, onion and celery to the water, as well as salt and vinegar or lemon juice. For a more flavorsome court-bouillon, add ½ bottle inexpensive dry white wine instead of vinegar, or half white wine and half water may be used. And if the fish tends to be dry, add 2 or more tablespoons olive oil.

A red court-bouillon can be made by substituting claret for the white wine to give the fish a bluish tinge.

A long, solid fish poacher, with a drainer to allow fish to be lifted out easily without being broken, is the best utensil to use for poaching fish. My poacher is 2 feet long, which is just large enough to hold a young salmon or a salmon trout comfortably. When poaching smaller fish or a center cut of a larger fish I always fasten the fish loosely to the drainer with a piece of string to prevent it floating about during cooking.

A large saucepan or ovenproof casserole can be used for poaching fish if a plate is placed on the bottom of the saucepan and the fish is tied in a piece of muslin or cheesecloth, with the end of the cloth hanging over the sides of the pan so that the fish can be lifted out of the water easily without being broken.

Do not use too much liquid to cook the fish or the skin will in all probability break. Just enough liquid to cover the fish by 1 or 2 inches is a good rule. And if I use a fish poacher with a tight-fitting lid, I use only enough court-bouillon to come halfway up the fish; the steam does the rest.

Allow the liquid to come to the boil again after the fish is put in; then reduce heat to a bare simmer and cook for the required time. If the fish is cooked too quickly, the outside will crack and break before the inside is ready. Remove all scum that rises, for if allowed to remain it will spoil the appearance of the fish.

Test the fish by flaking it with a fork before it is lifted from the water; the flesh ought to have lost its clear appearance and to have become white and opaque. It should also come away from the bone easily; a wooden skewer may be pushed in gently to try this. Overcooked fish is flavorless.

As soon as the fish is ready, lift it out of the cooking liquid and drain well. If it cannot be served at once, keep it warm on the drainer placed across the fish poacher and covered over with a hot clean cloth. Garnish with fresh parsley and lemon wedges, and serve sauce separately. Boiled or steamed potatoes are usually served with boiled fish.

To pan-poach fish

One of the most delicate ways of cooking fish fillets and small fish steaks or cutlets is to pan-poach them in equal quantities of well-seasoned fish stock and dry white wine. Butter a shallow, ovenproof *gratin* dish and place the fillets of fish in it; season with salt, freshly ground black pepper and a little lemon juice, and barely cover with fish stock and wine. Place a piece of well-buttered waxed paper over fish and cook in a hot oven (450°F) or on top of the stove until the fish is tender and opaque (about 8–12 minutes).

To serve: lift fish out carefully, draining it well, and place on a heated serving dish. Keep warm. Thicken pan liquids slightly with *beurre manié* (equal quantities of flour and butter kneaded together) or with an egg yolk mixed with a little heavy cream and lemon juice, to taste. Serve with the fish. This manner of cooking is guaranteed to bring out the flavor of the most delicate fish.

To oven-poach fish
The most effective method of poaching fish fillets isn't really poaching at all. It is oven-poaching, or poaching without liquid. Just place your fillets, or fish steaks, in a well-buttered ovenproof baking dish with a little finely chopped onion and mushroom, and salt and freshly ground black pepper, to taste; cover the dish with buttered waxed paper or foil, and cook in a moderate oven (375°F) until fish flakes with a fork. The fish may be served with or without sauce.

Blanching
Blanching is not, properly speaking, a method of cooking at all, but a preliminary preparation. To blanch vegetables, meat or fish, put the ingredient into a generous saucepan of cold water; bring the water to boiling point; remove the pan from the heat and drain the ingredient, which is then "blanched."

Almonds and chestnuts are blanched to facilitate the removal of their skins. Certain vegetables—onions, cabbage and even Brussels sprouts—are blanched to remove bitterness before they are tossed in butter. Diced fat bacon is usually blanched to remove excess salt before it is sautéed in butter and olive oil and used as a flavoring agent in many stews and ragoûts. Veal and lamb are blanched to preserve their whiteness for certain "white" stews such as *fricassées* and *blanquettes*.

Aioli *(Illustration, pages 60 and 61)*

1 Soak codfish overnight in cold water.

2 Boil fish and vegetables. Cook each vegetable separately—white and sweet potatoes in their jackets, whole zucchini, carrots and green beans, making sure they are tender but still quite firm, and on no account overcooked.

3 Serve hot vegetables, hard-boiled eggs in their shells and raw tomatoes on large serving dishes decorated with lettuce and sprigs of fresh herbs. Place fish in center. For best effect, group well-drained vegetables by color. Serve with *aioli* sauce, from which this famous dish gets its name.

Serves 4–6

Ingredients
1 lb. salt codfish
6 white potatoes in their jackets
6 sweet potatoes in their jackets
6 small zucchini
1 lb. small carrots
1 lb. green beans
6 hard-boiled eggs
6 ripe tomatoes
Lettuce
Fresh herbs (parsley, basil and so on), to decorate

Aioli Sauce *(Illustration, pages 60 and 61)*

1 Crush the garlic to a smooth paste in a mortar with a little salt; blend in egg yolks until mixture is a smooth homogeneous mass. Now take the olive oil and proceed (drop by drop at first, a thin trickle later) to whisk the mixture as for a mayonnaise. The sauce will thicken gradually until it reaches the proper stiff, firm consistency. The exact quantity of olive oil is, determined by the number of egg yolks used.

2 Season to taste with additional salt, a little freshly ground black pepper and lemon juice. This sauce is served chilled in a bowl. Guests help themselves.

Ingredients
4 fat cloves of garlic per person
Salt
1 egg yolk each for two persons
Olive oil (about ⅔ cup for each yolk)
Freshly ground black pepper
Lemon juice

Poached Salmon in Court-Bouillon

Ingredients

4 slices fresh salmon, about
  1 inch thick
Onion, thinly sliced
Canned clam juice, or fish
  stock
Salt and freshly ground
  black pepper
4 large peeled potatoes

SAUCE

1 tablespoon butter
1 tablespoon flour
⅔ cup canned clam juice, or
  well-seasoned fish stock
Salt
Cayenne pepper
1 egg yolk
⅔ cup heavy cream
Juice of ¼ lemon

GARNISH

8 heart-shaped croûtons
4 slices broiled bacon
2 tablespoons finely
  chopped parsley

It is not that easy to poach a salmon *really* well. First of all, you need a fish poacher, with a removable rack, to allow you to lower the fish into the court-bouillon, and, what's more important, to remove the fish without breaking it. Then you need to measure your fish poacher, so that you can be certain the salmon will fit into it.

1 Combine elements of court-bouillon in a fish poacher large enough to hold salmon; bring to the boil; skim; lower heat and simmer for 20 minutes.

2 Let court-bouillon cool slightly; place the cleaned salmon on the metal rack of the poacher, and lower the rack gently into court-bouillon.

3 Bring court-bouillon to the boil again (about 3 minutes); reduce heat to a simmer; cover poacher and simmer salmon gently for 35–45 minutes, or until fish flakes easily with a fork.

4 To make sauce: heat butter in the top of a double boiler; add flour and cook over water, stirring, until sauce is smooth and thick. Add canned clam juice, or fish stock; season to taste with salt and cayenne pepper, and simmer until smooth. Stir in egg yolk, heavy cream and lemon juice, and simmer until thickened, being careful not to let sauce come to a boil. Strain sauce through a fine sieve into a clean saucepan. Add potato balls to sauce and heat for 3 minutes, stirring from time to time.

5 To serve: place fish on a heated serving dish; garnish with *croûtons*, broiled bacon and finely chopped parsley, and serve accompanied by sauce.

Serves 4

Marinated Salmon Steaks

Ingredients

1 whole salmon (about 4
  lb.)
Cucumber slices
Pimiento strips
Aspic jelly

COURT-BOUILLON

10 cups water
1 bottle dry white wine
1 large onion, sliced
4 carrots, sliced
4 stalks celery, sliced
2 bay leaves
10 peppercorns
Salt
Bouquet garni

1 Marinate salmon slices for at least 4 hours in 4 tablespoons each olive oil and dry white wine seasoned with finely chopped garlic, and salt and freshly ground black pepper.

2 Place marinated salmon steaks in a saucepan on a bed of thinly sliced onion; add clam juice, or fish stock, and just enough water to cover fish; season to taste with salt and freshly ground black pepper; cover pan, bring to a boil; lower heat and simmer gently for 15 to 20 minutes, or until fish flakes easily with a fork.

3 Scoop balls from potatoes with a potato scoop; boil potato balls in salted water for 15 minutes. Drain and reserve.

4 Remove fish carefully from court-bouillon; transfer it to a board and remove the skin with a sharp knife, leaving head and tail intact.

5 To serve cold: arrange the salmon on a serving platter and garnish fish with overlapping "scales" of paper-thin halved cucumber slices and "fins" made of strips of cooked pimiento. *Note:* I always use tiny toothpicks to hold cucumber "scales" to fish until aspic glaze holds them in place.

6 Brush fish with liquid aspic jelly; allow jelly to set; remove toothpicks. Serve with a well-seasoned mayonnaise (see page 49).

2

I

3

4

Poached Salmon in Court-Bouillon. One of the most attractive ways of decorating a cold fresh salmon is to coat it with a thin layer of overlapping cucumber slices.
1 Place 4 lb. salmon on rack in fish poacher and cook in prepared court-bouillon for 35–45 minutes.

2 Remove fish on rack from court-bouillon; let it cool slightly and then carefully remove skin.

3 To make cucumber "scales": slice cucumber in half lengthwise and then cut each half cucumber into paper-thin half-rounds.

4 To cover fish with "scales": dip each "scale" in aspic jelly which is just beginning to set. Then, starting at the tail end, place cucumber slices in overlapping rows until fish is entirely covered. Half toothpicks are invaluable for holding "difficult" slices to sides of fish.

Smoked Haddock in Court-Bouillon

Ingredients

2 lb. smoked haddock
    fillets
Water and milk
Thin lemon slices
Sprigs of fresh parsley
Boiled new potatoes
½ cup butter
Juice of ½ lemon
Salt and freshly ground
    black pepper

1 Soak haddock in water for 2 hours.

2 Drain fish and put in a saucepan; cover with equal amounts of water and milk, and bring to a fast boil. Remove from the heat and allow to stand for 15 minutes. Drain haddock, reserving stock for some other use.

3 Serve haddock on a heated serving dish, garnished with thin lemon slices, sprigs of fresh parsley and boiled new potatoes. Serve with butter melted with lemon juice and seasoned with salt and freshly ground black pepper, to taste.

Serves 4–6

Filets de Sole du Pays Normand

Ingredients

2 Dover sole (1–1¼ lb.
    each)
2 shallots, finely chopped
1¼ cups reduced fish fumet
    (see below)
1¼ cups dry white wine

FISH FUMET

Butter
Bones and trimmings from
    sole
1 small piece turbot with
    bone
4 sprigs parsley
2 sprigs thyme
2 bay leaves
1 shallot, finely chopped
⅔ cup dry white wine
2 mushrooms, sliced
⅛ teaspoon fennel seed
6 peppercorns
Salt and freshly ground
    black pepper

GARNISH

12 poached mussels
24 small cooked shrimp
4 mushroom caps
    simmered in butter and
    lemon juice
Crescents of flaky pastry
    (optional)

1 Ask your fish dealer to fillet Dover sole. Reserve bones and trimmings.

2 To make fish *fumet:* butter the saucepan; combine bones and trimmings from sole with small piece of turbot, parsley, thyme, bay leaves, finely chopped shallot, dry white wine, ⅔ cup water, sliced mushrooms, fennel seed and peppercorns, and salt and freshly ground black pepper, to taste. Bring to the boil; skim and simmer for 10–15 minutes. Strain fish *fumet* and reduce to half of the original quantity (there should be about 1¼ cups).

3 To prepare fish: poach fillets of sole with finely chopped shallots in equal quantities of fish *fumet* and dry white wine until fish flakes easily with a fork (about 7 or 8 minutes). Remove fillets and keep warm in a low oven. Reserve liquids for Normandy cream sauce.

4 To serve: place sole fillets on a heated serving dish and keep warm. Prepare Normandy Cream Sauce (see below). Strain sauce over sole. Garnish with poached mussels, shrimp, and mushroom caps which you have poached in a little butter and lemon juice. Add crescents of flaky pastry, if desired.

Serves 4

Normandy Cream Sauce

Ingredients

Reserved poaching liquids
    from Filets de Sole du
    Pays Normand
⅔ cup heavy cream
4 mushroom stalks, finely
    chopped
1–2 egg yolks
Salt and freshly ground
    black pepper (optional)
Cayenne pepper or freshly
    grated nutmeg (optional)

1 Reduce poaching liquids from fish until they are syrupy.

2 Bring cream to the boil with finely chopped mushroom stalks and add reduced poaching liquid little by little, stirring briskly with a wooden spatula or whisk until sauce is well blended.

3 Remove saucepan from heat and stir in egg yolks, which you have first mixed with a little of the hot sauce. Whisk well, return to heat and simmer, stirring continuously, until sauce is smooth and thick. Do not allow the sauce to boil after the eggs have been added.

4 Correct seasoning.

Sole in Court-Bouillon with Herb or Caviar Tartlets

1 To make court-bouillon: butter an enamelled saucepan or baking dish; lay half the fish bones and trimmings on bottom of pan; add lemon juice, parsley, bay leaf, onion, mushrooms, and salt and freshly ground black pepper, and enough water and dry white wine in equal quantities to cover fish. Bring to the boil; add fish fillets; cover with remaining bones and simmer gently, covered with a piece of buttered paper, for 10–15 minutes, or until fish flakes easily with a fork. Remove fish fillets from court-bouillon and keep warm.

Cook court-bouillon over a high heat until reduced to about $1\frac{1}{4}$ cups. Strain. Reserve for Fish Velouté Sauce.

2 To serve: place fish fillets on a heated serving dish; pour over the Fish Velouté Sauce (see below); garnish with thin slices of lemon and sprigs of fresh watercress. Surround with tiny tartlets filled with sour cream and topped with finely chopped fresh fennel and chives, or, for a more extravagant occasion, black caviar.

Serves 6

Ingredients
2 lb. fillets of sole

COURT-BOUILLON
Butter
Bones and trimmings of sole
Juice of 1 lemon
4 sprigs parsley
1 bay leaf
1 medium onion, finely chopped
4 mushrooms, finely chopped
Salt and freshly ground black pepper
Water and dry white wine

GARNISH
6 baked 1-inch tart shells (see page 156)
Thinly sliced lemon
Sprigs of watercress
Sour cream
Finely chopped fresh fennel and chives, or black caviar

Fish Velouté Sauce

1 Melt butter in the top of a double boiler; stir in flour and cook over water, stirring continuously, until smooth.

2 Add strained court-bouillon and cook, stirring from time to time, until thick and smooth. Add heavy cream

and continue cooking until sauce is reduced to the desired consistency.

3 Correct seasoning, adding a little salt and freshly ground black pepper if necessary.

Ingredients
2 tablespoons butter
2 tablespoons flour
Reserved court-bouillon from Sole in Court-Bouillon
$1\frac{1}{4}$ cups heavy cream
Salt and freshly ground black pepper (optional)

Stuffed Fillets of Sole in Sauce Hollandaise

1 Lay fillets of sole out flat on a clean surface; brush with softened butter; season with salt and freshly ground black pepper; place 1 tablespoon shrimp on each fillet and roll fillets up, starting from head; fasten with toothpicks.

2 Place rolled fillets in a well-buttered gratin dish. Sprinkle with chopped shallots and mushroom stalks, add salt and freshly ground black pepper to taste, and cover with fish bones and

trimmings. Cover with buttered waxed paper and "poach" in a hot oven (450°F) for 10 minutes, or until fish flakes easily with a fork. Keep warm.

3 To serve fillets: place pastry shells on a baking tray; place 1 cooked fillet in each case and spoon over sauce Hollandaise. Heat in a hot oven for a few minutes until sauce bubbles.

Serves 4

Ingredients
2 sole, filleted
Butter
Salt and freshly ground black pepper
4 tablespoons shelled chopped shrimp
2 shallots, finely chopped
Mushroom trimmings
Fish bones and trimmings
4 baked pastry shells (see page 156)
1 recipe sauce Hollandaise (see page 49)

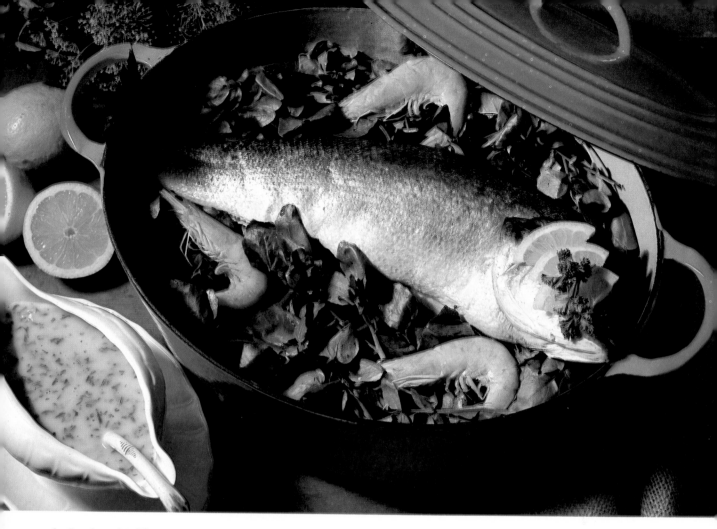

Sea Bass Steamed in Watercress is a nouvelle cuisine version of an age-old cooking process. The fish is at once tender and moist, impregnated with the flavors of watercress, lemon and shrimp. (Recipe, page 70)

Steaming

Steaming is one of the principal forms of Oriental cooking and one not to be by-passed in Western kitchens. It is rapid and also one of the most effective methods of cooking I know for preserving the maximum degree of original taste.

Season the water with salt, a clove of garlic or a few spring onion tops to give a subtle flavor to the steamed food. Or follow an ancient Arabian recipe and season your steaming bouillon with salt, powdered cumin, ginger, cinnamon, paprika and cayenne pepper.

Your cooking utensil should be large enough to hold comfortably, with a stand, the dish containing the food to be cooked.

Heat the dish; place the food in it and put the dish on the stand in the pan only when the water is actually boiling and steam is rising. To cook: cover the pan immediately and turn up the heat so that the steam is at its height.

Steamed food cooks quickly. It should be neither overdone nor underdone. All meat—except pork, which must be well done—should be a little pink when removed from the steamer.

Serve steamed food the moment it is considered cooked. Otherwise it will be overdone, for because of the intense heat it has absorbed the cooking process will continue away from the heat until the food cools. Steam-cooked food should be eaten hot, or it will lose its flavor and texture.

Steamed fish

Fish steaks or fillets—salmon, cod, sole, turbot—or whole small fish can be cooked to perfection by steaming.

To steam fish: place fish in a well-buttered oval baking dish; sprinkle with 1 or 2 tablespoons each finely chopped onion and mushrooms; moisten with 4–6 tablespoons dry white wine, canned clam juice or well-seasoned fish stock; season to taste with salt and freshly ground black pepper, and place over boiling water to which you have added a clove or two of garlic. Cover tightly and steam until fish flakes easily with a fork.

Steamed poultry

A whole chicken or duck (or even a lean leg of baby lamb) may be steamed in this way if your steamer is large enough. The legendary Alexandre Dumaine, often called the world's greatest chef when he was alive, used to serve a whole steamed chicken at his famous restaurant, *La Côte d'Or,* in Saulieu, Upper Burgundy. The chicken was marinated overnight in a few tablespoons of port or Madeira before being steamed in its own juices and a little butter in an ovenproof dish. The secret here? The chicken was steamed for an hour over a superbly flavored beef bouillon complete with onions, carrots, turnips and fresh herbs, which lent their flavors and juices to the finished dish.

Steamed vegetables

Most vegetables—cauliflower, peas, Brussels sprouts, green beans—steam to perfection in 15–20 minutes. Try steamed peas dressed with sautéed onion, diced ham, sugar and mint leaves; or dressed steamed cauliflower with lemon juice and fresh breadcrumbs or slivered almonds sautéed in butter. Serve steamed Brussels sprouts with a sprinkling of fresh breadcrumbs sautéed in butter until golden. Dress steamed green beans with butter, finely chopped parsley and crumbled bits of crisp-fried bacon.

Steaming equipment

There are special steamers on the market for whole chickens, whole fish or asparagus. These consist of a double boiler with a perforated bottom to allow the steam to rise. Or you can improvise with one of the folding round steamer attachments designed to fit almost any size saucepan or casserole. These handy little steamers fit easily into a round saucepan or casserole, with the water simmering below.

Whichever pan you use, cover it tightly so that the food is completely surrounded by steam and continues to cook in it until tender. Wet towels wrapped around the joint between the lid and pan help to prevent the steam from escaping.

Vegetable Couscous

I often serve *couscous* steamed on its own as a vegetable accompaniment for meats and poultry, the grains subtly flavored with my own version of a Moroccan spice blend.

Couscous should be light and fluffy and marvellously flavored. Season the broth with 1 large onion, 4 or 5 carrots, 4 stalks celery, 1 fat clove garlic, mashed with the point of a knife, some ground ginger, a little cayenne pepper and a little ground cumin seed. Put on the steamer top and then line it with a wet cloth so the steam can come right up through it, and the fine grains of *couscous* can't fall through. Dampen the *couscous* before putting it in the cloth-lined steamer top so that the steam can go through it more quickly.

Sea Bass Steamed in Watercress *(Illustration, page 68)*

Ingredients

1 sea bass (about 2 lb.)
2 bunches watercress,
 trimmed and washed
Lemon juice
Salt and freshly ground
 black pepper
2 cloves garlic
2 sprigs thyme
⅔ cup chicken stock (see
 page 37)
4 shrimp
Butter
Fennel seeds
Finely chopped parsley

1 Ask your fish dealer to scale and clean the fish and cut away its fins.

2 To steam sea bass: put a layer of half the watercress sprigs in an enamelled oval casserole large enough to contain the fish comfortably. Season the fish, inside and out, with lemon juice and salt and freshly ground black pepper, to taste. Lay fish on top of the layer of watercress. Add garlic cloves and thyme and top with remaining watercress (leaving a few sprigs for garnish). Add stock. Top with shrimp; cover casserole and cook over a fast heat for 20 minutes, or until fish flakes easily with a fork.

3 To serve sea bass: bring the fish to the table in the casserole, lifting lid so the full aroma of the dish escapes as you serve it. Then transfer fish to a serving platter and lift fillets away from bone. Season fillets with salt and freshly ground black pepper and arrange on hot plates. Garnish each plate with a few sprigs of fresh watercress and 2 shrimp. Serve with a hot butter sauce to which you have added fennel seeds, finely chopped parsley and salt, freshly ground black pepper and lemon juice, to taste.

Serves 2

Steamed Mussels in the Crock *(Illustration, page 69)*

Ingredients

48 mussels
3 shallots, finely chopped
1 tablespoon butter
⅔ cup dry white wine
⅔ cup chicken stock (see
 page 37)
4 slices of leek
1 small carrot, cut in
 quarters
1 small bay leaf
4 sprigs parsley
⅔ cup heavy cream
 (optional)
Salt and freshly ground
 black pepper
Lemon juice

1 Scrape and beard mussels; place in an ovenproof crock with shallots, butter, dry white wine and chicken stock. Add leek, carrot, bay leaf and parsley. Cover and steam for 5 minutes, or until mussels are all open.

2 Add cream, if desired, and salt and freshly ground black pepper, and lemon juice, to taste. Bring to the boil again and serve.

Serves 4

Steaming in the Chinese manner

Steaming in the Chinese manner is extremely simple: all you have to do is to slice the food concerned (a whole fish, fish fillets or steaks, a fillet of beef, a loin of pork, or breast of chicken or turkey) diagonally across the grain into thin strips. Season in the Chinese manner with 3 tablespoons dry white wine and 1 tablespoon soy sauce, with a little cornstarch added to thicken the sauce. Then add 6–8 thinly sliced button mushrooms for every pound of food used.

Place the meat, fish or poultry, and mushroom slices, in an ovenproof *gratin* dish or shallow casserole with 1 or 2 thinly sliced shallots or scallions and season to taste with salt and freshly ground black pepper. When ready to cook, set dish on a stand in a large pan containing about 2 inches rapidly boiling water. Cover pan and steam for 10–12 minutes. The sauce will be translucent, light and delicious.

Chinese Steamed Fish with Ginger and Scallions

1 Place cleaned fish in a flat dish large enough to hold them.

2 Slice mushrooms thinly. Add sliced ginger and sliced green beans.

3 Combine finely chopped garlic and chopped scallions with grated lemon peel, olive oil, soy sauce, cornstarch, dry white wine and salt and freshly ground black pepper, to taste. Mix well and pour over fish.

4 Place dish in a large steamer, or on a rack in a large saucepan wide enough to hold it, with about 2 inches of rapidly boiling water. Cover and steam for 15 minutes.

5 Remove to a hot platter and serve immediately, decorated with some of the mushrooms, ginger and green beans and lemon knots. Boiled rice (see page 140) or steamed sliced carrots (see page 135), new potatoes and green beans should accompany this dish.

Serves 2

Ingredients

2 whiting or sole (about ¾ lb. each)
1 cup button mushrooms
2–3 slices fresh ginger
12 green beans, sliced
1 clove garlic, finely chopped
2 chopped scallions
Peel of ½ lemon, grated
4 tablespoons olive oil
2 tablespoons soy sauce
1 tablespoon cornstarch
2 tablespoons dry white wine
Salt and fresh black pepper
2 strips lemon peel

Chinese Steamed Lobster *(Illustration, pages 72 and 73)*

1 Fill a large saucepan three-quarters full of salted water (1 tablespoon to 5 cups), or well-flavored court-bouillon, and bring to the boil. Plunge in the lobsters head first and boil quickly for 2 minutes. Remove lobsters from saucepan and slice over a shallow bowl into 1-inch slices, shell and all. Reserve juices.

2 Transfer enough of the salted water that you cooked the lobster in to cover the bottom of a large wok and bring to the boil. Reserve the rest of the liquid for stock.

3 Place spinach leaves in the bottom of a Chinese bamboo steamer. Arrange sliced lobster on this green "bed" and sprinkle with sliced fresh ginger and scallion segments.

4 Place bamboo steamer over water; cover steamer with bamboo lid and steam lobster over gently boiling water for 10–15 minutes, or until tender.

5 Transfer sliced lobster and spinach to a heated serving platter. Heat ginger and scallion segments in ⅔ cup stock with reserved lobster juices; add soy sauce and Tabasco, to taste, and spoon over.

Serves 4

Ingredients

2 live lobsters (about 2 lb. each)
Salted water or well-flavored court-bouillon (see page 64)
8–12 fresh spinach leaves
8–12 thin slices fresh ginger
8–12 scallions sliced in 1-inch segments
Soy sauce
Tabasco

Chinese Steamed Shrimp

1 Roll shrimp in cornstarch and place on a platter in steamer* with finely chopped shallots, finely sliced mushrooms and cucumber, soy sauce and white wine. Season with freshly ground black pepper, and cook over 2 inches fast-boiling water, covered, so platter is entirely confined in steam, until tender.

* If you do not have a steamer, place a trivet in the bottom of a casserole large enough to contain platter and cook, covered, over fast-boiling water.

2 Serve hot from the steamer on a bed of rice, garnished with fresh tomatoes.

Serves 4

Ingredients

1½ lb. shrimp
Cornstarch
4 shallots, finely chopped
¼ lb. (1 cup) mushrooms, finely sliced
½ cup cucumber, sliced
4 tablespoons soy sauce
4 tablespoons dry white wine
Freshly ground pepper
Rice
Tomatoes

Arabian Steamed Couscous

Ingredients

1 3–3½ lb. roasting chicken, or 2½ lb. shoulder of lamb
Salt and freshly ground black pepper
3 tablespoons olive oil
2 large onions, quartered
8 small turnips, quartered
8 small carrots, quartered
2 medium-sized green peppers, seeded, cored and quartered
2 teaspoons paprika
1 teaspoon ground ginger
½ teaspoon ground cinnamon
¼ teaspoon saffron strands
8 small zucchini
2 chicken stock cubes
2 tablespoons tomato purée
½ cup chick peas, soaked overnight
1 lb. couscous
½ lb. frozen broad beans (optional)
4 tablespoons chopped parsley
2 tablespoons butter
Ground ginger, cayenne pepper and tomato purée to finish sauce

BOUQUET GARNI

1 celery stalk, cut into 1-inch lengths
6 black peppercorns
3 cloves
1 bay leaf
1 clove garlic, peeled
½–1 teaspoon cumin seed

Preceding pages Chinese Steamed Lobster. The recipe is simplicity itself: take 1 Chinese wok, 1 Chinese steamer basket; add 2 sliced lobsters, 8–12 slices fresh ginger, 8–12 leaves spinach or escarole, 8–12 spring onion segments, and steam over bubbling water seasoned with ginger, scallion and soy. Delicious. (Recipe, page 71)

1 Cut chicken into serving pieces (or cut the lamb into chunks) and season with salt and freshly ground black pepper.

2 Collect ingredients for bouquet garni and tie them up in a square of muslin.

3 Place the bottom section of a *couscoussière* over a medium heat; or steamer which will fit it tightly. Heat 2 tablespoons olive oil in the *couscoussière* or saucepan, and sauté chicken or lamb steadily until golden brown all over, for 10–15 minutes. Transfer meat to a plate.

4 In the same oil, sauté quartered onions, turnips, carrots and green peppers for 15 minutes, or until golden. Sprinkle with paprika, ginger, cinnamon and saffron and mix well. Add meat.

5 Pour over 5 cups boiling water; add zucchini, stock cubes, tomato purée, the bouquet garni and soaked chick peas. Bring to the boil; reduce heat to a gentle simmer; cover and cook gently for 15 minutes.

6 Meanwhile prepare *couscous:* place the grain in a bowl and moisten with 6 tablespoons cold water, 1 at a time, working it in evenly with your fingertips, rather as though you were rubbing fat into flour to make pastry. The grain will absorb the water without any trouble, and look and feel almost as it did when it came out of the package.

7 Line steamer top with a piece of cheesecloth (wrung out in boiling water). Place *couscous* in this.

8 Remove lid from pan in which meat and vegetables are simmering. Fit steamer over the top and continue to simmer gently, uncovered. Steam *couscous* in this way for 30 minutes, occasionally drawing a fork through the grains to aerate them and ensure that they do not stick together in lumps.

9 After 30 minutes, remove *couscous* from steamer. Spoon grain into a heat-proof bowl that will fit snugly over the pan. Sprinkle with remaining tablespoon of olive oil and gradually add a further 6 tablespoons cold water, working it in evenly as before. Season to taste with salt.

10 Add frozen broad beans to stew, if desired. Stir in chopped parsley. Fit bowl over the pan; cover bowl with lid and continue to simmer for a further 30 minutes or until meat is tender.

11 Add butter to *couscous* and leave it to melt while you finish making sauce.

12 Strain off 1¼ cups liquid from stew. Pour into a small pan. Season with a further ¼ teaspoon ground ginger, a pinch of cayenne pepper and teaspoon of tomato purée. Taste and adjust the seasonings—sauce should be quite strong. Reheat to boiling point.

13 Toss *couscous* with a fork to mix in melted butter. Heap it around the sides of a large heated serving platter.

14 Arrange cooked chicken or lamb pieces in the center. Spoon over as much of the vegetables and juices as your dish will take and serve immediately, handing hot sauce around separately. Any remaining vegetables and juices can be kept hot, in reserve.

Serves 6

Note: sometimes, this wonderful combination is further garnished with hot little sausages called *merguez*, spicy little balls of minced lamb called *kefta* and chick peas and onions simmered in honey.

Basic Steamed Chicken

1 Rub cleaned and trussed chicken with cut side of ½ lemon; sprinkle with salt and freshly ground black pepper, to taste; place in a *gratin* dish just large enough to hold it.

2 Add butter, chicken stock and finely chopped onion to *gratin* dish; place dish in a large double steamer over 3 inches rapidly boiling water, and steam for 1–2 hours, according to size of chicken.

3 Serve chicken with pan juices and parsley sauce or celery sauce.

Serves 4

Ingredients

1 roasting chicken
½ lemon
Salt and freshly ground black pepper
4 tablespoons butter
4 tablespoons chicken stock
2 tablespoons finely chopped onion
Parsley sauce or celery sauce (see page 46)

Steamed Chicken with Béarnaise Stuffing

1 Rub cleaned and trussed chicken with cut side of ½ lemon; sprinkle inside and out with salt and freshly ground black pepper, to taste.

2 To make Béarnaise Stuffing: put chicken liver, prosciutto or ham, pork and garlic cloves through the finest blade of your blender. Moisten breadcrumbs with milk; combine with ground meats and add finely chopped parsley, dried tarragon, or chervil, mixed spice and eggs, and season to taste with salt and freshly ground black pepper. Mix well, adding more milk if necessary to make a fairly loose mixture.

3 Stuff chicken with Béarnaise stuffing and place in *gratin* dish just large enough to hold it. Add butter, chicken stock and finely chopped onion. Place *gratin* dish in a large double steamer over 3 inches of rapidly boiling water, and steam for 1½ to 2½ hours, according to size of chicken.

4 Serve chicken with pan juices and sauce of your choice.

Serves 4

Ingredients

1 roasting chicken with liver
½ lemon
Salt and freshly ground black pepper
4 tablespoons butter
4 tablespoons chicken stock
2 tablespoons finely chopped onion
parsley sauce, celery sauce (see page 46), or velouté sauce (see below)

BÉARNAISE STUFFING

Chicken liver (see above)
¼ lb. prosciutto, or cooked ham
¼ lb. fresh pork
1–2 cloves garlic
½ cup dry breadcrumbs
Milk
2–3 tablespoons finely chopped parsley
½ teaspoon dried tarragon, or chervil
Generous pinch mixed spice
2 eggs
Salt and freshly ground black pepper

Velouté Sauce

1 Melt butter in the top of a double boiler; add flour and cook for a few minutes to form pale roux. Add boiling chicken stock, and salt and white peppercorns, to taste. Cook, stirring vigorously with a whisk until well blended.

2 Add mushroom peelings or stems to sauce; reduce heat and simmer gently, stirring occasionally and skimming from time to time, until sauce is reduced to two thirds of the original quantity, and is thick but light and creamy.

3 Flavor sauce with lemon juice and strain through a fine sieve.

Ingredients

2 tablespoons butter
2 tablespoons flour
2½ cups boiling chicken stock
Salt
White peppercorns
Mushroom peelings or stems
Lemon juice

Roasting

Prime cuts of beef, veal, lamb or pork make successful roasts, but only the prime cuts. If you are ever in any doubt about the quality of a piece of meat, casserole it or pot-roast it instead.

A small cut of meat—anything 2 lb. or under—doesn't make a successful roast either, however good its quality. By the time the inevitable shrinkage has occurred, there will be little of it left. Again, settle for more gentle pot-roasting or casseroling instead.

The cuts of beef suitable for roasting are the ribs, the sirloin, the fillet and, in best-quality beef, the rump. Suitable cuts of lamb are the leg, the saddle, the loin and the shoulder. Pork roasts include the leg, the loin and the spare rib. The loin, the saddle, the leg, the shoulder, the rump and often the breast of veal can all be roasted.

The true secret of successful roasting is the even circulation of heat on all sides of the meat. It is best to roast meat on a rack set in a shallow roasting pan in the oven. Never use just a roasting pan without a rack, as the meat tends to stew in the fat and juices in the bottom of the pan as the top over-browns.

To test roasts for doneness
Take a sharp, *thin,* metal skewer or a long fork with no more than *two* sharp prongs to it. Push the skewer or fork into the thickest part of the meat—right through to the bone, if there is one—and pull it out again. You will be able to tell the state of the meat from the color of the juices that spurt out. The test spot in poultry is right through the thickest part of the inside leg (i.e., where the leg lies close to the body).

With roast beef, blood-red juice means that the meat is very rare, pink that it is medium done, and a clear liquid that it is well cooked. For pork or veal, the juices that run out should be perfectly clear. For lamb, the liquid should be clear or lightly touched with pink. With poultry, the juices should be perfectly clear.

One or two tests should be enough. Resist the temptation (understandable in a nervous novice) to jab your roast full of holes like a pin cushion.

Beef
I like to roast beef at a low temperature for an even texture. Roast beef in a moderately hot to fairly hot oven (400–425°F) for 15–30 minutes to seal it. Then reduce oven heat to 325°F and continue to cook until done.

Opposite page Roast Guinea Fowl with Aromatic Butter, photographed in the Long Hall at Hintlesham, is one of the house specialities. The guinea-fowl, farm-reared locally, are brushed inside and out with a pommade of softened butter seasoned with crushed juniper berries, thyme and rosemary, finely chopped onion, garlic and parsley and lemon and orange juice, before being roasted in the oven. (Recipe, page 79)

To serve a roast
To be at its best, roast meat should be served either really hot or really cold. Nothing is less appetizing than lukewarm meat. (The exception is delicate meat like veal which loses flavor if served too cold.)

Choose a large, flat serving platter that will give you plenty of room to carve without having to retrieve morsels from the table.

Make sure your platter, sauceboat and dinner plates are as hot as safety allows.

When the roast is ready, transfer it to the serving dish; *then leave it for 15–20 minutes in the turned off oven with the door ajar* to allow the cooking to subside and the juices, which were still flowing freely when you last pierced the roast, to be reabsorbed by the meat. You will find this "rest" makes the meat far easier to carve into slices, and it also gives you time to make the gravy and do any other last-minute preparation.

Finally, to avoid that awkward pause during carving, which usually results in a polite guest of honor being forced to watch his meat grow cold before him as he waits for the others to be served, it is a good idea to carve enough for the first round before serving. Second helpings can then be sliced to order as needed.

Veal
It is very important to roast veal slowly, too, so that it is still juicy with just a hint of firmness. Most cooks make the mistake of letting it go on to the stage of being stringy and dry. You'll be amazed at the difference if you try low-temperature roasting the next time you roast veal.

Always lard veal—or cover it with a protective layer of fat or bacon—before you roast it. Do not sear veal at a high temperature as you do beef. Cook it in a slow oven (325°F) for 20–35 minutes per pound. Veal is at its succulent best when well cooked but with a delicate hint of pink still in evidence.

Lamb and mutton
Lamb should never be overcooked. It is at its succulent best—moist and richly flavored—when it is a little pink on the inside. So do not roast it until it is a dull greyish-brown in color, with the meat falling off the bones, the flesh dry and tough. Instead, treat lamb gently in the French fashion, roasting it until the juices run pink. For maximum juiciness and minimum shrinkage, I like to cook it for 20–25 minutes per pound at a relatively low temperature (300–325°F) for roasting, and a bare simmer for cooking in liquid. Cook mutton at the same temperature for 40 minutes per pound.

Pork
Pork is best if roasted at about 300–325°F—with plenty of cooking time and basting to give the skin or crackling a nice flavor and texture. All cuts of pork, provided they are tender and fairly fat, can be roasted. Cook pork slowly in an uncovered shallow pan or casserole. Maximum flavor is reached only when the pork is slowly and well cooked. Cook it until the meat has lost its pinkish tinge and is pale beige in color. I like to roast pork in a slow to moderate oven (300–325°F) for about 35 minutes per pound.

To glaze pork roasts after cooking: increase the oven temperature to 425°F; sprinkle fat with 2–3 tablespoons brown sugar; return meat to oven to glaze.

Duck
There are two schools of thought on the cooking of duck. One widely held theory is that for maximum flavor and succulence duck should be roasted for 15–20 minutes per pound at a high temperature (450°F).

I find that cooking a duckling in a slow oven gives the best results, with a straight 350°F temperature right through the cooking time.

To roast duck
Place duck, breast side up, on a rack in a roasting pan. Cover breast of the bird with buttered foil and roast in a moderate oven (350°F) for 1½–1¾ hours. Baste frequently with butter or dripping. Remove foil 20 minutes before removing duck from the oven; dredge breast with flour and leave in oven until well browned. Transfer to a hot serving dish; remove trussing threads and strings, and keep duck warm while preparing gravy.

Goose

A plump, well-fattened goose is one of the most delectable birds there is. Like duckling, it needs slow roasting to bring it to the peak of succulent perfection. I like to place diced apple and onion, seasoned with a little finely chopped garlic and dried thyme or sage, in the cavity of the goose; rub it outside with coarse salt, dried thyme and freshly ground black pepper, and roast it in a moderately hot oven (400°F) for 15 to 20 minutes or until fat starts to run, then reduce temperature to 300°F, and continue cooking for 10–15 minutes per pound, basting occasionally with a little white wine, butter and dried thyme. The skin should be pricked from time to time during cooking to release melted fat.

To roast goose

Place goose, breast side down, on a rack in a shallow roasting pan. Prick fatty parts of goose with a fork to help draw out remaining fat during cooking. Roast goose at 400°F for 15 minutes, and then in a very slow oven (300°F) for 2 hours, pouring off fat during roasting as it accumulates. Then turn goose and cook for 1½–2 hours more, or until goose is nicely browned and the meat is very tender. You will find that long, slow cooking at this temperature will cook out excess fat and leave meat juicy and tender.

Turkey

To prepare a turkey for roasting, rub with softened butter and place the bird, breast side up, in a roasting pan. Cover breast with thin strips of unsmoked bacon and then cover bacon with a piece of muslin brushed with melted butter to prevent bird drying out during roasting.

To roast turkey

Roast stuffed turkey in a slow oven (325°F) for 3½–4 hours for a 10–12 pound oven-ready bird, allowing about 15 minutes per extra pound of weight for larger birds. To let turkey brown and crisp, remove bacon and muslin 20–30 minutes before turkey is done.

Roast Guinea Fowl with Aromatic Butter *(Illustration, page 76)*

1 Combine crushed thyme, rosemary, garlic and juniper berries in a mortar and pound until well blended. Add diced butter and lemon and orange juice, alternately, pounding again until well blended.

2 Stir in chopped onion and finely chopped parsley, a pinch of grated nutmeg or mace, and generous amounts of salt and freshly ground black pepper. Mixture should be highly flavored. Brush birds—inside and out—with this aromatic butter and allow meat to absorb flavors overnight.

3 To roast birds: place in a roasting pan and cook in a fairly hot oven (425°F) for 25–35 minutes, basting frequently with melted aromatic butter. Birds are cooked when juices run quite clear when you insert a skewer through the thickest part of the leg.

Serves 6

Ingredients

3 guinea fowl, poussins or partridges
1 teaspoon crushed thyme
½ teaspoon rosemary leaves
1 clove garlic
6 juniper berries
½ cup butter, diced
Juice of ½ lemon
Juice of 1 orange
1 large onion, chopped
3 tablespoons finely chopped parsley
Pinch of grated nutmeg or mace
Salt and freshly ground black pepper

Roast Rib of Beef

Ingredients

- 1 3-rib roast of beef
- 2 cloves garlic, cut in slivers
- 6–8 sprigs of rosemary
- 4–6 tablespoons beef dripping
- 1 tablespoon dry mustard

Freshly ground black pepper
- 2 tablespoons lightly browned flour
- 1 flattened piece beef suet

Red wine

Salt

Butter

Worcestershire sauce

1 To prepare beef for roasting: make 6–8 insertions in beef with the point of a sharp knife and insert slivers of garlic and sprigs of rosemary. Spread beef with dripping and sprinkle with a mixture of dry mustard, freshly ground black pepper and flour (which you have browned lightly in a frying pan or in the oven). Tie a flattened piece of beef suet over the top.

2 When ready to roast beef: place meat on a rack over a roasting pan and brown in a preheated fairly hot oven (425°F) for 15 minutes. Reduce oven to 325°F; add a little warmed red wine to the pan and continue to roast, basting frequently, allowing 15–18 minutes per pound if you like your beef rare, 20–24 minutes per pound for medium and 25–30 minutes per pound if you prefer it well done. *Note:* if desired, add a little more red wine or water to pan from time to time.

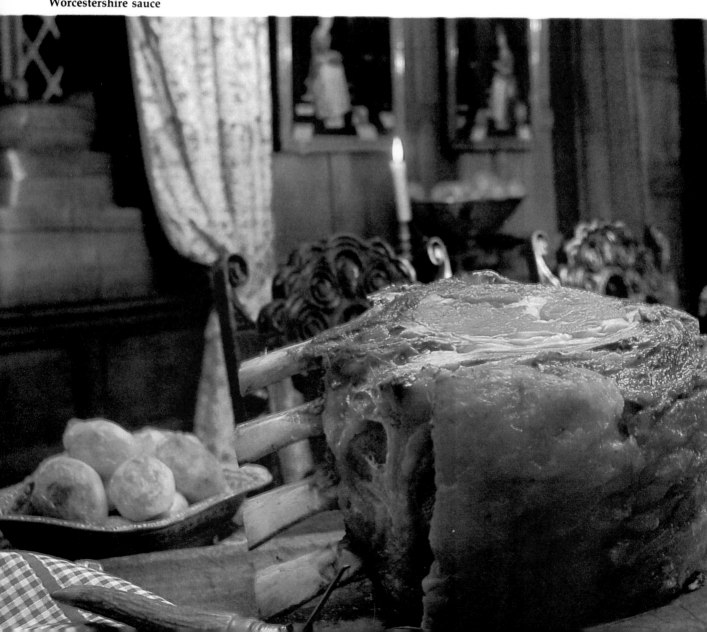

3 When meat is cooked to your liking, season to taste with salt and additional freshly ground black pepper. Remove beef to a warm serving platter and let it stand for 15–20 minutes at the edge of the open oven before carving. During this time the beef sets and the cooking subsides; the roast is then ready for carving.

4 In the meantime, pour off the fat in the roasting pan and use the pink juices that pour from the roast as it sets; stir all the crusty bits into it to make a clear sauce. Add a little more red wine, a little butter and a dash of Worcestershire sauce. Bring to the boil, reduce heat and simmer for 1 or 2 minutes. Strain and serve in a sauceboat with roast.

Serves 8–10

Roast ribs of beef with "attendant" vegetables. What could be better than a huge roast of beef, charred on the outside, meltingly rare on the inside, served with its traditional vegetables? **Main picture** *Roast potatoes and Brussels sprouts.* **Top right** *Buttered new potatoes and peas.* **Center right** *Carrot and turnip strips.* **Bottom right** *Creamed button onions with buttered breadcrumbs.*

Roast Loin of Veal

Ingredients

1 loin of veal (4–6 chops)
Salt and freshly ground
   black pepper
Crushed rosemary
2–4 tablespoons softened
   butter
⅔ cup dry white wine

1 Have your butcher bone and trim a loin of veal. Season to taste with salt and freshly ground black pepper and crushed rosemary. Spread with softened butter and roast the meat in a slow oven (325°F) for about 20–30 minutes per pound, or until it is well done, basting frequently. Add a little hot water if fat tends to scorch during cooking.

2 Remove veal from oven; add dry white wine and make sauce with the pan juices in the usual manner.

Serves 4–6

Rack of Lamb in Pastry with Walnuts

Ingredients

1 rack of lamb (8 chops)
Salt and freshly ground
   black pepper
Butter
1 large onion, finely
   chopped
3 tablespoons olive oil
2 cups mushrooms, finely
   chopped
½ cup cooked ham, finely
   chopped
½ cup coarsely chopped
   walnuts
½ lb. frozen puff pastry
1 egg yolk, beaten

1 Ask your butcher to trim off fat from rack of lamb, separate meat from bone, and chine bone.

2 Season lamb generously with salt and freshly ground black pepper; brush with softened butter and roast in a moderate oven (375°F) for 10 minutes, or until lamb is half cooked. Allow meat to cool.

3 Sauté finely chopped onion in 3 tablespoons each butter and olive oil until onion is transparent; add finely chopped mushrooms and continue to cook, stirring constantly, until mixture is almost dry. Add finely chopped ham and coarsely chopped walnuts; season with salt and freshly ground black pepper, to taste, and cook for 1 minute more. Allow mixture to cool.

4 Spread lamb generously with chopped onion, mushroom, ham and walnut mixture; brush with softened butter

5 Roll out puff pastry into a thin sheet and wrap the lamb in it, allowing bones to protrude from pastry. Decorate pastry with "leaves" and "tassels" cut from pastry, fixing them to pastry with a little beaten egg yolk. Brush pastry with water; cover "leaves" and "tassels" loosely with a little aluminum foil.

6 Increase oven temperature to hot (450°). Place lamb in pastry on a baking sheet and bake in oven for 15 minutes. Remove foil, brush pastry slightly with beaten egg yolk and continue baking until the crust is browned (about 10–15 minutes more).

Serves 3–4

Roast Loin of Pork

Ingredients

1 loin of pork (4–6 chops),
   chined
6 tablespoons softened
   butter
1½ tablespoons French
   mustard
2 bay leaves, crumbled
½ teaspoon dried rosemary
   or thyme
Salt and freshly ground
   black pepper
3–4 sage leaves, quartered
12–16 slivers of garlic
GARNISH

4–6 tomato halves
Sliced mushrooms

1 Preheat oven to hot (450°F).

2 With the point of a sharp knife, make 12–16 incisions all over the roast about 1 inch deep.

3 Blend butter with French mustard, crumbled bay leaves and rosemary or thyme.

4 Season pork with salt and freshly ground black pepper and spread with mustard butter, making sure it goes deep into the incisions.

5 Stick a quartered sage leaf and a sliver of garlic in each incision with the point of a sharp knife.

6 Roast in the usual way, lowering heat to 300°F after the first 15 minutes. Serve with tomato halves scooped out and filled with sliced mushrooms, which have been sautéed in butter.

Serves 4–6

Basic Roast Chicken

1 Loosen the skin at the neck end of a cleaned and trussed roasting chicken as much as possible from the breast; insert stuffing over the flesh of the breast and fill the loose skin of the neck with as much as it will hold. Fold the skin over and fasten with 1 or 2 stitches. Stuff body cavity as well.

2 Tie 1 or 2 slices of bacon over the breast, making 1 or 2 slits in the bacon to prevent it from curling. Cover the bird with waxed paper and roast in a slow oven (325°F), basting frequently with butter, for 1–1½ hours, according to the size and age of the bird. Test it by feeling the flesh of the leg; if it gives way to pressure it is ready. A few minutes before the end of cooking time, re-move the paper and bacon; sprinkle the breast lightly with flour; baste well, turn up the oven temperature to 400°F and brown quickly.

3 When ready to serve: put bird on a hot serving dish; remove the trussing string, and garnish with watercress seasoned with lemon juice and salt.

4 Pour away the fat from the roasting pan in which the bird was roasted; add chicken stock and stir over a high heat until boiling, scraping in any brown bits from sides of pan. Season to taste with salt and freshly ground black pepper, and serve in a sauceboat.

Serves 4

Ingredients
1 roasting chicken (3½–4 lb.)
Parsley stuffing
2 slices bacon
4–6 tablespoons butter
1 tablespoon sifted flour
Sprigs of watercress
Lemon juice
Salt
1¼ cups chicken stock (see page 37)
Freshly ground black pepper

Roast Chicken à la Provençale

1 Ask your butcher to clean and truss chicken.

2 Peel garlic and cut into 12 slivers.

3 Make 12 deep slits into chicken with the point of a sharp knife, and push a strip of garlic and a sprig of rosemary well down into each slit. Season meat generously with salt and freshly ground black pepper. Place it on a dish, cover with foil and leave at room temperature for 1 hour to absorb flavors.

4 Preheat oven to hot (450°F).

5 Transfer chicken to a roasting pan; add finely chopped onion, olive oil, butter and dry white wine and roast for 15 minutes; then reduce heat to 300°F and continue to roast until chicken is cooked through but still moist (37–38 minutes per pound), basting occasionally with pan juices plus a tablespoon or two of boiling water if juices are scarce.

6 To serve: transfer chicken to an oval heated serving dish and moisten with pan juices. Sprinkle with finely chopped herbs and serve immediately.

Serves 4

Ingredients
1 2-lb. chicken
2 large cloves garlic
12 small sprigs rosemary
Salt and freshly ground black pepper
1 medium onion, finely chopped
2 tablespoons olive oil
4 tablespoons butter
6 tablespoons dry white wine
2 tablespoons finely chopped parsley
½ teaspoon each finely chopped fresh tarragon and chives

Roast Goose with Baked Apples

1 Place the goose on a rack in a roasting pan and spread with 4 tablespoons butter which you have mixed with crumbled sage leaves and crushed juniper berries. Season generously with salt and freshly ground black pepper.

2 Place bird in a preheated hot oven (450°F), and roast for 30 minutes. Spoon off excess fat and baste goose. Return to oven and roast for 18 minutes per pound, removing excess fat from pan juices and basting every 15 minutes.

3 Forty-five minutes before goose is done, place peeled and cored cooking apples around bird; dot apples with remaining butter and continue to cook.

4 To serve: place goose on a large heated serving dish and surround with baked apples. Remove all fat from sauce; whisk in currant preserve and add calvados or cognac; correct seasoning and spoon a little sauce over goose and each baked apple.

Serves 8

Ingredients
1 oven-ready goose (8–10 lb.)
6 tablespoons softened butter
Crumbled dried sage leaves
Crushed juniper berries
Salt and fresh black pepper
8 cooking apples, peeled and cored
Red currant preserve
4 tablespoons calvados or cognac

Broiling

Broiling—the roasting of meat, poultry, game or fish on an open fire—was probably the starting point of all cooking.

Broiling is really only a matter of applying direct, intense heat to whatever you are going to cook. In other words, if you are going to cook a steak, a chop or a piece of game, all you want to do is get that piece of meat as hot and as charred on the outside and as moist and tender on the inside as you possibly can.

It is best to remember when broiling, whether over charcoal or under gas or electricity, that the metal grid of the broiler should always be very hot when the objects to be broiled are placed upon it, otherwise they tend to stick to the bars of the grid. I like to heat the grid thoroughly, wipe it clean with a damp cloth and then rub a bit of fat over the bars to prevent the meat from sticking.

Open-fire broiling

One of the hazards of open-fire broiling is that fat dripping from the meat causes the fire to flare up and smoke. So keep coals under the meat for a short time until the meat becomes brown, then spread the coals in a circle with none directly under the meat. If flames still flare up, put a dripping pan under the meat. You will find that the meat will cook sufficiently even though there is no fire under it. If after the meat is done you still want a little more charring, push coals back under the meat and cook until it is as brown as you wish.

If you want a fire that sears quickly—perfect for broiling small fish, minute steaks or skewered meats—the charcoal should be piled about two or three inches high. If you need a lazy, more controlled heat for a whole leg of lamb or a large duck, the charcoal should be spread out in a single layer, with the coals separated a little from each other.

Keep a circle of fresh charcoal at the outer edge of your fire and push it into the center as needed. Do not put fresh coals on top of the lighted charcoal, or you will find that you have set up a dense smoke screen. A bulb syringe filled with water should be kept handy to tame flames when necessary.

It is important not to start cooking too soon with charcoal. For perfect broiling, charcoal should look ash-grey by day and have a warm, red glow after dark. If your charcoal is still flaming, it is too early to start cooking.

Broiling meat (or fish) over an open fire

Always give meat (or fish) on the spit or grill a chance to warm up and relax over the coals before you start basting. The meat (or fish) will absorb the flavors of your basting sauce better this way. A word to the wise: if your sauce has a tomato base, do not begin to use it until the last 15 minutes of cooking time. This gives a rosy brown glaze to barbecued food and avoids unnecessary scorching.

When broiling steak or lamb, cut a garlic clove in half and toss it on the coals for a wonderful flavor. For pork or ham on the spit, wait until meat is almost done and then drop a spiral of orange or lemon peel in the fire. I like to use herbs in this way too: a sprig of rosemary, a bay leaf or two, or a sprig of sage or thyme, make all the difference.

Charcoal-broiled Sole, Coulis de Tomates à la Provençale *(Illustration, pages 84 and 85)*

Ingredients

2 large sole, 1¼–1½ lb. each, trimmed and cleaned
Olive oil
Salt and freshly ground black pepper

COULIS DE TOMATES À LA PROVENÇALE

6 ripe tomatoes, skinned, seeded and diced
6 tablespoons olive oil
4 tablespoons freshly chopped parsley
2 tablespoons freshly chopped tarragon
½ clove garlic, finely chopped
6 coriander seeds, crushed
4 fennel seeds, crushed
Salt and freshly ground black pepper

1 To prepare sole: wash fish and score the skins in a criss-cross pattern with the point of a sharp knife. Brush fish with olive oil and season with salt and freshly ground black pepper.

2 To prepare *coulis de tomates*: combine diced tomatoes with olive oil, chopped parsley and tarragon and finely chopped garlic in a frying pan. Add crushed coriander and fennel seeds and heat through. Season with salt and freshly ground black pepper, to taste. Keep warm.

3 To charcoal-broil sole: brush the charcoal grill rack with olive oil. Place fish on it, white skin down, lying diagonally across the ridges and broil for 2 minutes. Place fish diagonally across the rack in the opposite direction, to mark it. Then broil for a further 2 minutes. Turn the fish over and broil for 4–6 minutes on the other side, in the same manner.

4 To serve sole: lift the fillets from the fish in 4 unbroken pieces, cutting along the length of backbone with a sharp knife, and sliding the blade between flesh and bones to loosen the fillets. Serve with *coulis de tomates*.

Serves 4

Seafood Kebabs *(Illustration, page 88)*

Ingredients

6 sea scallops
9 slices of bacon, cut in half
¼ lb. large shelled shrimp
Finely chopped parsley

MARINADE

6 tablespoons olive oil
4 tablespoons dry white wine
2 shallots, finely chopped

1 Separate orange coral "tongues" from sea scallops and cut white sections in half. Trim.

2 Roll a small strip of bacon around each coral tongue and piece of scallop. Thread scallop and bacon rolls onto skewers alternately with shelled shrimp.

3 Place marinade mixture in a shallow bowl; brush kebabs with mixture and allow them to stand in the mixture for at least 2 hours.

4 When ready to cook: brush kebabs again lightly with marinade mixture and cook gently over charcoal, turning frequently, for 8–10 minutes. Sprinkle with finely chopped parsley.

Serves 3

Charcoal-broiled Chuletas *(Illustration, page 88)*

1 Pierce steaks with a thick barbecue skewer.

2 Combine remaining ingredients and brush steaks with this mixture, forcing mixture well down into holes in meat. Allow meat to marinate for at least 2 hours before cooking.

These may be spread on hot steak before serving.

DEVIL SPREAD
Cream 1 tablespoon Worcestershire sauce and 4 drops Tabasco with ½ cup butter.

3 To broil: rub hot grid with a piece of fat; place steaks on grid, brush with marinade and broil over charcoal for 5 minutes on each side for a rare steak; broil a few minutes longer if you prefer steak to be medium rare.

Serves 4–6

ROQUEFORT SPREAD
Cream ½ cup Roquefort cheese with ½ cup butter.

MUSTARD SPREAD
Cream 4 tablespoons Dijon mustard with ½ cup butter.

Ingredients

4–6 sirloin steaks, 1-inch thick
8 tablespoons olive oil
4 tablespoons dry white wine
1 tablespoon lemon juice
2 tablespoons coarsely chopped onion
2 cloves garlic, chopped
¼ teaspoon oregano
¼ teaspoon crumbled bay leaves
1 tablespoon chopped parsley
Salt and freshly ground black pepper

Old English Grilled "Skuets"

1 Cut beef and lamb into 2-inch cubes; cut kidney into thinner pieces.

2 Marinate meats in olive oil and lemon juice with finely chopped garlic and herbs for at least 1 hour.

3 When ready to broil: thread meats on skewers with mushroom caps and small parboiled onions.

4 Rub hot grid with a piece of fat; place "skuets" on grid; brush with marinade sauce and broil over charcoal for 5 minutes on each side for rare, a few minutes longer for medium rare.

Serves 4

Ingredients

½ lb. boned sirloin
½ lb. boned shoulder of lamb
½ lb. lamb's kidney
4 tablespoons olive oil
4 tablespoons lemon juice
1 clove garlic, finely chopped
½ teaspoon each dried thyme and sage
Mushroom caps
Small white onions, parboiled

Broiled Lamb with Oriental Spices

1 Cut lamb into 1-inch cubes and combine in a porcelain bowl with remaining ingredients. Mix well and allow lamb cubes to marinate in this mixture for at least 4 hours, turning lamb from time to time so that it becomes impregnated with all the flavors.

2 When ready to broil: drain and reserve marinade. Thread meat onto skewers, 4–6 cubes on each; brush with marinade and broil for 5 minutes about 3 inches from the coals. Turn lamb and baste with marinade every 5 minutes until done—20–25 minutes in all.

Serves 6

Ingredients

2½ lb. lamb, cut from leg
Salt and freshly ground black pepper
2 teaspoons coriander
2 teaspoons cumin seed
1 large onion, finely chopped
2 teaspoons brown sugar
4 tablespoons soy sauce
4 tablespoons lemon juice
¼ teaspoon powdered ginger

Broiling under gas or electricity

Broiling is a wonderfully quick way to cook, but because it is so quick, it is difficult to broil perfectly. A minute too long under the broiler or the wrong temperature—too hot for a thin slice of ham or a piece of chicken; not hot enough for a thick slice of beef—will ruin the end result.

Practice, of course, will teach you how to deal most successfully with your broiler. One easy rule to remember: thick cuts of meat and fish should be cooked at a greater distance from the heat, thinner cuts, near the heat.

To broil steaks or chops successfully: season meat with freshly ground black pepper and place on preheated broiler tray. The thicker cuts of meat should be "seized" on both sides with a very high heat to preserve their juices, before cooking at a more moderate heat to allow its gradual penetration into the juicy center of the meat. The smaller cuts—tournedos, chops, cutlets—can be cooked without lowering the heat once the juices have been sealed in. For best results, season meats to taste with salt after cooking.

Broiled Rump or Sirloin

Ingredients

**1 large rump steak (about
1½ inches thick) or 4
small sirloin steaks
(½ lb. each)**
**Freshly ground black
pepper**
Butter
Olive oil (optional)
**Cracked peppercorns
(optional)**
Salt

1 Remove meat from refrigerator at least 30 minutes before cooking; trim off excess fat and score remaining fat in several places around side to prevent meat from curling up during cooking.

2 Preheat broiler for 15 to 20 minutes.

3 Either sprinkle both sides of steak, or steaks, with freshly ground black pepper and spread with 4 tablespoons softened butter; or brush steak, or steaks, on both sides with olive oil seasoned with cracked peppercorns.

4 Rub hot grill with a piece of excess fat; place steak, or steaks, on tray, and broil for 8 minutes on each side for a rare steak; brushing with melted butter or olive oil from time to time; broil a few minutes longer if you prefer steak to be medium rare. Sprinkle with salt, to taste.

Serves 4

Previous pages *Michel Guérard is a superb cook who loves the down-to-earth simplicity of country food as well as the sophisticated artistry of* haute cuisine. *Nowhere is this more apparent than his own country-based, three-star restaurant at Eugénie-les-Bains. Here, among other delights, we tasted a superb sole broiled over the open fire. Photographer John Stewart lends his artistry to Michel's in this great shot.*

Open-fire broiling is one of the oldest and most delicious ways of dealing with top-quality beef, lamb, poultry and game. We use open-fired real charcoal grills in both my restaurants to give a superb flavor to cuts of beef, lamb, veal, poultry, game and seafood.

Broiled Steak "Fines Herbes"

Ingredients

1 rump steak (about 1½ inches thick)
Freshly ground black pepper
2–4 tablespoons softened butter
Salt
Slices beef marrow

SAUCE

6 tablespoons melted butter
1 tablespoon chopped chives
1 tablespoon chopped parsley

1 Remove steak from the refrigerator at least 30 minutes before cooking; slit fat in several places around side to prevent meat from curling during cooking.

2 Preheat broiler for 15 to 20 minutes.

3 Sprinkle both sides of steak with freshly ground black pepper and spread with softened butter.

4 Rub hot grill with a piece of fat; place steak on grid and broil for 8 minutes on each side for a rare steak, grill a few minutes longer if you prefer steak to be medium rare. Sprinkle with salt, to taste.

5 To make sauce: combine melted butter with chopped chives and parsley in a bowl.

6 Transfer thick steak to a heated serving platter and pour sauce over it. Top with slices of beef marrow poached for 4 minutes in salted water.

Serves 4

Broiled Steak with Roquefort Butter

Ingredients

1 rump steak (about 1½ inches thick)
Freshly ground black pepper
6–8 tablespoons softened butter
Salt
½ cup Roquefort cheese
Juice of ½ lemon
2 tablespoons finely chopped parsley, chervil, or chives

1 Remove steak from the refrigerator at least 30 minutes before cooking; slit fat in several places around side to prevent meat from curling during cooking.

2 Preheat broiler for 15 to 20 minutes.

3 Sprinkle both sides of steak with freshly ground black pepper and spread with 2 to 4 tablespoons softened butter.

4 Rub hot grill with a piece of fat; place steak on grid, and broil for 8 minutes on each side for a rare steak; broil a few minutes longer if you prefer steak to be medium rare. Sprinkle with salt, to taste.

5 Cream Roquefort cheese and 4 tablespoons butter with lemon juice and finely chopped parsley, chervil, or chives. Season to taste with salt and freshly ground black pepper.

6 Transfer thick steak to a heated serving platter and top with Roquefort butter.

Serves 4

Grilled Steak with Mushrooms

Ingredients

1 rump steak (about 1½ inches thick)
Freshly ground black pepper
6–8 tablespoons softened butter
Salt
½ lb. button mushrooms
Lemon juice
Finely chopped garlic

1 Remove steak from the refrigerator at least 30 minutes before cooking; slit fat in several places around side to prevent meat from curling during cooking.

2 Preheat broiler for 15 to 20 minutes.

3 Sprinkle both sides of steak with freshly ground black pepper and spread with 2 to 4 tablespoons softened butter.

4 Rub hot grill with a piece of fat; place steak on grid, and broil for 8 minutes on each side for a rare steak, broil a few minutes longer if you prefer steak to be medium rare. Sprinkle with salt, to taste.

5 Sauté button mushrooms in 4 tablespoons butter and a little lemon juice. Season with salt, freshly ground black pepper and a little finely chopped garlic, to taste.

6 Transfer thick steak to a heated serving platter and top with mushrooms.

Serves 4

Skewered Beef with Chinese Oyster Sauce

1 Cut beef into equal sized cubes 1- to 1¼-inches square and place in a large bowl.

2 Make Chinese oyster sauce, as in recipe below.

3 Pour sauce over meat. Mix well and let meat marinate in the refrigerator overnight, or at least for 2 hours.

4 When ready to cook: preheat broiler for 15 to 20 minutes or build charcoal fire and burn until flames have subsided.

5 Thread meat on long skewers. (*Note:* Two thin slices of preserved ginger between every 2 to 3 cubes makes an attractive and flavorful variation to this dish.) Brush meat with marinade sauce and cook under broiler or over charcoal until done, turning skewers and basting with sauce several times during cooking. When cooked to your taste, sprinkle brochettes with thinly sliced scallions and serve immediately. Cooked rice—either simply boiled, or a pilaff, makes a good accompaniment.

Serves 4

Ingredients
1½ lb. sirloin steak
1 recipe Chinese oyster sauce (see below)
Thin slices of preserved ginger (optional)
Green parts of 2 scallions, thinly sliced
Rice (optional)

Chinese Oyster Sauce

1 Combine first 6 ingredients in a bow and flavor with cayenne pepper, chil sauce, or Tabasco, to taste.

2 An excellent flavoring marinade for grilled beef, lamb, pork, chicken, or duck.

Ingredients
1 tablespoon oyster sauce
1 tablespoon soy sauce
1 tablespoon honey
2 tablespoons dry white wine
2 tablespoons peanut oil
2 tablespoons finely chopped onion
Cayenne pepper, chili sauce, or Tabasco

Broiled Pork Chops

1 Two hours before you are ready to broil pork chops, lay chops in a flat porcelain or earthenware rectangular baking dish just large enough to hold them in one layer. Season chops generously with salt and freshly ground black pepper and spoon over olive oil, dry white wine, finely chopped onion and crumbled bay leaves. Allow chops to marinate in this mixture, turning them once in the two hours.

2 Preheat broiler for 15 to 20 minutes.

3 Place chops on rack of broiler pan; slide pan under broiler so that chops are 3 inches away from heat and broil for 5 to 6 minutes on each side, basting with marinade juices from time to time.

4 Transfer pork chops to rectangular baking dish; pour over pan juices and give them about 10 minutes more in the oven, or until chops are cooked through.

Serves 4

Ingredients
4 tender pork chops, ¾–1 inch thick
Salt and freshly ground black pepper
4 tablespoons olive oil
2 tablespoons dry white wine
2 tablespoons finely chopped onion
2 bay leaves, crumbled

Brochettes of Halibut or Turbot

Ingredients

1½ lb. halibut or turbot (thick end of fillet)
4 firm medium-size tomatoes
3 small onions
Rice or shredded lettuce

BASTING SAUCE

8 tablespoons olive oil
4 tablespoons dry white wine
1 medium onion, finely chopped
2 bay leaves, crumbled
Salt and freshly ground black pepper

1 To make basting sauce: combine olive oil, dry white wine, finely chopped onion, crumbled bay leaves and salt and freshly ground black pepper, to taste, in a large shallow bowl.

2 Cut halibut or turbot into chunks (1–1½ inches square). You should have about 30 in all—any thin pieces should be rolled up into pieces the same size as chunks.

3 Slice tomatoes and onions ¼ inch thick.

4 Place fish pieces in bowl with basting sauce. Toss fish carefully in sauce; cover half the bowl with slices of tomato and the other half with slices of onion. Place bowl in refrigerator for at least 2 hours.

5 When ready to cook, thread six 8- or 9-inch metal skewers with alternate pieces of fish and tomato and onion slices, starting and ending with a chunk of fish, and dividing ingredients equally among skewers.

6 Preheat broiler for 15 to 20 minutes.

7 Line rack of broiler with foil. Arrange skewers on it; brush with half the basting sauce and place under a broiler. Reduce heat to moderate and broil for 4–5 minutes.

8 Turn skewers; baste with remaining sauce and continue to broil for 4–5 minutes longer, or until fish flakes easily with a fork.

9 Serve immediately on a bed of rice or shredded lettuce, spooning some of the cooking juices over skewers.

Serves 6

Broiled Turbot Steaks with Garlic Butter

Ingredients

6 turbot steaks, about 1 inch thick
2–3 tablespoons olive oil
Salt and freshly ground black pepper
Lemon juice

GARLIC BUTTER

6 tablespoons butter
2 large cloves garlic, crushed
1 tablespoon very finely chopped shallot
½ teaspoon very finely chopped parsley
Lemon juice
Salt and freshly ground black pepper

1 Prepare garlic butter in advance. Work butter in a bowl with a wooden spoon until slightly softened. Add crushed garlic and chopped shallot and continue to beat until thoroughly blended; then beat in finely chopped parsley and lemon juice, to taste. Season to taste with salt and freshly ground black pepper. Roll butter into a long thin sausage shape; roll in foil and chill until firm again.

2 Preheat broiler for 15 to 20 minutes. Line broiler pan with a large sheet of aluminum foil.

3 Brush both sides of each turbot steak with olive oil and sprinkle with salt and freshly ground black pepper; arrange steaks side by side on the foil in broiler pan; squeeze a little lemon juice over steaks.

4 When ready to cook steaks, turn broiler down to moderate and broil steaks for about 15–20 minutes, depending on their thickness, turning them once and squeezing a little more lemon juice over. They are ready when the fish can easily be moved away from the bone with a fork.

5 Transfer turbot steaks to a heated dish and top each one with a thin slice of chilled garlic butter. Serve immediately.

Note: this same recipe is also good for salmon steaks, tuna steaks or tournedos of beef.

Serves 6

Basic Broiled Chicken

1 Only very young and tender chickens can be cooked in this way. Split cleaned chickens open through the back, flatten and trim birds, cutting off feet and wing tips; wipe with a damp cloth, and season generously with salt and freshly ground black pepper, paprika and a little lemon juice.

2 When ready to cook; preheat broiler for 15 to 20 minutes or build charcoal fire and burn until flames have subsided.

3 Skewer birds open; brush both sides with melted butter and sprinkle with fine browned breadcrumbs. Broil under broiler or over charcoal for 25–30 minutes, turning the birds occasionally and basting frequently with melted butter. Serve very hot, garnished with watercress and lemon wedges.

Serves 4

Ingredients
2 tender poussins (young chickens)
Salt and freshly ground black pepper
Paprika
Lemon juice
Melted butter
4 tablespoons fine browned breadcrumbs
Sprigs of watercress
Lemon wedges

Broiled Chicken with Lemon and Garlic

1 Cut chicken into serving pieces. Place chicken pieces in a generously buttered shallow ovenproof baking dish. Sprinkle with grated lemon rind, finely chopped garlic and dried oregano and pour over strained lemon juice and olive oil. Season to taste with salt and freshly ground black pepper; dot with remaining butter and refrigerater for at least 2 hours.

2 Preheat broiler for 15 to 20 minutes.

3 Cook chicken under it for about 15 minutes, basting frequently with marinade juices, until chicken pieces are brown on one side. Turn pieces over and broil on other side until well browned.

4 Baste chicken pieces with pan juices; cover baking dish (or cover chicken pieces with aluminum foil) and continue to cook in a preheated slow oven (325°F) for 30–40 minutes, or until chicken is tender, basting from time to time. Sprinkle with finely chopped parsley and serve immediately.

Serves 4–6

Ingredients
1 roasting chicken
½ cup butter
Grated rind and juice of 1 lemon
2 cloves garlic, finely chopped
½ teaspoon dried oregano
2 tablespoons olive oil
Salt and freshly ground black pepper
2 tablespoons finely chopped parsley

Magret de Canard au Poivre Vert

1 To prepare *glace de canard:* chop duck carcass and trimmings coarsely with a chopper. Combine chicken stock cube and tomato purée with finely chopped carrot and onion and sauté in butter until ingredients are well browned. Add 2½ cups water and dry white wine and cook, skimming from time to time, until sauce is reduced to half its original quantity. Strain sauce into a small saucepan, pressing vegetables and bones to extract all juice. Continue to cook sauce over a low heat until it is reduced to about ⅔ cup. Season with freshly ground black pepper, to taste.

2 Preheat broiler for 15 to 20 minutes.

3 Brush duck breasts with melted butter and season generously with salt and freshly ground black pepper, to taste.

Broil for 10 minutes on each side.

4 Then, using a kitchen towel to protect your hands from the heat of the cooked duck, remove skin. Keep warm.

5 Place duck breasts on an ovenproof serving dish or shallow casserole (an oval enamelled iron *gratin* dish is very good for this as it can go directly onto the heat). Keep warm in oven. Make a new "skin" for each breast of duck by covering with overlapping thin slices of apple which you have sautéed in butter.

6 Place *gratin* dish on a medium heat and heat duckling; brush apple slices with a little *glace de canard;* add green peppercorns to remainder and pour around duck breasts in pan. Garnish with watercress and serve at once.

Ingredients
4 breasts of duck
Butter
Salt and freshly ground black pepper
2 tart eating apples
Green peppercorns
Sprigs of watercress

GLACE DE CANARD
Carcass and trimmings of duck
¼ chicken stock cube
1 tablespoon tomato purée
1 carrot, finely chopped
1 medium onion, finely chopped
6 tablespoons butter
⅔ cup dry white wine
Freshly ground black pepper

Pan broiling

An excellent method of broiling steaks at home is to broil them in an iron frying pan or in one of the special corrugated broiling pans made for this purpose. For best results, you need a heavy iron pan with a raised grid. The ridges mark meat in an appetizing way. You can use an ordinary old-fashioned iron frying pan, however, if you cover the entire bottom surface with a little coarse salt, just enough to keep the meat away from the actual pan so that it will not stick.

If the pan or broiler is hot enough, it should not be necessary to add fat. Season meat to taste with freshly ground black pepper, sear quickly on one side, reduce the heat and cook for a minute or two longer. Turn the steaks.

Baste all meats with butter or olive oil before placing them on the hot grid and repeat this operation several times during the cooking process to keep the meat from drying out during cooking. Little beads of blood on the outside surfaces indicate that the meat is done.

To broil meat

Meat is often marinated in olive oil and wine to tenderize and flavor it before cooking. Add salt and freshly ground black pepper, to taste, and one or more of the following: sliced onion, shallot, garlic, soy sauce, bay leaf, thyme or parsley. Marinate meat for at least 2 hours in this mixture, turning it occasionally to ensure maximum penetration. Pat dry with a paper towel before broiling.

Beef

Beef is the most popular meat for broiling. The best cuts to use for broiling are the fillet, the rump and the upper cut of sirloin. I like a good thick rib steak, cut from the sirloin, complete with bone. The most expensive cuts of beef for broiling are those cut from the fillet. Slices of fillet are usually named according to their thickness: a tournedo is a small piece of fillet about $1\frac{1}{2}$ inches thick; the famous filet mignon of restaurant parlance is a piece $1\frac{3}{4}$-2 inches thick; while a piece 2–3 inches thick is known as a Châteaubriand.

White meats

When broiling white meats—veal, lamb or chicken—a moderate heat will ensure that you cook and color the meat simultaneously. Baste white meats fairly often with butter, or butter and olive oil. They are done when the juices coming from them are colorless.

To grill fish

Wash and clean fish; dry lightly and score the skin across diagonally on both sides to prevent it cracking during cooking. Season with salt and freshly ground black pepper, and brush with olive oil or melted butter. Or marinate fish for 2 hours before cooking in equal quantities of olive oil and dry white wine with a little finely chopped garlic and a crumbled bay leaf or two. Or split open the fish, remove the bones, then lightly coat the fish with flour, egg and breadcrumbs, or fine oatmeal.

For best results, always heat the grid thoroughly and grease it well before you place the fish on it. Keep the fish rather close to the fire if cooking over an open fire or it will become flabby. Cook fish for 8–12 minutes according to thickness, and turn at least once during the cooking time. I like to serve broiled fish with lemon quarters and *fines herbes* butter, where butter is beaten with finely chopped parsley, chives, tarragon and a hint of marjoram and lemon juice.

Pan-grilled Tournedos with Corncakes *(Illustration, pages 96 and 97)*

1 Heat a large, heavy-bottomed grill pan over a moderately high heat until drops of water shaken onto the surface bounce and sizzle on contact.

2 Grease pan thoroughly with a piece of beef fat impaled on a fork, or with a wad of absorbent paper soaked in olive oil.

3 When pan is practically smoking, add fillet steaks and sear for just 2 minutes on each side or until steaks are well marked, turning once. Season generously with salt and freshly ground black pepper.

4 Reduce heat to very moderate and time carefully according to chosen degree of "doneness": 5–6 oz. (2 inches thick): 3½–4 minutes/blue; 5½–6 minutes/rare; 7 minutes/medium; 8½ minutes/well done.

5 Half a minute before steaks are due to come out of pan, add a good lump of butter. Let it froth and turn golden.

6 Transfer steaks to a heated serving dish.

7 Pour buttery pan juices over steaks. Place prepared corncakes in pan and heat through. Transfer corncakes to serving dish with steaks. Top each steak with a piece of "snail" butter and serve immediately.

Serves 4–6

Ingredients
4 small fillet steaks
Beef fat or olive oil to grease grill pan
Salt and freshly ground black pepper
4 tablespoons butter
Prepared corncakes (see page 102)
"snail" butter (see page 96)

Pan-broiled Steaks with Scallions

1 Flatten steaks with the side of a cleaver and season both sides with salt and freshly ground black pepper.

2 Heat a large heavy-bottomed broiler pan over a high heat until drops of water shaken onto the surface, bounce and sizzle on contact.

3 Brush with olive oil and sear steaks 2 at a time, on both sides over a high heat, 30–45 seconds per side. Return all steaks to pan. Remove from heat.

4 Add sherry and brandy to the pan; stand back and set alight with a match. When flames die down, transfer steaks to a heated serving platter and keep warm.

5 Add butter to broiler pan; return to heat and bring cooking juices to the boil again.

6 Sprinkle steaks with chopped scallions and pour sauce over. Serve immediately.

Serves 4

Ingredients
4 thin slices sirloin steak, about 6 oz. each
Salt and freshly ground black pepper
Olive oil
4 tablespoons dry sherry
2 tablespoons brandy
4 tablespoons butter
2 tablespoons chopped scallions

Pan-broiled Beefsteak—Southern Style

1 Brush steaks with olive oil and season with freshly ground black pepper, to taste.

2 Make a paste of the remaining ingredients, with freshly ground black pepper, to taste. Set aside.

3 Heat a large, heavy-bottomed broiler pan over a moderately high heat until drops of water shaken onto the surface bounce and sizzle on contact.

4 Brush ridges of broiler pan with olive oil and broil steaks on both sides for 3–4 minutes per side for rare, 5–6 minutes per side for medium, and a few minutes more for well done.

5 When steaks are done, spread with paste and serve immediately.

Serves 4

Ingredients
4 small sirloin steaks
Olive oil
Freshly ground black pepper
1 teaspoon dry mustard
1 teaspoon salt
2 teaspoons brown sugar
2 teaspoons grated onion
4 tablespoons butter

Pan-broiled Steak Satés

Ingredients

1½ lb. rump steak, 1 inch thick
2 tablespoons soy sauce
6 tablespoons olive oil
2 tablespoons lemon juice
1 small onion, finely chopped
1 clove garlic, finely chopped
1 tablespoon powdered cumin
Freshly ground black pepper

1 Cut steak into thin strips 3 inches long and marinate for at least 4 hours in a mixture of soy sauce, olive oil, lemon juice, finely chopped onion and garlic, and powdered cumin.

2 When ready to cook, thread the beef on skewers and brush with marinade.

3 Heat a large, heavy-bottomed broiler pan over a moderately high heat until drops of water shaken onto the surface bounce and sizzle on contact.

4 Broil kebabs, turning from time to time, until cooked through. Season to taste with freshly ground black pepper.

Serves 4

Pan-broiled Marinated Lamb Steaks

Ingredients

2 lamb steaks, cut from leg of lamb
4 tablespoons olive oil
4 tablespoons lemon juice
2 teaspoons ground cumin
1 teaspoon ground coriander
Freshly ground black pepper
Coarse salt

1 Place lamb steaks in a shallow *gratin* dish or baking pan.

2 Mix olive oil and lemon juice and pour over steaks. Sprinkle both sides of steaks with ground cumin and coriander and freshly ground black pepper, to taste. Rub spices in well. Cover dish with aluminum foil and refrigerate for 12–24 hours, turning steaks once or twice during this time so that they absorb all the flavors.

3 When ready to cook; heat iron broiler pan over a medium heat until drops of water shaken onto the surface, bounce and sizzle on contact. Place steaks on broiler pan and broil for 3–5 minutes on one side. Season with coarse salt, to taste; turn steaks, brush with marinade and broil on other side for 3–5 minutes. Test meat for "doneness" but cutting into edge of steak to check color. Serve immediately.

Serves 2

Pan-broiled Tournedos with Corncakes and "Snail" Butter. Pan-broiling is an age-old manner of cooking tender cuts of beef, lamb and poultry. Use a ridged iron pan to mark meat. The corncakes—a cross between fritters and pancakes—are first pan-fried and then broiled for a moment or two in the ridged pan to give them the added flavor of the meat juices. To make "Snail" Butter, combine ½ cup softened butter with 4 level tablespoons finely chopped parsley and chives and flavor with finely chopped garlic and lemon juice, to taste. (Recipes, page 95 and 100).

Pan-broiled Lamb's Kidneys en Brochette

1 Split kidneys in half from rounded edge; remove thin outer skin; open and run skewer through them to keep them open. Brush kidneys with melted butter; season with salt and freshly ground black pepper and sprinkle generously with breadcrumbs.

2 Heat a large, heavy-bottomed broiler pan over a moderately high heat until drops of water shaken onto the surface bounce and sizzle on contact.

3 Brush ridges of broiler pan with olive oil and broil kidneys until cooked through. Do not overcook kidneys, however, or they will be tough.

4 Just before serving, place a knob of garlic butter on each kidney half. Garnish with grilled bacon and sprigs of watercress. Serve with boiled new potatoes.

Serves 4

Ingredients
8–12 lamb's kidneys
4–6 tablespoons melted butter
Salt and freshly ground black pepper
Fresh breadcrumbs
Olive oil
Garlic butter
4 slices grilled bacon
Sprigs of watercress
Boiled new potatoes (see page 134)

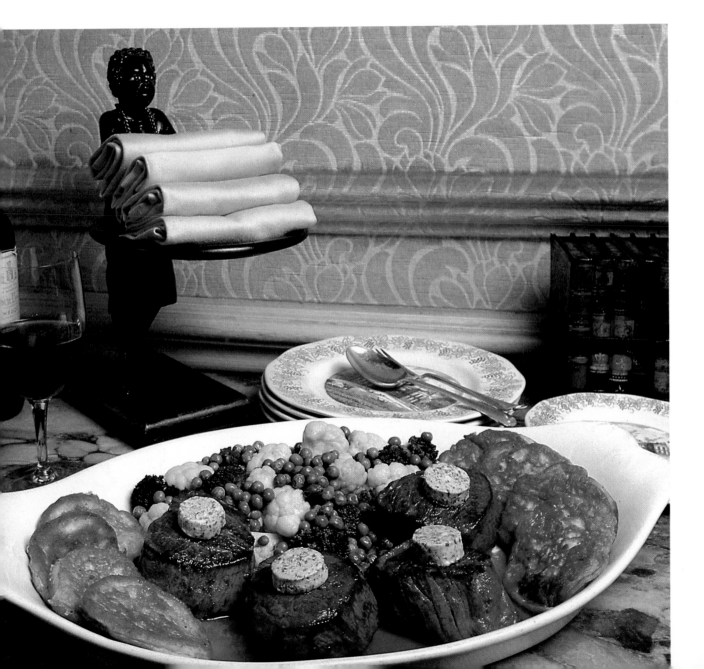

Pan-broiled Liver and Bacon

Ingredients

4 slices calf's liver, 6–8 oz. each
4 slices bacon
Melted butter
Salt and freshly ground black pepper
Béarnaise sauce (see page 48)

1 Heat a large, heavy-bottomed broiler pan over a moderately high heat until drops of water shaken onto the surface bounce and sizzle on contact.

2 Broil bacon slices until crisp on each side. Remove from pan.

3 Brush liver slices with melted butter and arrange slices in broiler pan, buttered side down. Cook until lightly browned; turn liver slices over; brush with melted butter and cook until lightly browned on the other side. Do not overcook. Liver should be pink on the inside.

4 Remote liver slices to a heated serving platter; sprinkle with salt and freshly ground black pepper. Garnish each liver slice with crisp bacon and serve with Béarnaise sauce.

Serves 4

Pan-broiled Veal Steak "Mode d'Içi"

Ingredients

4 veal steaks, ⅓-inch thick
Freshly ground black pepper
4 shallots, finely chopped
4–6 tarragon leaves, finely chopped
⅔ cup dry white Chablis
⅔ cup rich beef stock (see page 37)
4 tablespoons tomato purée
⅔ cup heavy cream
Salt
Butter
Oil
Fresh watercress

1 Remove veal steaks from refrigerator and season with freshly ground black pepper.

2 To make sauce: combine finely chopped shallots and tarragon leaves with dry white Chablis in a small saucepan and cook over a high heat until there are only 1 to 2 tablespoons liquid left in the bottom of the saucepan. Add rich beef stock and tomato purée; stir well; cover saucepan and simmer gently for 30 minutes over a very low flame.

3 Add cream and simmer for 10 more minutes; add salt and freshly ground black pepper, to taste; stir in 1 tablespoon butter and keep warm.

4 To cook veal: heat a heavy frying pan over a moderately high heat until drops of water shaken onto the surface bounce and sizzle away on contact.

5 Grease pan thoroughly with a thick wad of absorbent paper soaked in oil.

6 When pan is practically smoking, slap on the veal steaks and sear for just 2 minutes on each side, turning once.

7 Reduce heat to moderate and cook for a few more minutes on each side, until veal is cooked through and tender.

8 Just before steaks are due to come out of pan, add a good lump of butter. Let it froth and turn golden.

9 Transfer steaks to a heated serving dish.

10 Strain sauce through a fine sieve over steaks. Garnish with a few sprigs of watercress and serve immediately.

Serves 4

Pan-broiled Turkey

Ingredients

2 cooked turkey legs (drumsticks and thighs)
¾ cup softened butter
1 teaspoon dry mustard
1 teaspoon Dijon mustard
½ teaspoon curry powder
Cayenne pepper
Salt
Toasted breadcrumbs
Olive oil (optional)

1 Cut meat from turkey legs and thighs into cubes about ¾-inch in diameter.

2 Mix softened butter with mustards, curry powder, cayenne pepper and salt, to taste, and roll turkey cubes in this mixture. Let turkey marinate in this mixture at room temperature at least ½ hour before cooking.

3 When ready to cook, heat a large, heavy-bottomed broiler pan over a moderately high heat until drops of water shaken onto the surface bounce and sizzle on contact.

4 Toss turkey with toasted breadcrumbs and pan-broil turkey for 7–8 minutes, or until nicely browned on all sides, basting from time to time with a little melted butter or olive oil. Serve very hot.

Serves 4

Pan-broiled Chicken

1 Sprinkle chicken pieces with salt and freshly ground black pepper and marinate in Lemon Sauce (see below) for at least 4 hours.

2 Heat a large heavy-bottomed broiler pan over a moderately high heat until drops of water shaken onto the surface bounce and sizzle on contact.

3 To broil chickens: drain chicken pieces, reserving marinade juices. Pan-broil chicken pieces slowly until tender, turning and basting with marinade juices from time to time.

Serves 4

Ingredients

2 young frying chickens, quartered
Salt and freshly ground black pepper
Lemon sauce

Lemon Sauce

1 Combine olive oil, lemon juice, finely chopped mushrooms, onion, garlic and parsley and dried tarragon in a flat dish large enough to hold chicken pieces.

2 Season sauce to taste with salt and freshly ground black pepper. Add a dash of Tabasco for extra flavor.

Ingredients

4 tablespoons olive oil
4 tablespoons lemon juice
6 button mushrooms, finely chopped
3–6 tablespoons finely chopped onion
1 clove garlic, finely chopped
1 tablespoon finely chopped parsley
½ teaspoon dried tarragon
Salt and freshly ground black pepper
Tabasco

Pan-broiled Chicken with Paprika Sauce

1 Melt butter and chicken fat in a small saucepan; add garlic clove and simmer for 1 minute. Season generously with salt and freshly ground black pepper. Remove garlic clove and pour garlic-flavored fat into a shallow *gratin* dish.

2 Dip chicken pieces in garlic-flavored fat and sprinkle with freshly grated lemon peel and freshly ground black pepper.

3 Preheat oven to moderate (375°F).

4 Heat iron broiler pan to very hot until drops of water shaken onto the surface, bounce and sizzle on contact.

5 Place chicken pieces on pan and broil for 7 minutes on each side, turning pieces 2 or 3 times during cooking, basting each time with garlic-flavored fat. Finish cooking chicken pieces in preheated oven until tender, about 20 minutes.

6 In the meantime, make paprika sauce: sauté finely chopped onion and paprika in butter until onions are transparent. Add chicken stock and salt and freshly ground black pepper, to taste, and cook over a high heat, stirring constantly until stock is reduced to a glaze. Stir in sour cream and lemon juice, to taste. Keep warm.

7 To serve: arrange chicken pieces on a heated serving platter and strain paprika sauce over them.

Serves 4

Ingredients

2 tablespoons butter
2 tablespoons rendered chicken fat
1 clove garlic
Salt and freshly ground black pepper
1 3½-lb. chicken, cut up for frying
Freshly grated peel of 1 lemon

PAPRIKA SAUCE

1 medium onion, finely chopped
1½ tablespoons paprika
3 tablespoons butter
9 tablespoons chicken stock
Salt and freshly ground black pepper
1¼ cups sour cream
Lemon juice

Frying

Frying, strictly speaking, is simply the immersing of food in very hot fat or oil. In England, the term is also extended to pan-frying, which has come to mean the same as sautéeing, and in this country many foods are oven-fried, a new combination of sautéeing and baking which has much to recommend it for simple dishes.

Pan-frying

This popular method of cooking uses butter to sauté meat, fish or fresh vegetables in a frying pan. Finely chopped fresh parsley, lemon juice or slivered almonds are sometimes added to the sauce obtained. It is a good idea to add a little olive oil (but only a very little) to the butter at first; then, when what you are cooking begins to take on color, add more butter. This will prevent butter from browning during the cooking process.

For pan-frying, you need a good heavy frying pan or sauté pan and a little fat: lard, vegetable oil or a combination of vegetable oil and butter, or clarified butter. Professional cooks always clarify butter to get all the impurities and salt particles out of the butter, leaving a clear liquid which does not burn (see page 45).

Only very tender foods are suitable for pan-frying: fish, young chicken, chops, liver, beef fillets and vegetables. Thick slices of meat—other than fillet steak and chops—cannot be pan-fried successfully.

Do not crowd food in the pan and do not cover the pan when frying, because the steam thus held in will moisten the food and destroy its surface crispness.

Oven-frying

This process is a very useful method of cooking fish or chicken. Heat the oven to moderately hot (400°F). Use enough olive oil, or olive oil and butter, to cover the bottom of a shallow baking dish. Heat the dish in the oven for a minute or two and then put in the food, which you have first basted with melted butter and rolled in breadcrumbs mixed with chopped fresh herbs (parsley, chervil, chives, etc.) and a little grated lemon rind. Turn once during cooking time. Cook in the oven until tender.

Pan-frying is quick cooking at its gourmet best. Here we have—left to right—Pan-fried sea Scallops, Calf's Liver with Sage and Avocado, and Pan-fried Veal with Lemon. (Recipes, pages 105 and 106)

Pan-fried Tournedos

Ingredients

4 small fillet steaks
Beef fat or olive oil to grease frying pan
Salt and freshly ground black pepper
4 tablespoons butter
Prepared corncakes (see below)

1 Heat a large, heavy-bottomed frying pan over a moderately high heat until drops of water shaken onto the surface bounce and sizzle on contact.

2 Grease pan thoroughly with a piece of beef fat impaled on a fork (do not forget sides of pan), or with a wad of absorbent paper soaked in olive oil.

3 When pan is practically smoking, add 4 small steaks and sear for just 2 minutes on each side. Season generously with salt and pepper.

4 Reduce heat and time carefully according to chosen degree of "done-ness": 4–6 oz. (2 inches thick): $3\frac{1}{2}$–4 minutes/blue; $5\frac{1}{2}$–6 minutes/rare; 7 minutes/medium; $8\frac{1}{2}$ minutes/well done.

5 Half a minute before steaks are due to come out of pan, add a good lump of butter. Let it froth and turn golden.

6 Transfer steaks to a heated serving dish. Pour buttery pan juices over steaks. Place prepared corncakes in pan and heat through. Transfer corncakes to serving dish with steaks.

Serves 4–6

Variations on the tournedos theme:
TOURNEDOS IMAM BAYELDI
Sauté tournedos in butter and serve with half a small stuffed eggplant and a pilaff of rice (see page 140).

TOURNEDOS POMMES ANNA
Sauté tournedos in butter and serve on top of a small round of *pommes Anna* (see page 134) made in an individual tart tin. Serve with a small cooked artichoke heart mounded with puréed *foie gras* and a slice of truffle.

TOURNEDOS OPERA
Sauté tournedos in butter and accompany with individual tart shells filled with diced sautéed chicken livers mixed with Madeira sauce (see page 47).

Corncakes

Ingredients

1 small onion, finely chopped
4 tablespoons butter
1 small can sweet corn
1 egg, beaten
$\frac{2}{3}$ cup cold Béchamel sauce

Salt and fresh black pepper
Milk
Oil or fat, for frying

1 Sauté finely chopped onion in butter until onion begins to take on color. Stir in drained sweet corn, and continue to cook, stirring constantly, for 2 minutes. Stir in beaten egg and cold Béchamel sauce and season to taste with salt and fresh pepper.

2 Add just enough milk to make a loose batter which should be just enough to produce thin corn pancakes when fried in hot oil or clarified butter as detailed in Step following.

3 To make corncakes: pour 2–3 tablespoons of mixture into hot oil or clarified butter and fry until golden on both sides. Drain well and keep warm until ready to serve.

Serves 4–6

Fillet "Hare and Hounds"

Ingredients

4 fillet steaks
Salt and fresh black pepper
4 tablespoons butter
2 tablespoons olive oil
1 tablespoon Dijon mustard
2 tablespoons brown sugar

1 Season steaks generously with salt and freshly ground black pepper.

2 Heat butter and olive oil in a thick-bottomed frying pan. Sauté steaks on each side until tender. Spread mustard over top of steaks; sprinkle with brown sugar; transfer steaks to a *gratin* dish and glaze under preheated grill for a few minutes until golden brown.

3 Pour off fat from pan juices; heat remaining juices and pour over steak. Serve immediately.

Serves 4

Pan-glazed Sliced Sirloin

1 Trim fat from sirloin and slice into thin strips across the grain.

2 Heat 2–3 tablespoons butter and the olive oil in a large, thick-bottomed frying pan. When hot, add a quarter of the sirloin strips and sauté, stirring constantly, until beef browns and crusts slightly on the outside but remains rare and tender on the inside.

3 Remove strips from the pan and keep warm.

4 Continue to cook remainder of beef, in batches, as above. Keep warm.

5 Add chopped shallots to the pan and cook, stirring constantly, until they are just colored. Add lemon juice, dry sherry and red wine vinegar and continue to cook for a second or two more.

6 Add beef stock. Stir thoroughly and cook over a low heat until stock is reduced to a quarter of the original quantity.

7 Work in 5 tablespoons butter, tablespoon by tablespoon. Season to taste with salt and freshly ground black pepper; add finely chopped parsley and tarragon. Return beef strips to pan and reheat them in the sauce. Serve immediately.

Serves 4

Ingredients
2–2½ lb. sirloin steak, about 1½ inches thick
Butter
1 tablespoon olive oil
2 tablespoons chopped shallots
2 tablespoons lemon juice
2 tablespoons dry sherry
2 tablespoons red wine vinegar
1¼ cups beef stock (see page 37)
Salt and freshly ground black pepper
4 tablespoons finely chopped parsley
4 tablespoons finely chopped tarragon

Ham-and-Beefburgers

1 Form beef into 8 thin, oval-shaped patties.

2 Spread 4 patties with French mustard, and season generously with salt and freshly ground black pepper. Place a slice of ham on each patty, trimming ham to size of each patty with a pair of kitchen scissors. Place ham scraps on top of ham slice and top with remaining patties, pressing meat firmly together.

3 Sauté patties in equal quantities of butter and olive oil for 2 or 3 minutes on each side. Serve patties with knobs of anchovy butter, made by combining butter with anchovy paste, to taste.

Serves 4

Ingredients
1 lb. freshly ground beef
French mustard
Salt and freshly ground black pepper
4 thin slices ham
Butter
Olive oil

ANCHOVY BUTTER
2 tablespoons softened butter
Anchovy paste

Ham Hash

1 Boil potatoes in salted water. Drain thoroughly and toss in the dry pan over a moderate heat to evaporate excess moisture.

2 Put potatoes, cooked ham, quartered onion and green pepper through the coarse blade of a grinder. (Or chop them up together very finely indeed.) Season to taste with salt and freshly ground black pepper; add thyme and mix well.

3 Heat butter and olive oil together in a heavy, 8-inch frying pan. Add hash mixture; shape into an even cake with a spatula or the back of a spoon, and cook over a moderate heat for 5 minutes, or until cake is crisp and golden underneath.

4 Brown top under a hot broiler for 3–4 minutes.

5 Garnish with onion rings and a sprig of parsley. Serve immediately, cut into thick wedges.

Serves 2–4

Ingredients
4 medium-size potatoes
Salt
½ lb. cooked ham
1 small onion, quartered
½ green sweet pepper, seeded and cored
Freshly ground black pepper
¼ teaspoon thyme
2 tablespoons butter
1 tablespoon olive oil
Onion rings and a sprig of parsley, to garnish

Pan-fried Veal with Lemon *(Illustration, page 101)*

1 Slice veal into 8–16 pieces according to the size. Pound slices flat. Season veal on both sides with salt and freshly ground black pepper.

2 Heat olive oil and 2 tablespoons butter in a frying pan. When fat froths, add pieces of veal, lemon slices (they must be paper-thin), scallions and herbs and cook veal for 1 minute on each side, or until cooked through but still juicy.

3 Transfer veal and lemon slices to a heated dish with a slotted spoon. Keep warm. Add remaining butter to the pan, together with a little dry white wine (or water) and heat gently, scraping surface of the pan clean with a wooden spoon. Pour pan juices over hot veal and lemon and serve immediately.

Serves 4

Ingredients
1 lb. boneless veal, loin or fillet
Salt and freshly ground black pepper
1 tablespoon olive oil
4 tablespoons butter
8 thin slices lemon
4 scallions, sliced thinly
1 sprig fresh tarragon or rosemary
2 tablespoons finely chopped parsley
4 tablespoons dry white wine (optional)

Calf's Liver with Sage and Avocado *(Illustration, page 101)*

1 Peel avocados and remove pits; slice thinly. Brush each slice with a little lemon juice to preserve color.

2 Dip liver slices in flour well seasoned with salt and freshly ground black pepper.

3 Melt butter and olive oil in a frying pan; add sage leaves and sauté calf's liver very quickly on both sides. Add veal or beef stock and a squeeze of lemon juice to pan; top liver slices with sliced avocado; warm through and serve immediately.

Serves 4

Ingredients
2 avocados
Lemon juice
8 thin slices calf's liver
Flour
Salt and freshly ground black pepper
4 tablespoons butter
1 tablespoon olive oil
6 sage leaves
6 tablespoons veal or beef stock

Swiss Liver Brochettes

1 Cut thin slices of liver into 20 even-sized rectangles. Wrap each rectangle of liver in bacon piece and place each bacon-wrapped liver rectangle alternately with sage leaf on metal skewers, allowing 5 liver pieces to each skewer.

2 Peel potatoes and grate coarsely.

3 Heat 3 tablespoons butter and 1 tablespoon olive oil in frying pan. (I like to use an oval pan for this recipe as the brochettes look so attractive on an oval potato cake.) Add potatoes and season generously with salt and freshly ground black pepper. Simmer gently, covered, shaking pan from time to time to prevent sticking, until potato cake is crisp and brown on the bottom. Invert potato cake onto a plate and then slide cake into frying pan to brown other side. Transfer to an oval heated serving platter and keep warm.

4 Heat remaining butter and olive oil in another frying pan and sauté finely chopped onion until transparent. Add liver brochettes and sauté, covered, until brown and tender.

5 To serve: arrange brochettes on potato cake.

Serves 4

Ingredients
4–6 thin slices fresh calf's liver
10 slices bacon, cut in half crosswise
16 sage leaves
4–6 potatoes
6 tablespoons butter
2 tablespoons olive oil
Salt and freshly ground black pepper
1 medium Spanish onion, finely chopped

Opposite page *Sauté of Duckling with Wine Vinegar. Tender duckling sautéed in clarified butter until golden on all sides, splashed with sherry vinegar and then gently pan-simmered in a sauce enriched with wine and finely chopped shallots. (Recipe, page 106)*

Sauté of Duckling (Illustration, page 104)

Ingredients

1 tender duck (5–6 lb.), or 2 smaller ones
Salt and fresh black pepper
2 stalks celery, chopped
2 carrots, sliced
2 large onions, sliced
4 tablespoons cognac
2 cups dry red wine
¾ cup unsmoked bacon, diced
4 tablespoons olive oil
2 tablespoons dry sherry
1 tablespoon wine vinegar
2 tablespoons butter
1 tablespoon flour
Bouquet garni
2 cloves garlic

1 Cut duck into serving pieces and place in a porcelain or earthenware bowl. Add salt and freshly ground black pepper, chopped celery, sliced carrots and onions, cognac and red wine, and marinate the duck in this mixture overnight.

2 Remove duck pieces from the marinade; drain and pat dry. Reserve marinade.

3 Pan-fry diced unsmoked bacon in olive oil in a large frying pan until golden. Remove bacon bits and reserve. Pan-fry duck pieces over a low heat in remaining fat until brown on all sides. Return bacon bits to pan; cover frying pan and simmer gently for 20 minutes.

4 Skim excess fat from pan juices. Add sherry and wine vinegar and stir over high heat for 2–3 minutes.

5 To prepare sauce: while duck is cooking, make a roux. Strain marinade juices into roux mixture and stir over a low heat, until smooth.

6 Add marinade vegetables, bouquet garni and garlic to the thickened sauce and simmer over a very low heat for 20 minutes.

7 When ready to serve: remove bouquet garni; skim off excess fat; strain sauce through a fine sieve over duck and bacon pieces in pan, pressing vegetables well, to extract full flavor. Simmer duck pieces in sauce until tender. Serve with boiled noodles.

Serves 4–6

Basic Sautéed Chicken with Aromatics

Ingredients

1 tender chicken (2½–3 lb.)
Salt and freshly ground black pepper
2 tablespoons butter
2 tablespoons olive oil
Bouquet garni
1 medium onion, finely chopped
1 small clove garlic, finely chopped
⅔ cup dry white wine
⅔ cup heavy cream
4 ripe tomatoes, peeled, seeded and chopped
4 button mushrooms, simmered in butter and lemon juice

1 Cut chicken into serving pieces, reserving backbone. Season well with salt and freshly ground black pepper, and put chicken pieces, flesh side down, in a sauté pan or thick-bottomed frying pan just large enough to hold them comfortably. Add butter and olive oil and sauté chicken pieces until they are browned on all sides—about 10 minutes.

2 Add backbone and bouquet garni; cover pan and simmer gently for 20 minutes. Remove wings and breasts after 15 minutes. They are the most delicate, and cook most quickly. Keep warm.

3 Remove remaining chicken pieces and sauté finely chopped onion in pan juices until transparent. Add garlic and dry white wine, and continue cooking until wine is reduced to half the original quantity. Add heavy cream and chopped tomatoes and simmer gently for 5–10 minutes more. Do not allow sauce to boil.

4 Return sautéed chicken to the pan and allow it to steep gently, covered, over the lowest of heats for 5 minutes. Do not allow liquid to boil or your sauce will separate and the chicken will be tough. Garnish chicken with button mushrooms.

Pan-fried Sea Scallops (Illustration, pages 100 and 101)

Ingredients

8 sea scallops
2 eggs, beaten
4 tablespoons heavy cream
Salt and fresh black pepper
Cornmeal, or breadcrumbs
½ cup butter
⅔ cup oil, for frying
Lemon wedges

1 Wash and trim sea scallops; slice in half.

2 Combine beaten eggs and cream in a bowl. Add salt and freshly ground black pepper, to taste. Dip sea scallops in egg mixture, then in cornmeal or crumbs, and allow to set on aluminum foil for about 5 minutes before cooking.

3 Melt butter in a thick-bottomed frying pan. Add oil; bring to frying temperature and cook sea scallops in fat until they are golden brown. Serve immediately with wedges of lemon.

Serves 4

Deep-frying

The way you fry is more important than the fat or oil you use. If anyone asked me to define the quality of a fried food, I would say that its quality was in inverse proportion to the oil or fat absorbed by the food. Deep-fried food should never be greasy. *Thus, the temperature of the fat is of prime importance:* it must be hot enough to "carbonize" the exterior of what is being fried at the very moment of immersion. This prevents grease from penetrating the food, conserves the juices, and allows the food to retain all its taste. Deep-frying is simple and quick when you know how.

Vegetable fats and vegetable oils are good for all deep-frying. Rendered beef fat is a good choice for meats, fish croquettes and less delicate foods. Chicken fat and butter are not suitable for deep-frying because they scorch at low temperatures. *The quality and freshness of the oil or fat used is of great importance.*

A frying medium uses itself up quickly, especially when it is heated to excess. I have found that I can double the life of my frying oil if I never allow it to smoke or boil. Use the bread test instead: drop an inch cube of day-old bread in the hot oil. If your temperature is right for deep-frying (375°F) the bread should brown in about 60 seconds.

1 Do not allow fat to smoke or boil.

2 The temperature of the fat should vary as little as possible during cooking.

3 If you plunge food into the fat a second time, the temperature of the second cooking must be higher than that of the first.

To deep-fry fish

When properly fried, fish should be a light golden brown and dry and crisp in texture, as free from fat as if it had never touched it. I like to deep-fry fish in a combination of lard and oil to give added flavor; for pan-frying I use butter or olive oil, or a combination of the two.

Small fish are better fried whole, large ones should be filleted or cut into steaks or cutlets.

To fry well, fish should be perfectly dry. Always pat fish dry with a clean cloth or paper towel before coating with seasoned flour, fine oatmeal or cornmeal, beaten egg and dry breadcrumbs, or a frying batter. This serves two purposes: (1) to keep fat from entering the fish while it is immersed in the hot cooking fat or oil; and (2) to add a flavorsome, crunchy coating to the fried fish, which adds enormously to the delicately flavored flesh within.

If seasoned flour or flour and milk are used as a coating, apply just before the fish is to be cooked, or the flour will become moist and the fish will not fry well. Batter, too, should be applied only at the last moment.

Délices au Gruyère. Make a thick white sauce; season it with freshly grated Gruyère cheese and nutmeg; spread it out in a baking-pan to cool; cut into rectangles. Dip each délice in flour, in beaten egg and then in breadcrumbs. Then deep-fry them for a minute or two in deep fat.

Délices au Gruyère

1 Melt butter in the top of a double boiler; stir in 4 tablespoons flour and cook over water, stirring continuously with a wooden spoon, until smooth. Pour in boiling milk and mix with a whisk to make a thick sauce.

2 Simmer sauce for a few minutes longer; add freshly grated Gruyère cheese and a little freshly grated nutmeg, and continue cooking, stirring continuously, until cheese is completely blended into sauce.

3 Remove sauce from heat; stir in egg yolks; season to taste with salt and freshly ground black pepper, and more nutmeg if desired. Continue to cook over water, stirring continuously, for 2 or 3 minutes, being careful not to let mixture boil. Spread in a rectangular baking tin and allow to cool. Cover with paper or foil and chill in refrigerator for 3 hours, or until needed.

4 Just before serving, cut into rectangles; flour lightly and dip in egg beaten with milk and olive oil; drain, roll in fresh breadcrumbs and fry in hot oil (375°F) until golden. Serve immediately.

Serves 4–6

Ingredients
4 tablespoons butter
Flour
2 cups, scant, boiling milk
1 cup freshly grated
    Gruyère cheese
Freshly grated nutmeg
2 egg yolks
Salt and freshly ground
    black pepper
1 egg beaten with 2
    tablespoons milk and 1
    tablespoon olive oil
Fresh breadcrumbs
Oil, for frying

Délices aux Fruits de Mer

Deliciously different little deep-fried *délices* of crab, salmon or shrimp can be made in much the same way as *Délices au Gruyère*.

Simply drain the canned fish of your choice—crab, Alaska King crab, salmon or shrimp; chop finely; season to taste with salt, fresh black pepper, cayenne pepper and lemon juice. Add to sauce in Step 3 of above recipe at the same time as you add the egg yolks; proceed as above.

Batter-dipped Shrimp

Ingredients

1½ lb. shrimp
½ chicken stock cube
Juice of 1 lemon
Cayenne pepper
Salt and fresh black pepper
Oil, for frying
Mayonnaise (see page 49)
Lemon wedges

BEER BATTER

1¼ cups all-purpose flour
Pinch of salt
2 tablespoons olive oil
⅔ cup beer, preferably lager
1 egg white

1 Dissolve chicken stock cube in 2 tablespoons boiling water. Add lemon juice and a dash of cayenne pepper.

2 Season shrimp with salt and freshly ground black pepper and marinate in flavored lemon juice.

3 To make beer batter: sift flour and salt into a bowl, and make a well in the center. Pour in olive oil and gradually add beer, stirring with a wooden spoon to incorporate flour from sides of well. Batter should be completely smooth and slightly thicker than a crêpe batter. Leave to rest for 2 hours. When ready to use batter: whisk egg white until stiff but not dry, and fold in gently but thoroughly.

4 Preheat oven to very slow (275°F).

5 To cook shrimp: half-fill deep-fryer with oil and heat it to 375°F using bread cube test (see page 107). Dip shrimp, one at a time, in batter so that they become completely coated and lower them—4–6 at a time—into hot oil. Cook for 3–4 minutes, or until batter is puffed and golden brown.

6 To keep shrimp hot: as shrimp are fried, lift them from frying basket, let them drain for a minute or two on a baking sheet lined with paper towels and then keep warm in preheated oven.

7 Serve with mayonnaise and lemon wedges.

Deep-fried Fillets of Sole

Ingredients

8–12 fresh fillets of sole
½ chicken stock cube
Juice of 1 lemon
Cayenne pepper
Salt and freshly ground
    black pepper
Flour
1 egg, well beaten
Fresh breadcrumbs
Hot lard or oil, for frying
Lemon wedges

1 Dissolve chicken stock cube in 2 tablespoons boiling water in a large flat soup bowl or serving dish. Add lemon juice and a dash of cayenne pepper.

2 Season fillets of sole with salt and freshly ground black pepper and marinate in flavored lemon juice for 2 hours.

3 When ready to cook, remove fillets

from marinade; pat dry with a paper towel; dip in flour, then in lightly beaten egg, and then in breadcrumbs, pressing breadcrumbs into fillets with a spatula to make them adhere well.

4 Shake off loose crumbs and fry in hot lard or oil (375°F) until golden brown. Serve with lemon wedges.

Serves 4

Deep-fried Eggplants and Zucchini

Ingredients

2 eggplants
4 zucchini
Oil, for deep-frying
Flour
2–3 eggs, lightly beaten
Fine breadcrumbs
Salt and freshly ground
    black pepper

1 Do not peel eggplants or zucchini. Cut eggplants crosswise into ¼-inch slices; then cut each slice into strips ¼-inch thick. Trim ends from zucchini and cut each across into 2 equal-sized pieces. Cut each piece in 2 lengthwise and remove seeds. Then cut into ¼-inch thick strips.

2 Preheat oven to very slow (275°F).

3 Half-fill the deep-fryer with oil and heat it to 375°F using the bread cube test (see page 107).

4 Dip eggplant and zucchini strips, a

few at a time, into flour, then into lightly beaten eggs and then into breadcrumbs. Fry strips, 12–20 at a time, in hot oil until golden brown.

5 To keep vegetable strips hot: as vegetable strips are fried, lift them from frying basket; let them drain for a minute or two on a baking sheet lined with paper towels and then keep warm in preheated oven.

6 Season generously and serve at once.

Serves 4–6

Chinese stir-frying

Chinese cooking has much to recommend it when it comes to quick, easy dishes with a truly fabulous flavor. I often serve my friends a quickly prepared dish of strips of lean beef and green peppers, tossed for minutes only in a wok—a Chinese round-bottomed frying pan—before being steamed for a moment or two in a pungent sauce made of equal quantities of Chinese soy sauce, oyster sauce, dry white wine and peanut oil, softened in flavor with a little honey.

So, if you are like so many friends of mine—who admit that they love Chinese food but are afraid to cook it themselves because it is too different, too exotic, to try—change your mind, I beg of you. Chinese food *is* different, of course. But the stir-fry recipes I have chosen for you are simple, quick and easy.

The Canton school of cooking, one of the best known in the Western world, is famous for quick stir-frying of meats and vegetables together. The secret here is the cutting of the ingredients to the same size so that they not only look well together in the finished dish, but they cook more quickly in the hot oil.

Quick stir-frying is as easy as it sounds. All that is needed is a round-bottomed shallow frying pan or wok.

The foods to be stir-fried are cut into small, uniform pieces before they are cooked so that more surface is exposed to the heat. As a result the foods cook quicker and do not lose their character, flavor or vitamin content. Vegetables cooked in the *ch'ao* manner are cooked for minutes only (spinach, 3–5 minutes; green beans, 9 minutes). Thinly sliced pieces of meat are cooked through almost as soon as they touch the pan. Even pork can be cooked in a matter of minutes in this particular way.

To quick stir-fry beef: cut fillet or rump steak into pieces 2 inches square and then slice each square against the grain into thin strips $\frac{1}{16}$-inch thick. Marinate the slices for at least 30 minutes in a mixture of cornstarch mixed with water, soy sauce and saké, or sherry, to keep in juices and add flavor during cooking time.

Tender vegetables such as scallions and young leeks are cut across the grain. Carrots, celery and asparagus are usually cut diagonally so that a large area of the cut vegetable will be exposed to the heat during cooking.

All ingredients should be prepared before you start cooking. Cut vegetables and meats to size and place them near the stove on individual plates. You won't have time, once you start cooking, to chop or cut an extra ingredient. And remember, a high heat is essential for quick stir-frying. The wok has rounded sides which allow every part of it to become very hot.

In the Chinese meal, rice bowls are always individual. I like to use mine as a "dripping bowl," carrying each morsel of shrimp in oyster sauce, or pork ball in sweet and sour, or crisp stir-fried vegetables by the chopstickful (if there is such a word) from the central dish over my bowl to allow some of the juices to drip into the fluffy rice, adding their own subtle flavor to the rice in passing.

I find that food eaten in this manner actually tastes better than when it is served Western style, all on one plate and eaten with a fork. Enjoyed the Chinese way, in little morsels from the bubbling hot central dish, each single nugget is a small mystery, its flavor a nagging reminder of some subtle ingredient just beyond your palate's memory.

Stir-fried Duck with Mixed Vegetables

Ingredients

- 2 breasts of lightly roasted duck
- 2 tablespoons Chinese oyster sauce
- 1 tablespoon Chinese chili sauce
- 2 tablespoons soy sauce
- 2 tablespoons peanut oil
- 2 tablespoons honey
- 2 tablespoons dry white wine
- ¼ lb. green beans cooked in boiling salted water until just tender
- 4 canned water chestnuts, thinly sliced
- 1½ cups button mushrooms, thinly sliced
- 8 scallions cut into 2-inch segments

1 Cut duck into even-size cubes. Place in a large flat bowl and add Chinese oyster sauce, chili sauce and soy sauce (obtainable in some supermarkets and all Chinese grocery stores), peanut oil, honey and dry white wine. Toss and marinate duck in sauce for at least 2 hours.

2 When ready to cook, heat a Chinese wok, or a large thick-bottomed frying pan, over a high heat; add duck pieces and stir-fry until duck is crisp and heated through. Add marinade juices, green beans, thinly sliced water chestnuts and mushrooms, and scallion segments. Continue to cook, stirring constantly, for 1 minute more. Serve immediately.

Serves 4 as part of a Chinese meal, or 2 as a separate dish on its own.

Below *Chinese Stir-fried Rice. Toss cooked rice over a high heat with sausage or diced ham, chicken and pork and sliced mushrooms, and chopped onions. Top with thin strips of Chinese Omelette. (Recipe, page 114)*

Right *Stir-fried Duck with sliced mushrooms, water chestnuts, green beans and scallions is first marinated in a mixture of soy, oyster and chill with dry white wine, honey and peanut oil.*

Stir-fried Chicken with Zucchini and Walnuts

Ingredients

2 raw chicken breasts
1 tablespoon cornstarch
Dry white wine
1 egg white, unbeaten
16 walnut halves
4 tablespoons peanut oil
2 zucchini, thinly sliced
2 thin slices fresh ginger,
    cut into thin strips
1 small clove garlic, finely
    chopped
2 tablespoons soy sauce
1 tablespoon sugar

1 Slice raw chicken breasts lengthwise into ¼-inch slices. Cut each slice across into 3 sections and cut each section into strips ¼-inch thick.

2 Dissolve cornstarch in 1½ tablespoons dry white wine and combine with unbeaten egg white.

3 Place chicken strips in a large flat bowl; pour over egg white mixture and toss well.

4 Place walnut halves in a small frying pan; add cold water to just cover them and bring to the boil. As soon as water boils, drain and pat dry, removing any skins to take away bitter flavor.

5 Heat peanut oil in a Chinese wok, or large frying pan; add blanched walnut halves and stir-fry until they are lightly browned. Add zucchini and stir-fry for 1 minute more. Transfer walnuts and zucchini to a plate.

6 Add chicken, ginger strips and finely chopped garlic to wok or frying pan, and stir-fry until chicken pieces change color. When chicken pieces change color, add fried walnuts and zucchini, soy sauce, sugar and 2 tablespoons dry white wine and continue to cook for 1 minute more. Serve immediately.

Serves 4 as part of a Chinese meal, or 2 as a separate dish on its own.

Chinese Beef with Oyster Sauce

Ingredients

2 raw fillet steaks
2 green peppers
4 tablespoons Chinese
    fermented beans

CHINESE MARINADE

3 tablespoons Chinese
    oyster sauce
1 tablespoon Chinese chili
    sauce
3 tablespoons soy sauce
3 tablespoons peanut oil
3 tablespoons dry white
    wine

1 Trim beef fillets of fat and cut diagonally into thin strips.

2 Cut peppers in half and remove stems and seeds. Cut peppers into 1-inch squares.

3 Place meat in a shallow bowl and peppers in another. Combine Chinese marinade ingredients and pour half over peppers and half over meat. Toss each well and leave for 2 hours.

4 When ready to cook, heat a Chinese wok, or a large thick-bottomed frying pan, over a high heat; add pepper pieces and stir-fry until peppers are tender. Return cooked pepper pieces to bowl in which they were marinated.

5 Wipe wok, or frying pan, clean with a paper towel; add marinated beef pieces and stir-fry until tender; add green pepper pieces; pour over marinade juices and fermented beans and heat through. Serve immediately.

Serves 4 as part of a Chinese meal, or 2 as a separate dish on its own.

Chinese Stir-fried Rice *(Illustration, page 112)*

Ingredients

2 eggs
2 tablespoons water
Soy sauce
5 tablespoons vegetable oil
1 medium onion, chopped
2 cups cooked rice
½ cup diced cooked pork
½ cup diced cooked chicken
½ cup diced Italian sausage
6 mushrooms, diced
Salt and freshly ground
    black pepper

1 Make a thin omelette with eggs, water and ½ teaspoon soy sauce cooked in 1 tablespoon vegetable oil; cut in strips and set aside.

2 Heat remaining oil in wok or large frying pan; when it is very hot add finely chopped onion and sauté until golden. Add cooked rice that has been left to become cold, and diced pork, chicken, sausage and mushrooms and sauté gently for 3–5 minutes.

3 Just before serving, add egg strips, 2 teaspoons soy sauce and salt and freshly ground black pepper, to taste. Serve immediately.

Serves 4

Stir-fried Eggs with Soy Pork Sticks

1 Place a Chinese wok, or an omelette pan, over a medium heat; heat 1 tablespoon peanut oil; pour in beaten egg mixture and stir-fry until eggs begin to cook. Remove from heat and transfer half-cooked eggs to a dish.

2 Cut leeks into 1-inch segments and then finely slice each segment lengthwise.

3 Cut pork into matchstick-sized segments.

4 Cut scallions into 1-inch segments.

5 Heat 6 tablespoons peanut oil in wok, or omelette pan; add shredded leeks and cook for 2 minutes; add pork sticks and cook until pork changes color. When pork changes color, add scallion segments, soy sauce, sugar and dry white wine. Toss once; add stir-fried eggs and continue to cook, stirring constantly, until heated through. Serve immediately.

Serves 4 as part of a Chinese meal, or 2 as a separate dish on its own.

Ingredients

6 eggs, well beaten with 1 teaspoon each water and soy sauce
Peanut oil
2 leeks
2 cups lean pork
4 scallions
3 tablespoons light soy sauce
½ teaspoon sugar
2 tablespoons dry white wine

Stir-fried Shrimp and Asparagus Tips

1 Combine 1 tablespoon peanut oil, dry sherry and 1 tablespoon soy sauce in a shallow porcelain or earthenware bowl. Add shelled shrimp and toss well. Sprinkle with cornstarch and toss again.

2 Beat egg white in a small bowl until it begins to froth. Add to shrimp and toss. Refrigerate for 30 minutes.

3 When ready to cook shrimp, heat a wok or a large frying pan over a high heat until hot. Pour in just enough peanut oil to fry shrimp. Spoon in shrimp—5 or 6 at a time—and cook, stirring. Remove shrimp when they are pinky white. Drain fried shrimp on a paper towel until ready to finish dish.

4 To prepare asparagus: break off tough ends of asparagus and trim ends with a sharp knife. Rinse asparagus carefully to remove any sand and cut diagonally into 1½-inch segments.

5 To stir-fry asparagus: heat a wok or large frying pan over a high heat. Add 2 tablespoons peanut oil, ginger strips and finely chopped garlic and stir-fry asparagus segments, tossing them in oil over a high heat for 1 minute. Add 4 tablespoons water and stir for a few seconds more. Cover wok and steam asparagus over a high heat for 1 minute.

6 Add shrimp and stir; add 1 tablespoon soy sauce and sesame oil and stir-fry for 1 minute more.

Serves 4 as part of a Chinese meal, or 2 as a separate dish on its own.

Ingredients

1 lb. shelled shrimp, 1–1½ inches long
Peanut oil
1 tablespoon dry sherry
Soy sauce
1 tablespoon cornstarch
1 egg white
8–10 asparagus stalks
2 thin slices fresh ginger, cut in thin strips
1 clove garlic, finely chopped
1 tablespoon sesame oil

Stir-fried Shrimp with Snow Peas

1 Dissolve cornstarch in 1½ tablespoons dry white wine and combine with unbeaten egg white.

2 Pat shrimp dry and place in a large flat bowl. Pour over egg white mixture and toss well.

3 Heat peanut oil in a Chinese wok or large frying pan, and stir-fry shrimp until they change color. Add 2 tablespoons dry white wine, soy sauce, sugar and blanched snow peas. Toss over a high flame until heated through. Serve immediately.

Serves 4 as part of a Chinese meal, or 2 as a separate dish on its own.

Ingredients

½ lb. shrimp
1 tablespoon cornstarch
Dry white wine
1 egg white, unbeaten
6 tablespoons peanut oil
2 tablespoons soy sauce
1 tablespoon sugar
¼ lb. snow peas, cooked in boiling salted water until just tender

Cooking in a Casserole

Braising is simply a combination of roasting, stewing and steaming. The meat to be braised is sometimes (Step 1) larded; often (Step 2) marinated; always (Step 3) browned in fat and then (Step 4) cooked gently, covered, in a little liquid to preserve juices and flavor. In the classic French method, the casserole is lined with a layer of diced or sliced vegetables before slow simmering begins.

For the most part meat, poultry or fish to be braised is not cut up, but is braised in the piece, but the braising techniques listed below can also be used with great facility for cut-up pieces of meat, poultry or fish in the stews, ragoûts, daubes and casseroles of many countries.

1 Larding
Top-quality beef—rib or fillet—does not have to be larded, but it is usually wise to lard a rump or round of beef, a roast of veal or a leg of lamb with strips of bacon fat as long as the piece of meat to be cooked and about $\frac{1}{2}$ inch wide. Season these first with freshly ground black pepper and spices, sprinkle with chopped parsley and marinate for about 2 hours in a little brandy; then insert the strips into the meat with a special larding needle.

2 Marinating
The flavor of meat intended for braising is greatly improved by marinating it for a few hours in the wine which is to be the moistening agent in cooking. Roll the meat in a mixture of salt, freshly ground black pepper and finely choppped herbs, and place it in an earthenware casserole just large enough to hold it, on a bed of thickly sliced and fried carrots and onions, a generous bouquet garni, a clove or two of garlic, and some blanched, fried bacon. Cover the meat with wine and marinate for at least 2 hours in this mixture, taking care to turn it several times during this period.

3 Sautéeing
After marinating the meat, drain it well and wipe dry with a clean cloth. Sauté in a little olive oil, bacon fat, butter or lard, or a combination of these, to color it and seal in its juices. Then place the vegetables and herbs from the marinade in the bottom of a heavy casserole or braising pan just large enough to hold the meat; place the meat on this bed of aromatics and pour in enough of the juices from the marinade to cover the vegetables amply.

Raquoût of Lamb à la Provençale. Strips of orange peel and black olives add both color and flavor to this rustic casserole.

4 Casseroling

Add well-flavored beef stock; bring it to the boil; cover the casserole and cook gently on top of the stove or in a very slow to moderate oven (275°F-350°F) until the meat can be pricked deeply with a fork without giving blood. Remove the meat to another casserole just large enough to hold it; strain the sauce over meat through a piece of muslin and place casserole, covered, in the oven. Cook until

meat is tender, basting from time to time to keep the top moist. Before serving, correct seasoning and thicken the sauce, if necessary, with a *beurre manié* (equal quantities of flour and butter kneaded together).

Cook very slowly so that the meat will be tender and the fat will rise gradually to the surface of the liquid.

Vegetables—as well as meats, poultry and fish—can be braised in this way with excellent results.

Osso Bucco

Ingredients

4 thick slices shin of veal
Flour
Salt and freshly ground
   black pepper
2 tablespoons olive oil
2 tablespoons butter
2 cloves garlic, finely
   chopped
1 medium onion, finely
   chopped
⅔ cup boiling water or light
   stock
⅔ cup dry white wine
4 tablespoons tomato purée
4 anchovy fillets, finely
   chopped
4 tablespoons chopped
   parsley
Grated rind of ½ lemon or
   orange

1 Choose shin of veal with plenty of meat and have it sawed into pieces 2 inches thick.

2 Dredge veal pieces with flour; season with salt and freshly ground black pepper and brown them in olive oil and butter. Add half the finely chopped garlic and the onion; pour over boiling water or light stock, dry white wine and tomato purée; cover the pan and simmer gently over a very low heat for 1½ hours.

3 Add finely chopped anchovy fillets and remaining finely chopped garlic. Blend thoroughly, heat through and serve sprinkled with chopped parsley and grated lemon or orange rind, and accompanied by saffron rice (see page 140).

Serves 4

Ingredients

1 tablespoon lard
1 tablespoon olive oil
½ lb. fat salt pork, diced
1 onion, sliced
2 cloves garlic, chopped
2½ lb. lean beef, cut into
   bite-sized pieces
Salt and freshly ground
   black pepper
1 generous pinch marjoram
⅔ cup dry red wine
4 tablespoons tomato
   purée, diluted in water

Italian Braised Beef

1 Combine lard and olive oil in a thick pan or ovenproof casserole; when fat begins to bubble, add diced salt pork, sliced onion and chopped garlic and sauté until golden.

2 Add pieces of meat seasoned with salt and freshly ground black pepper and marjoram, and cook, stirring frequently, until meat is well browned on all sides. Now add dry red wine (one of the rougher Italian ones) and continue cooking until the wine has been reduced to half the original quantity.

3 Add diluted tomato purée and enough boiling water to cover the meat. Cover the pan and simmer gently over a very low heat for about 2 hours, or until the meat is tender and the savory sauce is thick and richly colored. A tablespoon or two of red wine just before serving will add extra bouquet to this dish, which should be served directly from the casserole.

Serves 4–6

Chicken in White Wine *(Illustration, page 121)*

1 Heat 2 tablespoons butter and olive oil in an iron *cocotte* or a heavy ovenproof casserole just large enough to hold chicken.

2 Sautée bacon pieces in fat until golden. Remove bacon; add coarsely chopped shallots and carrots and cook, stirring constantly, until vegetables "soften"; then add chicken and brown on all sides.

3 Return bacon bits to the pan; pour over cognac and flame. Then add bouquet garni, salt and freshly ground black pepper, to taste, dry white wine and chicken stock. Cover the bird with a piece of buttered waxed paper cut to fit the casserole, with a small hole in the center to allow steam to escape. Cover casserole and simmer gently over a very low heat until tender (1–1¼ hours). Add more wine or a little chicken stock if the sauce reduces too quickly during the cooking.

Serves 4

Ingredients
1 tender chicken (about 4 lb.)
Butter
2 tablespoons olive oil
¼ lb. fat bacon, diced
4 shallots, coarsely chopped
2 carrots, coarsely chopped
2 tablespoons cognac
1 Bouquet garni
Salt and freshly ground black pepper
1¼ cups dry white wine
⅔ cup chicken stock (see page 37)

Braised Chicken Mediterranean

1 Sauté chicken and diced slab bacon in butter and olive oil in an ovenproof casserole until chicken is golden on all sides.

2 Add pitted green olives, which you have previously soaked in hot water for 15 minutes to remove excess salt, and button mushrooms. Season to taste with a little salt and freshly ground black pepper. Moisten with cognac. Cover casserole and cook in a preheated slow oven (325°F) for 45 minutes.

3 Add sautéed potatoes and whole tomatoes and simmer gently for another 15 minutes, or until chicken is tender. Serve in the casserole or on a serving dish.

Serves 4

Ingredients
1 3½-lb. chicken
½ lb. slab bacon, diced
2 tablespoons butter
2 tablespoons olive oil
2 cups green olives, pitted
3 cups button mushrooms
Salt and freshly ground black pepper
6 tablespoons cognac
2 cups diced sautéed potatoes
4 tomatoes

Casserole of Duck with Red Wine

1 Cut duck into serving pieces and place in a porcelain or earthenware bowl. Add salt and freshly ground black pepper, to taste, chopped celery and carrots, sliced onion, cognac, lemon peel and red Burgundy, and marinate the duck in this mixture overnight.

2 Remove duck pieces from the marinade; drain and dry with a paper towel. Reserve marinade juices.

3 Dice bacon and sauté in olive oil until golden. Remove bacon bits and brown duck pieces in fat.

4 Place bacon bits and duck pieces with pan juices in a large ovenproof casserole and cook, covered, over a moderate flame for 20 minutes. Add the marinade juices and vegetables to the casserole; add rich duck stock, bouquet garni and garlic. Cook over a low flame for 1½ hours or until duck is tender. Remove bouquet garni, skim fat; correct seasoning; remove duck pieces and bacon to a serving platter; strain over sauce and garnish with boiled potatoes and sliced mushrooms which you have simmered in butter and lemon juice. Serve immediately.

Serves 4

Ingredients
1 tender duck
Salt and freshly ground black pepper
1 stalk celery, chopped
2 carrots, chopped
1 large onion, sliced
6 tablespoons cognac
1 strip of lemon peel
1¼ cups red Burgundy
¼ lb. bacon (1 piece)
2 tablespoons olive oil
⅔ cup rich duck stock, made with trimmings and giblets
Bouquet garni (parsley, bay leaf and thyme)
2 cloves garlic
12 small new potatoes
2 cups sliced mushrooms simmer in butter and lemon juice

Top left *Indian Lamb Curry.*

Bottom left *Lamb in Burgundy.*

Bottom right *Chicken in White Wine.*
(Recipes, pages 121, 122 and 123)

Indian Lamb Curry

1 Dust lamb with seasoned flour and sauté in butter and olive oil, stirring continuously, until meat is golden on all sides. Remove meat from pan with a slotted spoon; add sliced onion, garlic, green pepper and celery and sauté vegetables, stirring from time to time, until they are soft.

2 Mix *kari* blend thoroughly in a bowl and stir half the mixture into vegetables.

3 Make coconut milk by simmering a handful of dried coconut in ⅔ cup milk with 1 tablespoon butter. Press this mixture through a fine sieve; combine with stock and add to vegetables and spices. Now check flavor of sauce and add more *kari* until the sauce is of desired pungency. Cover and simmer for 15 minutes.

4 Add meat and raisins and continue cooking over a low heat or in a very slow oven (275°F) until meat is tender, stirring occasionally.

5 Remove from heat, stir in yogurt; correct seasoning and serve with boiled rice, *pappadoms,* and traditional curry condiments: mango chutney, apple chutney, preserved *kumquats,* chopped cooked bacon, etc.

Serves 4–6

Ingredients

2½ lb. boned lamb, cut into 1¼-inch cubes
Salt and freshly ground black pepper
4 tablespoons flour
4 tablespoons butter
2 tablespoons olive oil
1 large onion, sliced
1 clove garlic, sliced
1 green pepper, sliced
2 stalks celery, sliced
⅔ cup coconut milk (made with dried coconut, milk and butter)
1¼ cups well-flavored stock
½ cup seedless raisins
6 tablespoons yogurt
Boiled rice (see page 140)
Curry condiments

KARI BLEND

3 tablespoons curry powder
1 teaspoon each ground cumin and coriander
1 teaspoon each ground ginger and turmeric
¼ teaspoon each paprika and cayenne pepper
2 tablespoons flour
Coarse salt
Freshly ground black pepper

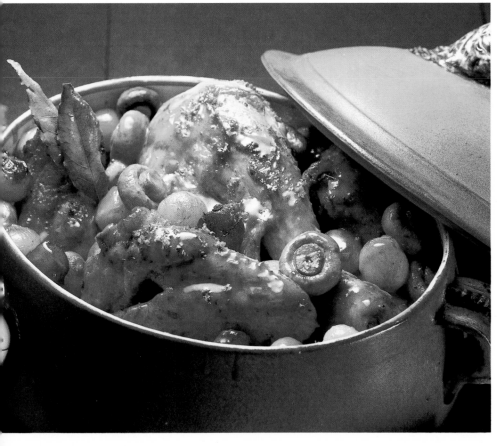

Lamb in Burgundy *(Illustration, page 120)*

Ingredients

2½ lb. lamb, trimmed and cut into 2-inch cubes
2 tablespoons butter
2 tablespoons olive oil
1¼ lb. small white onions
2 tablespoons flour
2 tablespoons tomato purée
1¼ cups Burgundy
Salt and freshly ground black pepper
1 bay leaf
¼ teaspoon dried thyme leaves
¼ teaspoon dried marjoram leaves
4 parsley sprigs
3 cups button mushrooms
Chopped parsley

1 Preheat oven to slow (325°F).

2 Heat butter and olive oil in a large, thick-bottomed casserole. Add onions and sauté in combined fats for 5 minutes; remove.

3 Add lamb, a third at a time, and brown well on all sides. Remove lamb with a slotted spoon and reserve.

4 Remove casserole from heat; discard all but 2 tablespoons fat. Stir in flour and tomato purée; return casserole to a low heat and stir until smooth. Gradually add Burgundy, stirring until smooth. Then add lamb, salt and freshly ground black pepper, herbs and mushrooms, stirring until well mixed. Cover casserole and cook in a preheated oven for 1½ hours.

5 Add onions; bake 1 hour longer, or until meat is tender. Sprinkle with chopped parsley. Serve with boiled rice (see page 140) or your favorite potato dish.

Serves 4

Braised Shoulder of Lamb with Herb Stuffing

Ingredients

1 shoulder of lamb
Olive oil
Salt and freshly ground black pepper
Lemon juice
Herb stuffing
Flour
2 tablespoons butter
6 tablespoons dry white wine
6 tablespoons chicken stock

1 Have your butcher bone and trim a shoulder of lamb ready for rolling. Do not have him roll this.

2 Brush lamb with olive oil and sprinkle with salt and freshly ground black pepper, to taste. Sprinkle with lemon juice.

3 Preheat oven to slow (325°F).

4 Spoon Herb Stuffing (see below) on meat; roll up and sew up with fine string. Dust the lamb roll with flour.

5 Melt butter and 2 tablespoons olive oil in an oval ovenproof casserole; brown stuffed shoulder of lamb on all sides over a medium heat; add dry white wine and chicken stock; cover casserole; transfer to preheated oven and cook for 1½–2 hours, basting from time to time with pan juices.

Herb Stuffing

Ingredients

½ lb. boneless lean pork
¼ lb. slab bacon, trimmed of rind
1 large onion, finely chopped
4 tablespoons butter
1 cup spinach, chopped
2 tablespoons finely chopped parsley
2 tablespoons finely chopped tarragon
¼ teaspoon dried oregano
2 eggs, beaten
Salt and freshly ground black pepper
Freshly grated nutmeg

1 Grind lean pork and trimmed bacon or process in a food processor.

2 Sauté onion until soft in butter. Add spinach and continue to sauté until spinach is well flavored.

3 Add finely chopped parsley, tarragon, dried oregano, beaten eggs and salt and freshly ground black pepper and freshly grated nutmeg, to taste. Mix well.

Ragoût of Lamb à la Provençale *(Illustration, page 116)*

1 Cut lamb into 1½-inch cubes and season generously with salt and freshly ground black pepper, rubbing seasoning well into meat with your fingers. Reserve bones and trimmings for stock.

2 Combine meat in a porcelain bowl with marinade ingredients and marinate in this mixture, turning from time to time, for at least 8 hours.

3 Drain meat (reserving marinade juices and vegetables) and season again with salt and freshly ground black pepper.

4 To make stock: place bones and trimmings in a baking tin; moisten with olive oil and brown in a preheated hot oven, (450°) turning bones from time to time. Place bones and pan juices in a large ovenproof casserole with marinade vegetables and cook over a high heat, stirring constantly, until vegetables are browned. Dust with flour and continue to cook for 5 more minutes. Add tomato purée, mashed garlic, well-flavored stock, leeks, celery, parsley, bay leaf, thyme, rosemary and sage. Simmer gently for 1½ hours, adding a little more liquid if necessary. Strain stock through a fine sieve; allow to cool, remove fat; dot with butter and reserve.

5 To cook lamb: heat 3 tablespoons butter in an ovenproof thick-bottomed casserole until it sizzles; place all lamb pieces in casserole and sauté over a reasonably high heat until lamb is golden on all sides; place casserole in a preheated moderate oven (350°F) and simmer gently for 1 hour, or until lamb is almost tender. Transfer lamb to a clean casserole and keep warm in a low oven.

6 Add strained stock to casserole in which you have cooked lamb cubes and cook over a high heat, stirring in all the crusty bits from the sides of the pan, until sauce is reduced to half the original quantity. Add remaining 2 tablespoons butter, diced, and whisk until sauce is smooth. Correct seasoning and pour over lamb pieces. Bring to the boil; reduce heat and simmer gently for 30–40 minutes, or until tender. Serve immediately garnished with black olives, sliced cooked carrots, glazed button onions and button mushrooms, and sprinkled with finely chopped tarragon and parsley.

Serves 4–6

Ingredients

3 lb. young lamb taken from shoulder and leg
Salt and freshly ground black pepper
5 tablespoons butter

MARINADE

2 large onions, finely chopped
6 carrots, finely chopped
3 tablespoons olive oil
2 cups dry white wine

STOCK

Bones and trimmings from lamb
3 tablespoons olive oil
Marinade vegetables
1 tablespoon flour
2–3 level tablespoons tomato purée
2 cloves garlic, mashed
1¼ cups well-flavored stock
2 leeks, white parts only
2 stalks celery
4 sprigs parsley
1 bay leaf
1 sprig thyme
1 sprig rosemary
4 sage leaves
Butter

GARNISH

24 black olives
4 carrots, peeled, sliced and simmered in butter with 2 strips of orange peel
12 button onions, simmered in butter and lemon until tender
12 button mushrooms, simmered in butter and stock until tender
1 tablespoon finely chopped tarragon
1 tablespoon finely chopped parsley

Cooking au Gratin

The term *au gratin* (from the French verb *gratiner:* to brown) applies to oven-cooked dishes—macaroni, noodles, *gnocchi,* meats, fish and vegetables—which are baked in shallow, ovenproof *gratin* dishes, usually covered with a sauce, sprinkled liberally with breadcrumbs, dotted with butter and browned in the oven or under the broiler until a crisp *gratin* coating forms. Cooking *au gratin* is associated in most people's minds with cheese, but although dishes *au gratin* often contain cheese, this is not an essential ingredient.

In order that there may be plenty of the characteristic crisp, golden brown top, a shallow ovenproof dish is used, hence the familiar term *"gratin* dish."

When browning in the oven, it is wise to set the dish in a pan half full of water. This prevents the sauce from spoiling or separating.

Left-overs—poached fish, chicken or turkey and sliced hard-boiled eggs—make an excellent luncheon or supper dish when cooked *au gratin.*

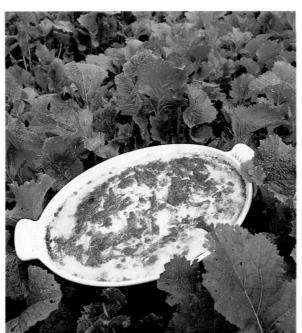

Left *Most vegetables can be gratinéed. Perhaps the most famous of these is Gratin Dauphinois: thinly sliced new potatoes and grated cheese, browned in the oven until smooth and flavorful, with a crisp golden crust.*
Near left *Gratin of Baby Turnips is a modern version.*
(Recipes, pages 126 and 127)

125

Fish and shellfish

Gratins can be made with either raw fish or leftovers. The most common raw *gratins* are made of whole fish, fish fillets or fish steaks. These can be sautéed in butter or poached in a little concentrated fish stock for a few minutes. They are then covered with a sauce *duxelles* (finely chopped mushrooms, onion and parsley, sautéed until smooth in butter) or a well-seasoned cream or cheese sauce, then sprinkled with freshly grated breadcrumbs and Parmesan cheese. Or, a little sauce Béchamel (see page 45) or Velouté sauce (see page 16) may be poured around the fish before it is dotted with butter and sprinkled with chopped parsley, mushrooms, shallots and cheese.

Vegetables

Most vegetables can be *gratineéd*. Perhaps the most famous of these is *gratin dauphinois* (thinly sliced new potatoes, cream and grated cheese, browned in the oven until smooth and flavorful, with a crisp golden crust), a wonderful accompaniment to steaks and roasts (see opposite). *Gratin savoyard* exchanges beef stock for cream in an equally delicious variation of this great dish. Try adding diced celery, finely chopped onions or shallots, or a hint of garlic to this basic recipe. You will be delighted with the result.

Larousse Gastronomique talks of a delicious *gratin languedocien* of peeled and sliced eggplants and tomato halves sautéed in olive oil and then placed in alternate layers in a buttered baking dish. The vegetables are covered with a mixture of fresh breadcrumbs and finely chopped garlic and parsley, sprinkled with olive oil (or dotted with butter), brought to the boil on the top of the stove and then baked slowly in the oven till the top is crisp and well browned.

Other vegetables—green beans, broccoli, endive, celery, leeks, onion and zucchini—can be *gratineéd* in a similar fashion.

Gratin of Baby Turnips or Carrots *(Illustration, page 125)*

Ingredients

1½ lb. long thin turnips, or
    baby carrots
Butter
1 egg
⅔ cup heavy cream
8 tablespoons freshly
    grated Gruyère cheese
4 tablespoons freshly
    grated Parmesan cheese
Salt and freshly ground
    black pepper

1 Peel or scrape turnips (or carrots) and slice them very thinly (about 1/16th-inch thick). Rinse thoroughly and leave to soak in a bowl of cold water for 15 minutes.

2 Select a shallow ovenproof dish about 9 × 5 inches. Grease with 1 tablespoon butter.

3 Preheat oven to very slow (300°F).

4 Drain turnip (or carrot) slices and dry them thoroughly with a cloth or paper towel.

5 Whisk egg and cream together until well blended.

6 Arrange a quarter of the turnip (or carrot) slices in the dish in overlapping rows; pour over 2 tablespoons egg and cream mixture; sprinkle with 2 tablespoons Gruyère cheese and 1 tablespoon Parmesan cheese; dot with 1 teaspoon butter; and, finally, season to taste with salt and freshly ground black pepper.

7 Repeat layers exactly as above, making four in all, and ending with grated cheese and butter.

8 Bake *gratin* for 1 hour 20 minutes, or until vegetables feel tender when pierced with a sharp skewer and are golden and bubbling on top. Allow to "settle" for a few minutes before serving.

Serves 4

Note: if top browns too quickly, cover with a sheet of aluminum foil.

Gratin Dauphinois *(Illustration, pages 124 and 125)*

1 Peel and slice potatoes thinly and soak in cold water for a few minutes. Drain and dry thoroughly with a paper towel.

2 Butter a shallow ovenproof casserole or deep *gratin* dish.

3 Place a layer of sliced potatoes on bottom of dish in overlapping rows; pour over a quarter of the cream, sprinkle with 2 tablespoons grated cheese (mixed Gruyère and Parmesan), dot with butter and season to taste with salt and freshly ground black pepper. Continue this process until dish is full, finishing with a layer of grated cheese. Dot with butter and cook in a preheated moderate over (350°F) for about 1 hour, or until potatoes are cooked through. If top becomes too brown, cover with aluminum foil. Serve very hot.

Serves 4

Ingredients
1½ lb. new potatoes
Butter
⅔ cup heavy cream
8 tablespoons freshly grated Gruyère cheese
4 tablespoons freshly grated Parmesan cheese
Salt and freshly ground black pepper

Creamed Eggs au Gratin

1 Melt 2 tablespoons butter in a saucepan; add flour and cook until the roux just starts to turn golden. Add milk and cook, stirring constantly, until sauce is reduced to half the original quantity. Stir in heavy cream.

2 Add 1¼ cups of this sauce to sliced hard-boiled eggs; season to taste with a little salt and freshly ground black pepper and pour into an ovenproof *gratin* dish.

3 Combine the remaining sauce with the beaten egg; fold in whipped cream and spread over creamed egg mixture. Sprinkle with fresh breadcrumbs and freshly grated cheese; dot with butter and brown in a hot oven (450°F) or under the broiler.

Serves 2

Ingredients
4 hard-boiled eggs, sliced
Butter
2 tablespoons flour
⅔ cup milk
⅔ cup heavy cream
Salt and freshly ground black pepper
1 egg, beaten
2 tablespoons whipped cream
Fresh breadcrumbs
Freshly grated cheese

Gratin of Sea Scallops and Leeks

1 Remove sea scallops from their shells. Wash them in cold running water to rid them of sand and trim. Drain and dry carefully.

2 Separate the white section of each sea scallop from the orange coral and cut in half.

3 Clean leeks and plunge into boiling salted water; when water comes to the boil again, cook for 3–5 minutes, according to size of leeks. Leeks should still be firm. Drain. Press dry with a paper towel to remove excess moisture.

4 Cut leeks into 1-inch pieces and arrange in the bottom of a well-buttered *gratin* dish.

5 Arrange coral and sliced sea scallops on top of leeks. Moisten with heavy cream and season generously with salt, freshly ground black pepper, cayenne pepper and grated nutmeg, to taste. Spoon over 1 tablespoon melted butter and cook in a hot oven (450°F) for 7–10 minutes. Serve immediately.

Serves 4–6

Ingredients
16 sea scallops
1¼ lb. leeks
Salt
Butter
½ cup heavy cream
Freshly ground black pepper
Cayenne pepper
Grated nutmeg

Cooking en Papillote

Cooking *en papillote* is not as difficult as it sounds. It is only half-cooking really, for when you enclose an ingredient in a *papillote* it is already half-cooked, or has at the very least been "seized" in hot fat before being folded into the little parcel of kraft paper, foil or parchment which gives this process its name.

There is nothing magic about this *haute cuisine* phrase: a *papillote* is just a piece of thin, strong paper or aluminum foil, about 8½ × 11 inches, cut into an oval or heart shape, greased with olive oil or butter and folded to enclose the ingredient to be cooked.

Cooking *en papillote* is not only colorful but gastronomic, for the ingredient cooked in this way simmers gently in its own juices, hermetically sealed, so that it loses none of its special flavor and aroma. It is almost always necessary to color the ingredient to be cooked in butter or olive oil before enclosing it in its casing, but it is important not to cook it too much in the process or you will lose the advantages and virtues of this exciting cooking method.

Nothing adds more glamour to a meal than individual servings of trout, mullet, or sole, veal cutlets, veal chops, or fat slices of salmon or turbot, first colored in a little butter or olive oil and seasoned with freshly ground black pepper, salt, fresh herbs and chopped shallots and mushrooms, then enclosed in their prepared paper cases, fried for a moment in hot oil to color and puff the cases, and cooked in the oven to succulent and savory goodness. Serve your *papillotes* in their puffed paper shells and let your guests cut them open at the table with a knife. (Aluminum foil cases are cooked in the oven only.)

To cook en papillote:

1 Cut kraft paper, parchment or foil in oval or heart shapes large enough to enclose, when folded, the food to be cooked.

2 Brush the insides of the shapes with melted butter or olive oil.

3 Sauté the food for a few minutes to color it before placing on shapes.

4 Place food on bottom half of shape; add butter and aromatics—finely chopped onion, shallot and mushrooms—or a *julienne* of lightly poached vegetables; season to taste with salt and freshly ground black pepper.

5 If *papillote* is kraft paper or parchment: fold shapes and crimp edges together and puff up shells by frying for a minute or two in hot oil in a frying pan. Then put shells on a baking sheet in the oven (at 375°F) where they will keep their puffed up appearance while the ingredients continue to cook.
If *papillote* is foil: fold shapes and seal edges well by crimping them together. Put shells on a baking sheet in the oven where the food will continue to cook.

Saumon en Papillote. Cooking **en papillote** *is not only colorful but gastronomic, for the ingredient cooked in this way simmers gently in its own juices, hermetically sealed, so that it loses none of its special flavor and aroma. (Recipe, page 130)*

Saumon en Papillote *(Illustration, pages 128 and 129)*

Ingredients

2 thick salmon steaks
Salt and freshly ground
   black pepper
Butter
16 thin strips of carrot, 3
   inches long
16 thin strips of cucumber, 3
   inches long
Peanut oil
16 strips of scallions (green
   parts only), 3 inches long
4–6 fresh tarragon leaves
4 tablespoons dry white
   wine
2 tablespoons reduced
   chicken stock (see note)
Sauce Hollandaise (see page
   49) or fresh lemon
   wedges

1 Season salmon steaks with salt and freshly ground black pepper and sauté steaks in 6 tablespoons butter until seared on both sides. Remove from heat. Cool.

2 Add strips of carrot and cucumber to pan and sauté vegetables for 5–8 minutes, or until vegetables are just crisp, stirring constantly with a wooden spoon to prevent them from browning or sticking to the pan. Season with salt and freshly ground black pepper, to taste. Remove from heat. Cool.

3 Cut 4 large oval sheets of kraft or parchment paper, approximately 7 × 11 inches. Brush paper ovals on one side with peanut oil. Place 2 paper ovals, oiled side up, on working surface; place half the carrot and cucumber strips in the center of each oval. Then place a salmon steak on top of vegetables. Arrange half the scallion strips in cavity of each steak and top each steak with 2 thin slices of butter and 2–3 fresh tarragon leaves. Add 2 tablespoons dry white wine and 1 tablespoon reduced chicken stock for added flavor.

4 Close the *papillotes* by placing the remaining paper ovals, oiled side down, over the salmon and vegetables, and crimping the edges of the paper ovals together carefully, making sure that each *papillote* is well sealed.

5 Oil a baking sheet with peanut oil and put it into a preheated moderate oven (375°F) for 5 minutes; place the *papillotes* on the heated sheet; brush with peanut oil and cook for 20 minutes.

6 To serve salmon steaks: bring *papillotes* to the table and open each *papillote* with a pair of sharp scissors or a very sharp knife. Place each salmon steak on a heated dish; surround with vegetable strips; spoon over fish juices and serve immediately. Accompany with sauce Hollandaise or fresh lemon wedges.

Note: to reduce chicken stock, cook 8 tablespoons well-seasoned chicken stock in a small saucepan until it is reduced to a quarter of the original quantity.

Serves 2

Mullets en Papillote

Ingredients

4 small mullets, 4–5 oz.
   each
Olive oil
Salt and freshly ground
   black pepper
4 bay leaves
4 slices bacon, broiled
Fat or oil, for frying
4 slices lemon
4 anchovy fillets

SAUCE

4–5 egg whites
1¼ cups heavy cream
4–5 anchovy fillets, mashed
Salt and freshly ground
   black pepper
Freshly grated nutmeg

1 Sprinkle fish with olive oil; season to taste with salt and freshly ground black pepper; place 1 bay leaf on one side of fish and a slice of broiled bacon on the other side.

2 Cut 4 pieces of kraft or parchment paper, approximately 8½ × 11 inches; fold each piece in half and cut into "heart" shape. Open; brush with olive oil and place prepared fish, bay leaf and bacon on one half. Fold paper shape over and seal edges well by crimping them together.

3 Sauté *papillotes* in deep fat or oil for about 18 minutes.

4 To make sauce: beat egg whites until stiff; whip cream; combine the two and add mashed anchovy fillets and salt and freshly ground black pepper and grated nutmeg, to taste. Cook over simmering water, stirring constantly, until sauce is just heated through. Strain and keep warm.

5 When *papillotes* are cooked, arrange them on a serving dish; open each carefully; decorate fish with a slice of lemon and an anchovy fillet. Serve with sauce.

Serves 4

Caneton en Papillote

1 Cut each duck into quarters, reserving livers; place in a roasting pan; season to taste with salt and freshly ground black pepper and roast for about ½ hour in a preheated moderate oven (375°F) until half cooked. Allow to cool and then bone duck pieces.

2 Put shallots, duck livers, garlic, chopped parsley, chervil and dried thyme through the finest blade of your grinder twice. Combine with Dijon mustard and dry white wine in a saucepan and bring slowly to the boil. Thicken with a little *beurre manié* (made with 1 tablespoon each flour and butter) and "finish" sauce by beating in 2 tablespoons butter.

2 Cut 16 heart shapes out of sheets of kraft of parchment paper, each one big enough to enclose one portion of duck; place paper "hearts" on table in pairs and brush lightly with melted butter. Place a little sauce on buttered side of one of each pair of "hearts"; place a boned portion of duck on the sauce; cover with sauce. Top with other paper "hearts," butter side down; roll and pinch edges together very firmly.

4 Bake *papillotes* in a preheated moderate oven (375°F) for about 20 minutes. Serve with remaining sauce in a sauceboat.

Serves 8

Ingredients
2 **ducks (about 2¼ lb. each)**
Salt and freshly ground
  black pepper
8 **shallots**
4–6 **cloves garlic**
4 **tablespoons chopped**
  parsley
4 **tablespoons chopped**
  chervil
2 **teaspoons dried thyme**
1 **tablespoon Dijon mustard**
½ **bottle dry white wine**
1 **tablespoon flour**
Butter

Vitello al Cartoccio (Italian Veal Chops in a Paper Case)

1 Sauté sliced mushrooms in 2 tablespoons each butter and olive oil in a large heavy-bottomed frying pan for 3 minutes, stirring constantly. Add diced tomatoes, strips of ham, oregano, salt and freshly ground black pepper to taste, and cook for a minute or two more.

2 Add dry white wine; bring to the boil; lower heat and simmer for 10 minutes.

3 Season veal chops with salt and freshly ground black pepper. Heat 2 tablespoons olive oil in a large clean frying pan and sauté chops until they are brown on both sides.

4 Cut 4 pieces of kraft or parchment paper large enough to contain veal chops. Brush paper on both sides with olive oil. Place 1 veal chop in the center of each piece of oiled paper and cover with the sauce. Sprinkle with finely chopped parsley and anchovy and grated lemon rind and fold over paper, sealing edges well.

5 Place veal packets on a baking sheet; bake in a preheated moderate oven (375°F) for 20 minutes, or until chops are tender.

Serves 4

Ingredients
4 **veal chops, 1 inch thick**
8–12 **button mushrooms,**
  thinly sliced
2 **tablespoons butter**
Olive oil
4–6 **ripe tomatoes, peeled,**
  seeded and diced
2 **slices cooked ham, cut in**
  matchstick-length strips
¼ **teaspoon dried oregano**
Salt and freshly ground
  black pepper
4 **tablespoons dry white**
  wine
2 **tablespoons finely**
  chopped parsley
2 **tablespoons finely**
  chopped anchovies
Grated rind of ½ lemon

Success with Vegetables

Vegetables are a very important part of our diet as far as nutrition and vitamin content are concerned. In addition to tasting better, well prepared vegetables retain more of these important nutrients and vitamins than those soaked in water. The key to successful vegetable cookery is a minimum of water and cooking time in order to retain maximum flavor and texture. To me the overcooking of vegetables is the eighth deadly sin . . . and should be punished accordingly.

So, do *not* drown vegetables in water. Instead, cook them in a little butter or olive oil, with just enough water, chicken stock, white wine or even steam to bring out their delicate flavors and textures. And serve them slightly crisp, not reduced to a pulpy, colorless mass.

Of course, the care and selection of your vegetables are of the utmost importance. Cooks who have their own kitchen gardens are to be envied, for new potatoes brought in fresh from the garden, peas picked an hour before serving, tomatoes still warm from the vine all add so much to the savor of good eating. But if this is not the case—and it rarely is today—great care must be exercised when shopping. Select vegetables that are crisp, fresh-looking and colorful. No amount of cooking and attention will revive limp, tired vegetables. They will have lost their texture and a great deal of their flavor and most of their goodness.

Don't peel vegetables unless it is absolutely necessary. It *is* true that most of the goodness is right under the skin, or in the skin itself. I usually wash vegetables with a stiff vegetable brush, or, in the case of mushrooms, tomatoes and very new potatoes, I just wipe them with a damp cloth. They are then stored in plastic bags or boxes in the refrigerator to keep them crisp and fresh until ready to be used. Parsley and other herbs will keep green and fresh in this way for weeks.

Keep a vegetable juice jar. Then if any liquid is left over, unwanted, after cooking your vegetables, strain it into the jar, kept covered and in the refrigerator for this purpose. Vegetable juices preserved in this way are wonderful flavor additives for soups, sauces and stews.

Cooks who have their own kitchen gardens are to be envied. For new potatoes and sweetcorn brought in fresh from the garden, peas picked an hour before serving, tomatoes still warm from the vine, all add so much to the savor of good eating.
Opposite page *Three Hot Vegetable Purées.*
Above *Corn and Bacon Soufflé.*
(Recipes, pages 136 and 137)

Boiled New Potatoes

Ingredients

1 lb. small new potatoes (20–24)
Coarse salt
Butter

1 Wash potatoes and either wipe, scrape or peel them.

2 Put potatoes in a pan. Cover with cold water; add a small handful of coarse salt and bring to the boil.

3 Simmer potatoes until they feel soft when pierced with a fork. The small ones specified in this recipe will take about 18 minutes.

4 Drain well and serve with plenty of butter and coarse salt, to taste.

Serves 3–4

Country-fried Potatoes

Ingredients

2 lb. large new potatoes
1 medium-sized onion, finely chopped
4 slices bacon, finely chopped
1 tablespoon butter
3 tablespoons olive oil
Salt and freshly ground black pepper
2 tablespoons finely chopped parsley

1 Scrub potatoes clean. Peel them and cut them into ¼-inch dice.

2 Sauté finely chopped onion and bacon in butter and 1 tablespoon olive oil until onion is golden, 4–5 minutes. Put aside.

3 In a large, heavy frying pan, heat remaining olive oil and sauté diced potatoes over a high heat until they are crisp and golden on all sides. Season to taste with salt and freshly ground black pepper.

4 Return sautéed onion and bacon to the pan; toss lightly to mix thoroughly with the potatoes and sauté for 1 minute longer. Serve immediately with finely chopped parsley.

Serves 4–6

Pommes Anna

Ingredients

1 lb. new potatoes
4–6 tablespoons softened butter
Salt and fresh ground black pepper

1 Peel and slice potatoes thinly and soak in cold water for a few minutes. Drain and dry thoroughly.

2 Butter a shallow ovenproof copper or enamelled iron casserole with lid (French chefs use a special thick copper *"pommes anna"* pan) and place in it a layer of sliced potatoes overlapping around sides of casserole. Spread potatoes with 1 tablespoon softened butter and season to taste with salt and freshly ground black pepper.

3 Repeat layers as above, with a final spreading of butter on top.

4 Cover casserole and cook in a fairly hot oven (425°F) for 45 minutes to 1 hour, or until potatoes are brown around outside edges.

5 To serve: invert golden brown potato "cake" onto a heated serving dish.

Serves 4

Buttered Glazed Vegetables

Ingredients

1 lb. small white onions, small carrots or small turnips
4 tablespoons butter
4 tablespoons chicken stock
1 tablespoon sugar
Salt

1 Peel onions, carrots or turnips and place them in a small saucepan; cover with cold water and cook over high heat until water boils. Remove from heat and drain.

2 Replace blanched onions, carrots or turnips in saucepan; add butter and chicken stock; season with sugar and salt, to taste, and simmer over low heat until vegetables have absorbed the liquid without burning and have taken on a little color.

Serves 4

134

Steamed Carrots

1 To prepare carrots: trim tops and tails of carrots. If they are young, you need only scrub or scrape them. Old carrots should be peeled. Average-size carrots (about 8 to the pound) can be left whole or cut into quarters. Small carrots (the finger-thick ones that come about 25 to the pound) should be left whole.

2 To steam carrots: place carrots on a rack over boiling salted water and cover steamer tightly with a lid. Steam over rapidly boiling water for about 15 minutes for average-size carrots. If you prefer them to be softer, cook for 4–5 minutes longer.

3 To serve: toss steamed carrots with melted butter and season to taste with salt and freshly ground black pepper and add a pinch of sugar to bring out their natural sweetness. Garnish with chopped parsley and serve immediately.

Serves 4

STEAMED GREEN BEANS

Cook as above, substituting a squeeze of lemon for sugar.

STEAMED BRUSSELS SPROUTS

Cook as green beans.

Ingredients
1 lb. carrots
Salt
4 tablespoons melted butter
Freshly ground black
   pepper
Pinch of sugar
2 tablespoons chopped
   parsley

The overcooking of vegetables is the eighth deadly sin. Garden-fresh vegetables should be simmered for minutes only in clarified butter; tiny new potatoes and green beans should be simmered for several minutes in boiling salted water before being tossed in butter.

Italian Cauliflower Sauté

Ingredients

1 medium-size cauliflower
Salt
Lemon juice
4 tablespoons olive oil
Freshly ground black
    pepper
2 tablespoons finely
    chopped parsley
Lemon quarters

1 To prepare cauliflower: cut off stem and remove green leaves from a medium-size cauliflower. Soak the head for ½ hour in cold water to which you have added ½ teaspoon salt and the juice of ½ lemon to free it from insects. Drain, and break or cut cauliflower into flowerets.

2 To cook cauliflowerets: fill a deep saucepan with enough water to cover cauliflowerets; add ½ teaspoon salt and bring to the boil. Put cauliflowerets in boiling water and simmer gently for 8–10 minutes. Drain.

3 Heat olive oil in a frying pan; add drained cauliflowerets and sauté until lightly colored. Season with freshly ground black pepper and lemon juice, to taste.

4 Serve cauliflowerets immediately garnished with finely chopped parsley and lemon quarters.

Serves 4

Sautéed Tomatoes

Ingredients

4–6 ripe tomatoes
2 tablespoons olive oil
2 tablespoons butter
Salt and freshly ground
    black pepper
Finely chopped parsley
Finely chopped scallions

1 Wipe tomatoes clean and slice crosswise into even slices.

2 Combine olive oil and butter in a large frying pan and heat until butter is melted.

3 Add sliced tomatoes and sauté for a minute or two on each side, turning tomatoes carefully with a spatula. Season generously with salt and freshly ground black pepper; sprinkle with finely chopped parsley and scallions and serve immediately.

Three Hot Vegetable Purées *(Illustration, page 132)*

Ingredients

3¼ cups frozen peas 3 cups
    frozen sweet corn or 4
    cups fresh carrots, thinly
    sliced
4 tablespoons chicken stock
4 tablespoons butter
1–2 tablespoons instant
    mashed potatoes
1–2 tablespoons heavy
    cream
Salt and freshly ground
    black pepper
Lemon juice and sugar
    (optional)

1 Place frozen peas or sweet corn on thinly sliced raw carrots in a pan. Add chicken stock and butter.

2 Bring to the boil; push a sheet of waxed paper down into pan on top of vegetables; reduce heat to moderate and simmer until very tender—about 5 minutes for frozen vegetables, 10–12 minutes for carrots.

3 Pour contents of pan into a blender. Add instant mashed potatoes. Turn to maximum speed and blend for 2 minutes, stopping occasionally to scrape down sides of container with a spatula. (If a blender is not available, put vegetables through a mouli or rub through a sieve. In the case of sweet corn, return contents of sieve to purée to give it bulk and texture.)

4 Return purée to pan. Beat vigorously with a wooden spoon over a moderate heat until purée is thoroughly hot again, adding enough cream so that it just holds its shape. Season to taste with salt and freshly ground black pepper. In addition, pea purée will be improved by a squeeze of lemon juice, sweet corn purée by ½ teaspoon sugar. Serve immediately.

Serves 4–6

Note: if you wish, you can reserve a tablespoon or two of the cooked peas or sweet corn kernels for garnish. Carrot purée looks well with a garnish of finely chopped parsley.

Corn and Bacon Soufflé *(Illustration, page 133)*

1 To prepare soufflé dish: grease base and sides of a 5-cup dish generously with butter, and coat with a mixture of freshly grated Parmesan cheese and stale white breadcrumbs, shaking out excess.

2 Preheat oven to moderate (375°F).

3 To prepare soufflé mixture: melt 3 tablespoons butter in a heavy pan, blend in flour and stir over a low heat for 2–3 minutes to make a pale roux. Remove pan from heat.

4 Bring milk just to boiling point in a separate pan. Add to roux very gradually, stirring vigorously to avoid lumps. When sauce is smooth, return pan to a moderate heat; bring to the boil, stirring constantly, and simmer 3–4 minutes longer until sauce is very thick and no longer tastes of raw flour.

5 Remove pan from heat and allow to cool slightly. Beat in egg yolks, one at a time; then turn mixture into a large bowl and allow to cool to lukewarm.

6 Sauté corn niblets with finely chopped onion in 3 tablespoons butter until onion is transparent. Add mixture to cooling sauce and stir with a wooden spoon until thoroughly blended. Then stir in crumbled cooked bacon and season with salt and freshly ground black pepper, and a pinch each of freshly grated nutmeg and cayenne pepper.

7 Add a pinch of salt to egg whites in a large bowl and whisk until stiff but not dry. Fold into lukewarm sauce as quickly and as thoroughly as possible, using a metal spoon.

8 Pour mixture into prepared soufflé dish and level off with back of spoon.

9 Place soufflé in the oven. Reduce temperature to 325°F and bake for 30–35 minutes, or until soufflé is well-puffed and golden-brown. Halfway through baking time, open oven door and sprinkle top of soufflé with freshly grated Parmesan cheese without removing it from the oven. Serve immediately.

Serves 4–6

Ingredients
SOUFFLÉ DISH

Butter
1 tablespoon freshly grated Parmesan cheese
1 tablespoon stale white breadcrumbs

SOUFFLÉ MIXTURE

Butter
3 tablespoons all-purpose flour
2 cups hot milk
4 egg yolks
1 6-oz. can corn niblets
1 medium onion, finely chopped
¼ lb. sliced bacon, cooked until crisp, then crumbled
Salt and freshly ground black pepper
Freshly grated nutmeg
Cayenne pepper
6 egg whites

TOPPING

1–2 tablespoons freshly grated Parmesan cheese

Corn Fritter Pancakes

1 To make fritters: mix first 6 ingredients together in a bowl, and stir lightly until well blended.

2 Melt butter in a frying pan. Drop in batter, using 2 tablespoons for each small flat fritter, and spacing them well apart to allow them to spread. Fry over a moderate heat, turning fritters once only with a spatula, for about 3 minutes, or until golden brown.

3 Drain fritters on paper towels.

Serves 4–6

Ingredients
1 12-oz. can whole-kernel corn, drained
2 eggs, lightly beaten
½ teaspoon salt
Freshly ground black pepper
1 teaspoon sugar
3 tablespoons all-purpose flour
About 4 tablespoons butter

Marinated Mushrooms

1 Trim stems and wash mushrooms thoroughly. Drain and place in a saucepan with just enough cold water to cover them; add lemon juice and salt, to taste, and bring gently to the boil. Lower heat and simmer for 10 minutes. Pour off liquids.

2 Combine remaining ingredients in an enamelled saucepan; bring to the boil; lower heat and simmer for 20 minutes. Pour marinade over blanched mushrooms and bring gently to the boil. Correct seasoning and serve immediately.

Serves 4–6

Ingredients
4 cups small mushrooms
Juice of ½ lemon
Salt
2 tablespoons wine vinegar
½ cup olive oil
1–2 cloves garlic, crushed
Sprigs of thyme and parsley
1 bay leaf
5 peppercorns
10 coriander seeds
Freshly ground pepper

Cooking with Rice and Pasta

Pasta, *polenta,* rice and beans—according to an old Roman friend of mine—were all God's gifts created specially to give pleasure and sustenance to the Italian poor. When I lived in Italy just after the war, in the teeming, narrow streets of old Rome around the Pantheon, we used to rely on these basic foods as the delicious mainstays of living. Wonderful dishes of spaghetti and *tagliatelle* served with a hundred delicate sauces were the order of the day; or *ravioli* or *tortellini,* tossed with thick, hot cream and freshly grated Parmesan cheese.

On feast days it was a steaming hot mound of golden *polenta* (yellow cornmeal simmered in boiling water and enriched with butter and Parmesan cheese) and stuck with dozens of diminutive grilled birds on little skewers, while on more simple occasions the boiled *polenta* was cooked and then sliced and grilled until golden, and served with a wild mushroom and tomato-flavored sauce.

Then there were *risottos,* great dishes of Italian rice simmered gently with chicken stock subtly flavored with saffron, onion and beef marrow and spiked with wild mushrooms or diced sweetbreads. *Risotto al frutti di mare,* saffron rice tossed with tiny nuggets of fresh seafood—lobster, shrimp or tiny squid—was a favorite, too.

Finally there were the great rustic casseroles based on red kidney beans, white kidney or *cannellini* beans, large flat beans from Siena or the delicate pink-colored beans called *borlotti,* soaked overnight and then simmered with olive oil and wine, finely chopped garlic and onion, fresh herbs and dried orange peel, and enriched with every kind of pork product imaginable. I liked, too, the Italian way with dried lentils, cooked in the same way, with olive oil and seasonings, and studded with fat slices of *cotechino* or *zampone* sausage, or a fine fat partridge.

It is my firm belief that no household today should be without its Italian-inspired emergency store, well stocked with these age-old "convenience" foods that were well known even in the time of the Caesars.

Rice

In Northern Italy, rice and *polenta* are usually served in preference to pasta—but never the pallid boiled rice so often served in this country. Instead the Italians toss their rice with butter and finely chopped onion, until it begins to be translucent. Then they add a rich chicken stock and simmer it gently until it is wonderfully tender—neither mushily soft nor unpleasantly hard, but *al dente,* just like their

Pasta is primarily a dough that is made to absorb a sauce. There are over a hundred different shapes and forms of pasta—and each has its own characteristic way of absorbing the sauce with which it is served. **Above** *Spaghetti and* conchiglie *with two imaginative new sauces: Spaghetti with Black Truffles and* conchiglie con le verdure. *(Recipes, page 145)* **Right** *Tiny shapes are used in soups and* brodi *only.*

spaghetti. And then they flavor it with the heady taste of saffron, the earthiness of wild mushrooms, or the crisp texture of golden fried pine nuts.

For the best results, rich should be cooked in only as much liquid as it can absorb, and special care is required when serving. The grains mash very easily, so they should never be stirred with a spoon, once cooked, but tossed lightly with a fork. Always serve your rice as soon as it is cooked.

Basic Boiled Rice

Ingredients

1¾ cups long-grain rice
Salt
4 tablespoons lemon juice
Butter
Freshly ground black
   pepper

1 Bring a large pan of salted water (at least 2 quarts) to the boil with lemon juice.

2 When water is bubbling vigorously, dribble in rice gradually through your fingers so that water does not come off the boil.

3 Stir once to dislodge any grains stuck to bottom of pan and boil rice for 15–18 minutes, or until tender but not mushy.

4 Drain rice in a colander and rinse thoroughly with hot water. Shake out all excess moisture. Toss rice gently with a little butter seasoned with salt and freshly ground black pepper. Serve immediately.

Serves 4–6

Simple Rice Pilaff

Ingredients

1¾ cups long-grain rice
1 medium onion, finely
   chopped
Butter
2 cups well-seasoned stock
Thyme
Salt and freshly ground
   black pepper

1 Wash rice; drain and dry with a cloth.

2 Sauté finely chopped onion in 4 tablespoons butter until a light golden color. Add rice and continue to cook, stirring constantly, until rice is translucent. Pour in hot stock, and season to taste with thyme and salt and freshly ground black pepper.

3 Cover saucepan and place in a moderate oven (350°F) for 15–20 minutes, or until the liquid has been absorbed and the rice is tender but not mushy. Serve with additional butter.

Serves 4–6

Simple Saffron Rice

Ingredients

½ teaspoon powdered
   saffron
6 tablespoons dry white
   wine
3¾ cups hot hot chicken
   stock (see page 37)
1¾ cups rice
Salt and freshly ground
   black pepper
4 tablespoons butter
Finely chopped parsley

1 Dissolve saffron in white wine; add it to hot chicken stock and combine in a large saucepan with rice and salt and freshly ground black pepper, to taste. Cover pan and simmer until all the liquid is absorbed and the rice is tender (about 30 minutes).

2 Add butter to hot saffron rice; garnish with finely chopped parsley and serve immediately.

Serves 4–6

Risotto Provençal

Heat olive oil in a thick-bottomed saucepan and sauté finely chopped onion until golden. Stir in rice and cook, stirring continuously with a wooden spoon, until rice becomes translucent. Moisten with 1¼ cups rich chicken stock in which you have dissolved saffron and simmer gently, stirring from time to time, adding more chicken stock as the liquid is absorbed by the rice. Season to taste with salt and freshly ground black pepper. Continue cooking in this way until rice is cooked through, but not mushy. Serve with risotto sauce.

Serves 4

Ingredients
1¾ cups long-grain rice
4 tablespoons olive oil
1 large onion, finely chopped
2 cups chicken stock (see page 37)
¼–½ teaspoon saffron
Salt and freshly ground black pepper

Sauce for Risotto

1 Sauté finely chopped onion and garlic in olive oil until transparent. Stir in dry white wine and peeled, seeded and chopped tomatoes. Season to taste with salt and freshly ground black pepper; add finely chopped parsley and simmer gently for 10 minutes.

2 Add diced green pepper and simmer for a further 10 minutes.

Ingredients
4 tablespoons finely chopped onion
2 cloves garlic, finely chopped
4 tablespoons olive oil
⅔ cup dry white wine
4 ripe tomatoes, peeled, seeded and chopped
Salt and freshly ground black pepper
4 tablespoons finely chopped parsley
1 green pepper, seeded and diced

Pasta

Pasta is really just a dough that is made to absorb a sauce. It is a serious matter in Italy, however, with its own philosophy, its own traditions and its own shapes and sauces for each area. The many shapes arise from the fact that each different form has its own characteristic way of absorbing the sauces with which it is served.

Although there are over 100 different varieties (all members of the same family), they break down roughly into these groups: (1) ropes or strings—including spaghetti, *spaghettini* and *vermicelli.* The sauce for these is usually thick, since the pasta absorbs it from the outside only. (2) Tubes—hollow shapes like macaroni and *rigatoni.* These come in all sizes, and are best with a thinner sauce that flows through the center hollows. (3) Flats or ribbons—*fettucine, tagliatelle* and all kinds of noodles and *lasagne* (4) Envelopes—*ravioli, tortellini, manicotti* and *cannelloni,* usually stuffed first and then cooked with a sauce. (5) *Pastine*—innumerable fancy shapes. The tiny ones are used in soups only.

Properly served in the Italian way, pasta is not fattening. Always serve it in flat soup bowls, designed to keep in the heat, with only ¼ lb. pasta per person, delicately sauced—almost dry in fact. Never drown it in a calorie-laden "soup." Pasta has an almost magic quality of being able to absorb and magnify anything it is served with. Even a simple sauce of olive oil with finely chopped flat-leafed parsley and garlic becomes a thing of beauty when warmed and tossed with a bowl of piping hot spaghetti.

To cook pasta perfectly

Pasta should be cooked in a lot of boiling water. Add a tablespoon or two of olive oil to keep the pasta from sticking together or sticking to the bottom of the pan, and 2 good handfuls of salt to flavor it. And no, that is not a lot of salt to use, because we are going to rinse the pasta in a colander to rid it of excess starch.

Pasta has an almost magic quality of being able to absorb and magnify anything with which it is served. Here, one of my childhood favorites— a steaming dish of Spaghetti with Meatballs. (Recipe, page 144)

The Italians have a wonderful expression, *al dente,* which means that the pasta is firm and resistant "to the tooth", not mushy, but still cooked through. The best way to see whether pasta is done is to pick up a piece on a fork and bite it.

Drain pasta by putting it in a colander, then run cold water through it to get rid of excess starch. If you don't do this, the strands are apt to stick together. Then have another pot ready with some butter or olive oil in it, so that you can toss your drained pasta in it to warm up again.

Fettucine alla crema

One of the easiest pasta dishes I know—and one of the most delicious—is *fettucine alla Crema,* wide ribbon noodles with a wonderful creamy sauce made with heavy cream and egg yolks.

Shop-bought *fettucine,* or egg noodles, will be cooked *al dente* in 12–15 minutes. Home-made *fettucine* would take only 5–8 minutes to cook. One pound of *fettucine* is enough for 4 people as a first course. For the sauce, blend 2 egg yolks in a small saucepan with 6–8 tablespoons heavy cream, flavored with freshly milled salt and freshly ground black pepper.

Toss drained *fettucine* in butter until it is heated through, adding more salt and freshly ground black pepper, then add the uncooked "sauce" of egg yolks and double cream. Stir the egg yolks and cream into the pasta, allowing the heat to cook the egg yolks so that they become a rich sauce for the pasta. All you need to complete the dish is a generous amount of freshly grated Parmesan cheese.

Pasta con le verdure

Pasta con le Verdure is a new light pasta dish that is currently taking pasta lovers in Italy and America by storm. The restaurants that serve it call it *primavera* for springtime, or *verdure* for green.

The recipe is simplicity itself: chop a clove or two of garlic finely, then simmer for a moment in butter and oil. Sauté thinly sliced raw zucchini in the garlic-flavored butter for a minute only; add lightly poached green beans, poached cauliflowerets and broccoli flowerets. Just give them a toss or two in the butter before you add frozen peas, which you have defrosted in a cup of hot water.

Toss cooked pasta over a medium heat in equal quantities of butter and olive oil. Then, add the *verdure* and its pan juices. Toss well and sprinkle generously with freshly grated Parmesan cheese, a bit more pepper, and then a big piece of butter to show that you mean business.

Pasta all'Uovo (Home-made Egg Pasta)

1 Sift 4 cups flour and salt onto a pastry board. Make a well in the center and into it put the eggs, the oil and 1 tablespoon cold water.

2 Work in the flour with your fingers until a firm dough is formed. Add a little more water if necessary to make dough hold together as you knead, but remember dough will soften quite a lot after kneading.

3 Knead the dough until very smooth and elastic. This will take 10–15 minutes.

4 Cover dough with an overturned bowl and leave to relax at room temperature for 30 minutes to 1 hour. This makes it easier to roll.

5 Divide the dough into 3 pieces. Lightly flour a board and roll out each piece of dough as thinly as possible. The thinner the better. Roll up each sheet of thin dough into a long roll, then cut the roll crosswise into strips. The strips can then be gently unfolded and cut to the correct lengths.

This amount of dough makes 1 lb. homemade egg pasta. Tossed with a sauce or butter, it will serve 4 as a main course, 6 as a first course.

Fettucine

Sprinkle the dough lightly with sifted flour and cut into 1/4-inch-wide strips. Spread on a clean cloth—or hang over a broomstick suspended between the backs of two kitchen chairs—and let dry overnight. Cook in a deep pot of boiled salted water. Drain well and serve with a sauce or melted butter.

Tagliatelle

Proceed as above, but cut into 3/4-inch-wide strips.

Cannelloni

Cut the dough into 4-inch squares. Do not dry the dough as above, but cook a few squares at a time in deep boiling salted water for 2 minutes. Remove with a perforated spoon and drop into cold water. Drain and dry on a clean kitchen towel.

Lasagne

Cut the dough into strips 6 × 2 inches. Cook a few strips at a time in boiling salted water for 4 minutes. Drain and dry as above. Use as directed.

Ingredients
4 cups flour
1 teaspoon salt
4 eggs
1 tablespoon oil

Tagliatelle alla Crema

Ingredients

1 lb. tagliatelle
Salt
Butter
4 egg yolks
⅔ cup heavy cream
Nutmeg
Freshly grated Parmesan
    cheese

1 Bring 4 quarts well-salted water to the boil in a large saucepan. Add *tagliatelle* and cook until tender but still firm.

2 Melt 4 tablespoons butter in a large saucepan. Drain the pasta and, while it is still very hot, toss in the butter.

3 Beat the egg yolks with the cream and pour over the pasta; add a grating of nutmeg. Stir for a minute; remove from heat and add 4 more tablespoons butter. The sauce and eggs should not begin to solidify. Serve with freshly grated Parmesan cheese and additional butter.

Serves 4

TAGLIATELLE ALLA CREMA CON TARTUFI BIANCHI

1 lb. *tagliatelle*, cooked as above, tossed just before serving with 2 canned white truffles, thinly sliced.

TAGLIATELLE ALLA CREMA CON FUNGHI

1 lb. *tagliatelle*, cooked as above, tossed just before serving with 2¼ cups thinly sliced button mushrooms which you have sautéed in butter.

TAGLIATELLE ALLA CREMA CON PROSCIUTTO E PISELLI

1 lb. *tagliatelle*, cooked as above, tossed just before serving with 1 cup frozen peas, defrosted and sautéed in butter with diced *prosciutto*.

Italian Spaghetti with Meatballs *(Illustration, page 142)*

Ingredients

1 lb. spaghetti
Salt
Freshly grated Parmesan
    cheese
Butter

MEATBALLS

¾ lb. finely chopped veal
½ lb. finely chopped
    prosciutto
2 slices bread, soaked in
    milk and shredded
1 clove garlic, finely
    chopped
2 tablespoons finely
    chopped parsley
Salt and fresh black pepper
1 egg, lightly beaten
Flour
4 tablespoons olive oil

SAUCE

1 large onion, chopped
1 clove garlic, finely
    chopped
2–4 tablespoons olive oil
1 small can mushrooms,
    sliced
1 large can peeled tomatoes
6 tablespoons tomato pureé
1 bay leaf
1 small strip lemon peel
1 beef stock cube
Salt and fresh black pepper
1 tablespoon
    Worcestershire sauce

1 To make meatballs: combine meat, bread (soaked in milk and shredded), finely chopped garlic and parsley, salt and freshly ground black pepper and lightly beaten egg. Mix well and shape into small meatballs. Dredge meatballs with flour and brown on all sides in hot olive oil. Remove from pan.

2 To make sauce: sauté finely chopped onion and garlic in olive oil in a large, thick-bottomed frying pan until transparent. Add sliced mushrooms and sauté for a minute or two more. Then add peeled tomatoes, tomate purée, bay leaf, lemon peel and beef stock cube,

and season to taste with salt and freshly ground black pepper. Simmer gently, covered, for 1 hour, stirring from time to time. Just before serving, stir in Worcestershire sauce.

3 Add meatballs to sauce and simmer gently for 20 minutes.

4 Cook spaghetti in boiling salted water until just tender. Drain.

5 Serve spaghetti with sauce and freshly grated Parmesan cheese and butter.

Serves 4

Spaghetti with Black Truffles *(Illustration, pages 138 and 139)*

1 Cook spaghetti in boiling salted water until just tender. Drain.

2 While spaghetti is cooking, make truffle sauce: slice canned black truffles as thinly as you can and sauté for a minute or two in butter with finely chopped garlic. This is not to "cook" the truffles, but just to give them a little added flavor. Add truffle juice, Madeira and port and keep warm over a very low heat.

3 To serve: return drained spaghetti to a clean saucepan; add butter, and egg yolks mixed with heavy cream, and toss over a medium heat until spaghetti is warmed through. Add truffle sauce; season with salt and freshly ground black pepper, to taste. Sprinkle with finely chopped fresh herbs and serve immediately, accompanied by freshly grated Parmesan cheese.

Serves 4

Ingredients
1 lb. spaghetti
Salt
½ cup butter
2 egg yolks
⅔ cup heavy cream
Salt and freshly ground black pepper
2–4 tablespoons finely chopped fresh herbs
Freshly grated Parmesan cheese

TRUFFLE SAUCE
2–3 canned black truffles
4 tablespoons butter
½ clove garlic, finely chopped
2 tablespoons truffle juice
2 tablespoons Madeira
2 tablespoons port

Pasta con le Verdure *(Illustration, pages 152 and 153)*

1 Wash and prepare vegetables, as below.

2 Cook broccoli and cauliflower in boiling salted water for 3–5 minutes. Drain and run under cold water. Cook asparagus and beans (or snow peas) in boiling salted water for 3–5 minutes. Drain and run under cold water. Cook zucchini in boiling salted water for 3 minutes. Drain.

3 Melt 8 tablespoons butter in a large saucepan; add garlic, finely chopped parsley, basil, nutmeg, freshly ground black pepper and chopped mushrooms and cook for 5 minutes. Then add pre-pared vegetables and frozen peas and cook for 5 minutes longer.

4 Bring 1 large pan salted water to the boil. Add pasta of your choice and cook—*conchiglie* for 20 minutes, other pasta for 6–12 minutes, depending on the pasta. Drain.

5 Melt remaining butter and toss drained pasta in it. Add vegetables and cream, and stir well, for 2–3 minutes, or until bubbling hot. Serve immediately with freshly grated Parmesan cheese and freshly ground black pepper.

Serves 6–8

Ingredients
1 small bunch broccoli
8 flowerets cauliflower
½ lb. asparagus
½ lb. green beans or snow peas
2 medium-sized zucchini
Salt
Lemon juice
⅔ cup butter
1–2 cloves garlic, finely chopped
1 tablespoon finely chopped parsley
3–6 large fresh basil leaves, chopped (or ½ teaspoon dried basil)
Pinch of nutmeg
Freshly ground black pepper
4 pieces dried mushroom, soaked and chopped
1 cup frozen peas, defrosted
1½ lb. very large shell macaroni (conchiglie, or pasta of your choice)
⅔ cup heavy cream
1 cup freshly grated Parmesan cheese

To Prepare Vegetables for Pasta con le Verdure

Broccoli and Cauliflower: **trim stem and remove outer leaves from broccoli and cauliflower; cut into flowerets, leaving 1-inch steams. Wash and leave for half an hour in cold salted water to which you have added a little lemon juice.**

Asparagus: **remove stray leaf points from asparagus stems below the head. Trim stalks; scraping the lower ends with the back of a knife. If stalks are woody, break off the woody part—you will find that the stalk snaps off right at the point where the tender part begins. Trim broken edge of stalk with a knife. Cut asparagus into ½-inch pieces and put pieces into cold water as you prepare them.**

Green Beans **(or snow peas): top and tail beans; rinse in cold water and cut them into ½-inch pieces.**

Zucchini: **slice thinly.**

The Nine-Herb Salad of Hintlesham is a salad in the Elizabethan manner: sprigs of fresh herbs and baby greens tossed in a well-flavored mustard vinaigrette dressing. (Recipe, page 149)

Salads

I know of no shop in the world other than Fauchon's in the Place de la Madeleine in Paris which has a greater variety of salads and salad herbs than I have growing in my kitchen garden at Hintlesham. I like to use as many fresh greens as I can, to ensure the utmost variety in my salads. Not just ordinary lettuce; young spinach leaves, chicory, endive, corn salad (*mâche*), dark Cos lettuce (romaine), Salad Bowl lettuce with its light green, crinkly leaves, and, of course, fresh herbs, all add immeasurably to the pleasure of salad-making.

For the purist, a salad evokes a beautiful vision of wonderful green leaves carefully dried, leaf by leaf, in a clean towel or in a salad basket or in one of those new machines that you just push down and the lettuce leaves dry by centrifugal force. I don't know why, but I prefer drying my salad greens by hand, perhaps because I always have since I was a very small boy. My job in the family, during the Depression years, when we had no help in the house, was to dry the lettuce, leaf by leaf, with a clean kitchen towel. So easy to do.

Oscar Wilde once compared the making of a salad dressing to diplomacy. He said it really was only a question of how much oil you put with your vinegar. I like French olive oil, Italian olive oil or oil from Tunisia or Morocco. If your olive oil does not have that typical fruity olive taste, here is a trick. Just put 2 or 3 black olives in oil (not in a salt water solution) in your bottle of olive oil to give a wonderful fruity flavor to your dressing.

Making a salad dressing is really very easy: all we need is a level teaspoon Dijon mustard and 2 tablespoons wine vinegar. We don't put the olive oil in yet because mustard won't dissolve in oil; it has to dissolve first in the wine vinegar to a smooth consistency. Then we flavor the vinegar and mustard mixture with salt and freshly ground black pepper. Finally we add fruity olive oil. The perfect formula is 3 to 1 (3 parts olive oil to 1 part wine vinegar or lemon juice), or, if your vinegar is very strong, 4 parts oil to 1 part vinegar. I like to use red wine vinegar to give a nice healthy outdoors look to the vinaigrette. For a thicker dressing add an ice cube. We can add many many things to this dressing: chopped chives, or a combination of chopped basil, tarragon and chives, for example. Or we could make the dressing for Caesar's salad: just sprinkle a little freshly grated Parmesan cheese over the dressing, with garlic *croûtons,* finely chopped anchovies and a coddled egg (poached for 1 minute). Finely chopped anchovies, onion and fresh herbs make a very good salad dressing, too. And perhaps one of my favorite tricks is to add a bit of crumbled Roquefort cheese, chopped walnuts and fresh herbs to the dressing for a salad of spinach, watercress, corn salad and lettuce. It's really a peasant salad, which makes a very good first course.

Salads can be served as a first course—or even as a luncheon or supper dish on their own, if they are more substantial. Add sliced tomatoes, diced tuna fish, or sieved hard-boiled eggs. There's a whole world of salads, and each and every one is a delicious adjunct to good dining.

Tossed Green Salad

Ingredients
2 small heads lettuce
1 bunch watercress
Vinaigrette dressing (see below)

1 Wash lettuce leaves well in a large quantity of water.

2 Drain leaves well and dry thoroughly in a cloth or a salad basket so that there is no water on them to dilute the dressing.

3 Wash watercress and cut off stems. Shake dry. Remove any yellowed or damaged leaves.

4 To serve: pour vinaigrette dressing into salad bowl and arrange prepared lettuce leaves and watercress sprigs on top. At the table, give a toss to ensure that every leaf is glistening with dressing. Check seasonings and serve.

Serves 4–6

Variations:
1 Add other salad greens in season—Cos lettuce (romaine), endive, chicory, escarole, young spinach leaves, watercress and French *mâche* (lamb's lettuce or corn salad).

2 Add finely chopped garlic and shallots to salad dressing.

3 Add orange segments and curry powder to salad dressing.

4 Add crumbled Roquefort cheese and chopped walnuts to salad dressing.

5 Add chopped peanuts, soy sauce and a dash of Tabasco to salad dressing.

6 Add 1 tablespoon each mayonnaise and heavy cream to salad dressing and sprinkle generously with fresh chives and fennel.

7 For crunch appeal, add diced celery, green pepper or fennel.

Eighteenth-century Dressing

Ingredients
1 small boiled potato, peeled
2 anchovy fillets
2 hard-boiled egg yolks
1 teaspoon Dijon mustard
2 tablespoons wine vinegar
6 tablespoons olive oil
1–2 tablespoons finely chopped onion
Salt and fresh black pepper

1 Pound boiled potato, anchovy fillets and hard-boiled egg yolks through a fine sieve into a bowl.

2 In a small bowl stir Dijon mustard into wine vinegar until well blended. Add olive oil, finely chopped onion and salt and freshly ground black pepper, to taste.

3 Pour over sieved ingredients and mix well. Add to tossed green salad (see above) and toss well.

Cucumber Salad with Fresh Herbs

1 Peel and slice cucumber thinly—a mandolin cutter is best for slicing cucumber. Place cucumber slices in a glass bowl and toss with salt and freshly ground black pepper, to taste.

2 Prepare a dressing by beating half the wine vinegar and half the Dijon mustard until well mixed; add half the olive oil and salt and freshly ground black pepper, to taste, and beat again until they form an emulsion. Pour over cucumber slices; toss and chill for at least 30 minutes. Drain juices from cucumbers.

3 Make a second vinaigrette dressing with remaining wine vinegar, Dijon mustard and olive oil. Season to taste with finely chopped tarragon and chives. Pour dressing over salad and toss well.

4 Whip heavy cream until stiff. Add salt to taste and spoon over salad.

Serves 4–6

Ingredients

1 large cucumber
Salt and freshly ground black pepper
2 tablespoons wine vinegar
1 tablespoon Dijon mustard
6 tablespoons olive oil
2 tablespoons finely chopped tarragon
1 tablespoon finely chopped chives
4–6 tablespoons heavy cream

Italian Tomato Salad

1 Peel tomatoes.

2 Wash Cos (romaine) lettuce, discarding any yellowed or damaged leaves, and cut leaves into 1½-inch strips. Shake dry and chill.

3 To make Italian dressing: combine wine vinegar, dry mustard and olive oil in a small bowl and mix well. Add finely chopped garlic and parsley, dried oregano, and salt and freshly ground black pepper, to taste.

4 When ready to serve: arrange peeled whole tomatoes and lettuce strips in a salad bowl; pour over dressing and toss well before serving.

Serves 4–6

Note: if tomatoes are too large, cut in half.

MEXICAN TOMATO SALAD
As above, but substitute guacamole dressing (see below).

Ingredients

8–12 whole small tomatoes
1 head Cos (romaine) lettuce
2 tablespoons wine vinegar
½ teaspoon dry mustard
6 tablespoons olive oil
1 clove garlic, finely chopped
2 tablespoons finely chopped parsley
1 teaspoon dried oregano
Salt and freshly ground black pepper

Nine Herb Salad of Hintlesham *(Illustration, page 147)*

1 Wash lettuces well. Drain well. Wash *mâche* carefully in a large quantity of water, snipping off root ends. Drain.

2 Cut fresh herbs—tarragon, basil, purple basil, *pourprier, roquette* and flat-leafed parsley—into tiny sprigs about 1-inch long. Wash well. Drain.

3 Shake lettuces, *mâche* and herbs dry in a salad basket.

4 Arrange salad in a salad bowl. Pour over dressing; sprinkle with coarsely chopped fennel, chives and parsley and toss well.

Serves 4–6

Ingredients

1 salad bowl lettuce
1 Cos (romaine) lettuce
Mâche (corn salad)
12 sprigs tarragon
12 sprigs basil
12 sprigs purple basil
12 sprigs pourprier (purslane)
12 sprigs roquette
12 sprigs flat-leafed parsley
Vinaigrette dressing (see above)
Coarsely chopped fennel
Coarsely chopped chives
Coarsely chopped parsley

Guacamole dressing
Cut in half 2 avocados and remove pits. Scoop out flesh with a sharp spoon; sprinkle with juice of ½ lemon and purée through a fine sieve.
    Rub 1 medium-sized onion, grated, into avocado purée through the same sieve; season to taste with salt, cayenne pepper and a pinch of ground ginger, and gradually beat in 4 tablespoons olive oil until mixture has consistency of mayonnaise. Chill before using.

Provençal Hors d'Oeuvre Salad

Ingredients

2 large green peppers
2 large sweet red peppers
6 firm ripe tomatoes
6 hard-boiled eggs
24 anchovy fillets
24 ripe olives

CAP D'AIL DRESSING

2 cloves garlic, finely
    chopped
1 tablespoon each finely
    chopped parsley,
    tarragon, chervil and
    chives
6–8 tablespoons olive oil
3 tablespoons wine vinegar
Salt and freshly ground
    black pepper

1 Prepare *Cap d'Ail* dressing by combining finely chopped garlic and fresh herbs with olive oil, wine vinegar and salt and freshly ground black pepper, to taste.

2 To prepare peppers: wash and dry whole peppers; place under broiler, as close to flames as possible. Cook, turning peppers continually, until skin on all sides has charred. Remove charred skin under cold water. Cut peppers into pieces lengthwise—4–6 pieces to each pepper—and wash off seeds and excess fiber; drain on paper towels.

3 Slice tomatoes thickly and cover bottom of a large flat serving dish with slices. Sprinkle with a quarter of the salad dressing; add a layer of green pepper slices; sprinkle with salad dressing; add a layer of red pepper slices and sprinkle with dressing.

4 Shell eggs and slice into rings; cover red pepper slices with a layer of sliced eggs and pour over the rest of the dressing. Arrange anchovies in a latticework on top and place a ripe olive in the center of each latticework square. Chill in the refrigerator for at least 30 minutes before serving.

Serves 4

Two fresh-tasting salads for summer:
Left *Provençal Hors-d'Oeuvre Salad with Cap d'Ail dressing.* **Right** *Spanish Appetizer Salad.*

Spanish Appetizer Salad

1 Peel tomatoes in the following manner: place each one on the end of a kitchen fork, and hold in boiling water for a minute or two (until skin of tomato begins to crack); remove from water and with a sharp knife gently peel skin from tomato. Cut in thick wedges.

2 Peel potatoes and cut into thick slices.

3 Peel and pit avocado and cut crosswise in thick slices. Brush slices with lemon juice to preserve color.

4 Cut boiled pepper into thick strips.

5 Wash lettuce leaves well in a large quantity of water. They should be left whole, never cut. Drain well and dry thoroughly in a cloth or a salad basket so that there is no water left on them.

6 Line a salad bowl with lettuce leaves. Toss prepared vegetables lightly in French dressing and arrange in lettuce-lined bowl. Pour remaining dressing over salad and garnish with thinly sliced onion rings.

Serves 4–6

Ingredients

4 ripe tomatoes, peeled
4 new potatoes, boiled
1 avocado
Juice of 1 lemon
1 green pepper, seeded and boiled
1 head lettuce
²/₃ cup French dressing (see page 147)
1 small onion, cut into thin rings

Pasta and Bean Salad

1 Cook macaroni in boiling salted water until tender. Drain, rinsing off excess starch with cold water.

2 Fry bacon until crisp. Crumble and set aside.

3 Make dressing by combining wine vinegar with dry mustard, salt and cracked peppercorns. Add olive oil, crumbled bacon, finely chopped onion, celery and parsley and mix well. Then add cooked, drained macaroni and drained beans. Toss until well mixed.

4 Just before serving, correct seasoning, adding a little more wine vinegar, olive oil and seasonings, if necessary.

Serves 4–6

Ingredients

1½ lb. elbow macaroni
Salt
¼ lb. bacon, sliced
3 tablespoons wine vinegar
1 teaspoon dry mustard
1 teaspoon cracked peppercorns
9 tablespoons olive oil
4 tablespoons finely chopped onion
4 tablespoons finely chopped celery
2 tablespoons finely chopped parsley
1 can cannellini (white kidney beans) drained

Opposite page *One salad to go. A portable picnic-hamper with everything for a super picnic salad meal—hard-boiled eggs, salad greens and vegetables, oils and vinegars and even a touch of Bordeaux mustard to give it zip. (Salad recipes begin on page 148)*

Japanese Salad

Ingredients

1 head lettuce
1 bunch watercress
1 bunch radishes
1 clove garlic, finely
    chopped
1 scallion, thinly sliced

SHOYU DRESSING

2 tablespoons wine vinegar
2 tablespoons soy sauce
Dry mustard
6–8 tablespoons olive oil
Freshly ground black
    pepper

1 Wash and trim lettuce and watercress. Dry thoroughly. Trim radishes and slice paper-thin. Chill.

2 To assemble salad: arrange lettuce leaves in a salad bowl and spread watercress on top. Scatter thinly sliced radishes over this.

3 Make *shoyu* dressing by combining wine vinegar, soy sauce and mustard in a small bowl. Add olive oil and freshly ground black pepper, to taste.

4 Just before serving pour the dressing over the salad; sprinkle with finely chopped garlic and thinly sliced scallion and toss until every ingredient glistens.

Serves 4–6

Provençal Salad Sandwich

Ingredients

4 rolls or 1 round loaf of
    bread
Olive oil
2 cloves garlic
8 lettuce leaves
4 large ripe tomatoes, sliced
1 small can pimiento,
    drained
2 green peppers, seeded
    and sliced
2 hard-boiled eggs, sliced
Salt and freshly ground
    black pepper
Lemon juice
4 tablespoons finely
    chopped parsley
16 small black olives
16 anchovy fillets

1 Slice rolls or bread in half lengthwise; pull out soft center of rolls or bread with your fingers. Brush insides of crusts liberally with olive oil in which you have crushed garlic cloves.

2 Place 1 lettuce leaf on bottom half of each roll, or place a layer of lettuce leaves on bottom half of bread. Cover lettuce with tomato slices, canned pimiento slices, green pepper slices and hard-boiled egg slices. Season with salt and freshly ground black pepper. Add lemon juice, to taste, to remaining garlic oil; add salt, freshly ground black pepper and finely chopped parsley.

3 Dribble dressing over sliced vegetables and eggs; garnish with black olives and anchovies; top with remaining lettuce leaves and cover with top half of rolls or bread.

4 Wrap rolls in foil, or cut round loaf into 4 wedges and wrap in foil; weight with a plate and chill for 1 hour before serving.

Serves 4

Summer Fruit Salad

Ingredients

1 ripe cantaloupe
Juice of 1 lemon
1 red apple, unpeeled
1 pear, unpeeled if skin is
    attractive
½ cup ripe cherries, pitted
½ cup strawberries, hulled
1 peach, peeled and sliced
1 orange, peeled and sliced
    and slices halved
About 8 sprigs of mint

PAPRIKA DRESSING

6 tablespoons pineapple
    juice
4 tablespoons lemon juice
1 egg, beaten until pale
½ cup sugar
¾ teaspoon paprika

1 Cut ripe cantaloupe melon about ⅔ of the way down into 6 or 8 sections so that it opens out slightly, taking care not to cut too far through top of melon. Remove seeds carefully with a spoon; brush melon segments with lemon juice; cover with aluminum foil and chill in the refrigerator until ready to use.

2 To make paprika dressing: combine all ingredients in the top of a double boiler and cook over boiling water until thick, whisking constantly. Chill.

3 Dice apple and pear and place in a bowl with remaining lemon juice; cover and chill. Chill remaining fruits.

4 Just before serving, drain diced apples and pears and combine with other chilled fruits. Place cut melon on a large serving platter. Pile in fruits attractively and use any remaining fruit to surround base of melon. Garnish with sprigs of mint and serve with paprika dressing. When serving melon, cut a wedge for each person to accompany salad.

Serves 6 to 8

Moroccan Orange Salad

1 Peel oranges, removing all pith. Squeeze 1 orange and combine with lemon juice in a bowl. Extract any juice from ends of peel and add to lemon and orange juice. This makes about ⅔ cup.

2 Thinly slice remaining oranges into a bowl and sprinkle with sugar and orange flower water. Pour orange and lemon juice over oranges and chill for 2 hours, or until ready to serve.

3 Just before serving: place 7 to 8 slices of orange on each individual small flat dessert plate and pour over 1 to 2 tablespoons of juice. Decorate center of each orange slice with a piece of coarsely chopped date. Finish salad with a dusting of ground cinnamon and a light sprinkling of flaked almonds.

Serves 8

Ingredients

6 ripe oranges
Juice of ½ lemon
2 tablespoons sugar
2 tablespoons orange
   flower water
6 dates, pitted and coarsely
   chopped
Ground cinnamon
2 tablespoons flaked
   almonds

Mediterranean Fruit Salad

1 Peel oranges, removing all white pith, and slice into rings. Wash and hull strawberries. Wash grapes and remove stems. Combine fruits in a serving dish and chill.

2 To make honey and lemon dressing: stir honey into lemon juice and add olive oil and salt and freshly ground black pepper, to taste.

3 Just before serving, garnish fruits with ripe olives and a few sprigs of fresh mint and pour over honey and lemon dressing.

Serves 6–8

Note: this Old English salad dressing is excellent with sliced fresh fruits, or a combination of fruit and green salad, or with thickly sliced cucumbers and coarsely chopped mint.

Ingredients

6–8 oranges
1 pint strawberries
1 lb. white grapes
Ripe olives
Fresh mint

HONEY AND LEMON DRESSING

1 tablespoon honey
2 tablespoons lemon juice
6 tablespoons olive oil
Salt and freshly ground
   black pepper

Fresh Fruit Compote

1 Peel oranges and grapefruit, cutting through to flesh with a sharp knife removing all pith and cut away from membrane into segments; remove seeds. Combine in a large bowl with honey and lemon juice.

2 Peel and slice kiwi fruit ⅛-inch thick; add to bowl and toss well.

3 Peel and slice banana; add to bowl and toss fruit together to preserve color. Chill.

4 Just before serving, garnish with whole strawberries, chopped pistachio nuts, and sprigs of mint around edge.

Serves 4

Ingredients

2 oranges
1 grapefruit
2 tablespoons honey
3–4 tablespoons lemon juice
2 kiwi fruit
1 banana
1 cup strawberries
2 tablespoons shelled
   pistachio nuts, chopped
Sprigs of mint

Pastries

Making pastry is child's play. After all, a good *pâte sablée* (rich shortcrust pastry) is just a combination of flour, butter, sugar and salt and a little cold water and egg yolk to hold it together. Yet the variations on this basic pastry mix—once you have acquired a little know-how—are limitless. I like to serve French savory tarts as a perfect beginning to a special dinner, or as a main course for a summer luncheon or picnic. The basic pastry can be used for all kinds of savory tarts and quiches—and, with a little more confectioners' sugar added—for rich dessert tarts and flans.

The confectioners' sugar is the "catalyst" here—the secret ingredient that combines with all the other ingredients into a smooth, buttery, crumbly whole.

But remember: there is no guesswork when it comes to making perfect pastry. Use *measuring spoons* for accurate measures; a *measuring cup*—marked in cups and fluid ounces—for all liquid measurements; a *wire pastry blender* to blend butter and flour quickly; and an *electric timer* to remind you when to take your pastry out of the oven.

Always use French pastry tins with false bottoms. Line with dough and bake according to instructions. Then remove fluted ring, leaving tart or flan invisibly supported on loose metal bottom. No need to serve tarts, flans and quiches in pastry tins any longer.

Fingertip pastry

My favorite kind of pastry for quiches and tarts is *pâte sablée,* a crumbly pastry which I call "fingertip" pastry because it is so rich that you literally just press it together in the tart tin.

To make fingertip pastry you will need 2 cups sifted all-purpose flour, 10 tablespoons diced butter, 1 tablespoon confectioners' sugar (the secret ingredient that holds the whole thing together), a little salt to counteract the sweetness of the sugar, an egg yolk and a little iced water.

First, mix the diced butter, the sifted flour, the sugar and the salt with a pastry blender, or even more simply with two knives held scissor-fashion, so that the butter can be cut into the flour without the mix getting heavy or greasy. Cut the butter into the flour until the pieces are about pea size, then you can use your fingers to work the butter further into the flour, lifting your hands high, until the mixture resembles coarse sand.

Combine the egg yolk with an equal amount of iced water; mix well and add to the pastry in the bowl. Now, mix the dough with a spoon, as it will be a little more difficult to handle at this point. When the dough is well blended, roll into a ball; wrap it closely in a clean kitchen towel and put it in the refrigerator for 30 minutes so that it will mature and the flour will absorb the butter into one nice homogeneous mass. Fingertip pastry is as easy as that.

To roll out pastry

Flour the working surface so that the pastry will not stick to the surface, and flour the rolling pin too. Start rolling out the pastry, always rolling from the center, turning the dough over occasionally so that the surface is always floured a bit on each side. When rolling out the pastry from the center, try not to stretch it in any way, because if you stretch it—either in rolling it out or in fitting it into the pastry tin—you will find that when baked it pulls back again into its own original shape and leaves the sides of the pastry tin. If the pastry breaks apart or splits while you are handling it, don't worry, because fingertip pastry is so rich a mix with its confectioners' sugar and egg yolk that you can patch it up in a second by just pressing it together with your fingers.

To line pastry tin with pastry

To line pastry tin with pastry, just roll the pastry gently over your rolling pin and lift it over the pastry tin. If you are using individual pastry tins, cut rolled out pastry into appropriately sized pieces to cover tins, leaving about 2 inches to spare. Then ease the pastry gently over the pastry tin (or tins) and press it loosely down into the sides of tin (or tins), using a little too much pastry. Press it against the sides of the pastry tin (or tins) and up, until it is of the thickness required. Then roll your rolling pin quickly across the top of the tin (or tins) to cut off the excess pastry neatly.

Prick the base and sides of your pastry shell (or shells) all over with the prongs of a dinner fork and chill pastry for 30 minutes in the refrigerator to minimize the danger of it "running down" the sides of the tin (or tins) when it is first put into the oven.

To bake "blind"

The bottom layer of pastry of tarts, quiches or flans that are to contain a creamy or liquid filling can become soggy if they are not half-baked before they are filled. This process is called baking "blind."

Line an 8- or 9-inch flan ring or tin with pastry, fluting the edges if necessary, and chill. Prick bottom with a fork, cover bottom of pastry with a piece of waxed paper or foil, and cover with dried beans. Bake in a preheated hot oven (450°F) for about 15 minutes, just long enough to set the crust without browning it. Remove beans and paper or foil and allow to cool. Fill with desired filling and bake in a moderate oven (375°F) until cooked. The beans can be reserved in a storage jar and used again.

To bake pastry case only

Bake "blind" as above for 15 minutes, remove beans and foil. Reduce oven temperature to moderate (375°F) and bake for 10–15 minutes. If crust becomes too brown at edges, cover rim with a little crumpled foil.

To bake pastry

A fairly hot oven is required for pastry. If it is not hot enough the butter will melt and run out before the starch grains in the flour have had time to burst and absorb it. If the oven is too hot, however, the pastry will burn before it has risen properly. When baking pastry, open and close the door as gently as possible and never more often than is absolutely necessary.

If pastry becomes too brown before it has cooked sufficiently, cover it over with a piece of foil or a double sheet of waxed paper that has been lightly sprinkled with water.

Italian Zucchini and Bacon Tart

1 Preheat oven to slow (325°F).

2 Chop onion finely and sauté in olive oil with crumbled stock cube until onion is soft, stirring constantly so that it does not take on color. Remove onion from pan with a slotted spoon and reserve.

3 Cut bacon into ¼-inch slices and then cut each slice into "fingers" about ¼-inch thick. Sauté in the same pan until golden. Remove from pan with slotted spoon and reserve.

4 Wash zucchini and cut off tops and bottoms. Slice zucchini as thinly as you can and sauté slices in remaining fats until lightly colored. Season to taste with salt and freshly ground black pepper. Remove from pan with slotted spoon and reserve.

5 Combine eggs, cream and milk in a mixing bowl and mix thoroughly. Season generously with salt, freshly ground black pepper, cayenne pepper and freshly grated nutmeg.

6 Sprinkle 2 tablespoons grated Gruyère cheese on the bottom of prepared pastry case. Combine sautéed onion, bacon and zucchini and spoon into pastry case; sprinkle with 2 tablespoons grated Gruyère cheese and pour in egg and cream mixture.

7 Sprinkle with remaining Gruyère cheese and bake in preheated oven for 30–40 minutes or until the custard is set and golden brown.

Serves 6–8

Ingredients

1 9- or 10-inch fingertip pastry shell, baked blind (see page 156)

FILLING

1 medium onion
2 tablespoons olive oil
½ chicken stock cube, crumbled
¼ lb. slab bacon
4–6 small zucchini
Salt and freshly ground black pepper
4 eggs
1¼ cups heavy cream
⅔ cup milk
Cayenne pepper
Freshly grated nutmeg
6 tablespoons freshly grated Gruyère cheese

Curried Egg, Cheese and Onion Tart

1 Beat egg yolks in a bowl.

2 Line a pastry tin with pastry. Prick bottom with a fork; brush with a little beaten egg and bake "blind" in a preheated hot oven (450°F) for 15 minutes.

3 Add cream to egg yolks and beat; flavor to taste with salt and freshly ground black pepper, curry powder and grated nutmeg.

4 Sauté finely chopped onion and diced bacon in butter until onion is transparent.

5 Arrange diced cheese in pastry shell. Spoon over sautéed onion and bacon and pour over the cream and egg mixture; bake in a preheated slow oven (325°F) for about 30 minutes.

Serves 4–6

Ingredients

4 egg yolks
Fingertip pastry for 8-inch pastry tin (see page 156)
1¼ cups light cream
Salt and freshly ground black pepper
Curry powder
Freshly grated nutmeg
1 large onion, finely chopped
¼ lb. bacon, diced
2 tablespoons butter
¼ lb. Gruyère cheese, diced

157

Shrimp and Lobster Quiche

Ingredients

PASTRY

2 cups all-purpose flour
1 tablespoon confectioners' sugar
Generous pinch of salt
10 tablespoons softened butter, diced
1–2 tablespoons iced water

QUICHE FILLING

½ small cooked lobster
¼ lb. small shrimp
2 tablespoons cognac
1 tablespoon lemon juice
Salt
Cayenne pepper
⅔ cup heavy cream
⅔ cup milk
⅔ cup fish stock, or canned clam juice
4 eggs

1 To make pastry: sieve flour, sugar and salt into a mixing bowl. Rub in softened butter a little at a time with the tips of the fingers until mixture resembles fine breadcrumbs. Do this very gently and lightly or mixture will become greasy and heavy. Add just enough iced water to make a good dough. Shape dough lightly into a flattened round, wrap in foil or plastic and put in refrigerator for at least 1 hour to ripen and become firm. If chilled dough is too firm for handling, leave at room temperature until it softens slightly. Then turn out onto a floured board and roll out in usual manner; place in a 9-inch pie tin and press out with fingertips.

2 Prick bottom of pastry shell with a fork; cover with a piece of foil; fill with dried beans and bake "blind" in a preheated hot oven (450°F) for 15 minutes. Remove beans and foil. Allow pastry shell to cool.

3 Remove lobster meat from shell and dice. Place diced lobster and shrimp in a dish and add cognac, lemon juice and salt and cayenne pepper, to taste.

4 Beat cream, milk, fish stock or clam juice and eggs with a whisk. Place diced lobster and shrimp on the baked pastry shell. Pour the beaten egg mixture over the lobster and shrimp.

5 Bake quiche in a slow oven (325°F) for 30 to 40 minutes, or until the custard is set and golden brown.

Serves 6–8

French Raspberry Tart

(Illustration, page 154)

Ingredients

1 9-inch fingertip pastry shell unbaked (see page 156)
French raspberries, to cover
1 recipe crème pâtissière (see page 160)
1 recipe raspberry fruit glaze (see page 160)

1 To bake prepared pastry shell: bake "blind" in a preheated hot oven (450°F) for 15 minutes. Reduce oven temperature to moderate (350°F) and bake for 30 minutes. If crust becomes too brown at edges, cover with a little crumpled foil.

2 Make *crème pâtissière*.

3 Make Raspberry fruit glaze.

4 To assemble tart: half-fill baked pastry shell with *crème pâtissière* and arrange raspberries in circles on top. Coat with raspberry fruit glaze. Serve chilled.

Serves 4–6

Orange Tart with Dates and Almonds

1 Prepare a 9-inch pastry shell.

2 Bake pastry shell (see page 156).

3 Make *crème pâtissière*.

4 Peel 4 small oranges, removing all pith, and slice thinly. Fill shell with pastry cream. Arrange orange slices on top of the cream in an overlapping circle. Fill center with finely chopped dates. Brush orange slices with a little sieved apple jelly or greengage conserve and sprinkle with slivered almonds.

Serves 4–6

Ingredients

1 **recipe fingertip pastry (see page 156)**

1 **recipe crème pâtissière (see page 160)**

ORANGE, ALMOND AND DATE TOPPING

4 **small oranges**
12 **dates, pitted and chopped**
Apple jelly or greengage conserve, sieved
Slivered almonds

My favorite recipes for pastry—shortcrust and fingertip—can be used for all kinds of savory tarts and quiches, and, with a little more confectioners' sugar added, for rich dessert tarts as well. (Recipe for Fingertip Pastry, page 156)

Crème Pâtissière

Ingredients

2 cups milk
2-inch piece of vanilla bean, split
5 egg yolks
½ cup sugar
2 tablespoons all-purpose flour, sifted
1 tablespoon cornstarch, sifted
Butter
Few drops of vanilla extract

1 Pour milk into a medium-sized pan and add split vanilla bean. Bring to boiling point over a low heat. Cover pan and put aside to infuse until needed.

2 In a bowl, beat egg yolks with sugar until thick and light. Gradually beat in flour and cornstarch.

3 Remove vanilla bean from milk and gradually pour milk into egg yolk mixture, beating until well blended.

4 Pour mixture back into the pan and bring to the boil over a moderate heat, stirring constantly. Then simmer for 3 minutes longer, beating vigorously.

5 Remove pan from heat; beat in 1 tablespoon butter and beat a little longer to cool the pastry cream slightly before adding the vanilla extract.

6 Put cream in a bowl and cover with a sheet of lightly buttered waxed paper to prevent a skin forming on top. Allow to become quite cold, then chill until required.

Creamy Peach Pie

Ingredients

1 recipe fingertip pastry (see page 156)
2 lb. peaches
Juice of ½ lemon
¾ cup sugar
¼ cup flour
¼ teaspoon salt
¼–½ teaspoon cinnamon
1¼ cups heavy cream

1 Prepare a 9-inch unbaked pastry shell.

2 Bake "blind" (see page 156).

3 Peel, core and thickly slice enough peaches to fill the shell. Put them in a large mixing bowl.

4 Combine lemon juice, sugar, flour, salt and cinnamon and add to peaches. Toss lightly and turn into pastry shell. Pour in heavy cream and bake in a preheated hot oven (450°F) for 35–45 minutes, or until firm. Serve warm.

Serves 4–6

Chocolate Tarts

Ingredients

6 individual baked pastry shells (see page 156)

CHOCOLATE CREAM

2 oz. unsweetened chocolate
1 cup sugar
2 tablespoons cornstarch
¼ teaspoon salt
2 cups milk
2 eggs, well beaten
4 tablespoons butter
½ teaspoon vanilla extract

DECORATION

1¼ cups heavy cream
¼–½ cup confectioners' sugar
½ teaspoon vanilla extract
Glacé cherries and angelica

1 To make chocolate cream: melt chocolate over hot water in the top of a double boiler. Combine sugar, cornstarch and salt in a bowl. Gradually stir in milk; then stir mixture into melted chocolate. Cook over boiling water, stirring constantly, for 10 minutes, or until thick. Pour hot mixture into well-beaten eggs, a little at a time, stirring after each addition. Return to top of double boiler and cook, stirring occasionally, for 5 minutes. Remove from heat; add butter and vanilla extract.

2 Pour mixture into baked pastry shells.

3 Whip cream and blend in the confectioners' sugar and vanilla extract. Decorate tarts with whipped cream, glacé cherries and angelica. Chill and serve.

Serves 6

Cakes

There is no branch of cooking where greater care and accuracy are required than in cake-making. I recommend strongly that if you are new to baking you should follow cake recipes carefully, without altering quantities of cooking times, until you have made the recipe at least twice. Then experiment as you like.

The handling of the cake has much to do with its lightness. Some cooks seem to have a knack of turning out light cakes and pastry, while others have to practice before their creations are a success.

Always preheat your oven before making your cake, especially for those cakes which include baking powder. They will spoil if they have to stand waiting for the oven to heat, and even more so if they are put into an oven that is not hot enough. You will find a moderate oven is best for most cakes; rather hotter for small and light cakes than for thicker fruit cakes.

Assemble all ingredients and cake pans before you start to make the cake. If fruit is included in the recipe, prepare it in advance.

In some cake mixtures—especially the plainer ones—the butter or fat is rubbed into the flour; in others, it is beaten to a cream before the other ingredients are mixed with it; and in still other mixtures, the eggs or egg yolks are creamed with the sugar, and the butter is added in a melted form. And in some sponges no fat at all is used.

1 When a cake rises in a cone in the center, this indicates that your oven was too hot when you started baking. As a result, the sides of the cake hardened with a crust before the mixture had time to rise.

2 If the cake rises at one side, your oven is hotter on one side than the other. Correct this by turning the cake from time to time during baking.

3 Do not open the oven door for at least 5 minutes after the cake has been put in, and then only with the greatest care. Do not slam the oven door; it can be fatal to the successful rising of the cake. Handle a cake carefully during baking. Moving or shaking it during baking is almost certain to cause it to fall.

Preparation of cake pans
Always prepare cake pans before mixing ingredients for your cake. Most cakes spoil if the mixture has to wait while you prepare pans.

To keep cakes
Do not store cakes until cold. Large cakes keep best if wrapped in paper and put in a tin with a tight-fitting lid. Fruit cakes which have to be kept for any length of time should be wrapped in waxed paper and then in a sheet of ordinary paper or a clean cloth.

(A)

(B)

(C)

(D)

To line a round cake pan with paper

Cut a double band of paper 2 or 3 inches deeper than the cake pan and rather longer than the circumference. Fold up an inch of this band on the double fold and make a mark. Open out and make cuts along the marked off inch of the paper an inch or so apart. Arrange this band inside the cake pan, making the notched section of paper lie flat on the bottom of the pan. Then cut a double round of paper to fit inside the pan and lay it smoothly on the bottom.

If the pan is very shallow, the paper will not need to be shaped, but just pressed in smoothly and folded or snipped at the corners.

If the cake mixture contains a fair amount of butter, no grease is required, but if there is little or no fat in the cake ingredients, the paper in the pan should be brushed lightly with clarified butter.

4 Be sure the cake is sufficiently cooked before removing it from the oven. Small cakes are ready if they feel firm when gently touched with the finger. Larger cakes should be tested by running a cake tester into the center. If the tester comes out sticky, the cake is not cooked enough; if it is dry, the baking is finished.

5 Allow cakes to stand for a minute or two before removing them from the cake pans; you will find that they come out more easily.

6 Always cool cakes on a wire cake rack so that the air gets around the bottom and sides.

For biscuits or small cakes: butter a baking sheet and sprinkle with flour. Knock edges of the sheet against table after flouring to shake off surplus flour.

For sponge cakes: tie a double band of paper around outside of pan to project 2 or 3 inches above top edge. Coat inside of tin and paper with melted butter. Dust lightly with equal quantities of flour and sugar to give sponge cake a light, dry coating. Shake off surplus flour and sugar.

Small cake pans: brush pans with clarified butter and dust with flour and sugar.

Sponge Cake (step-by-step)

1 Preheat oven to moderate (375°F).

2 Brush two 7-inch cake pans with melted butter. Line bases with circles of waxed paper and brush these with melted butter as well.

3 In a large bowl, cream ½ cup butter, sugar and flavoring together until light and fluffy.

4 In another, smaller bowl, whisk eggs until frothy (A). Add to creamed mixture a few tablespoons at a time, beating well between each addition. (B)

5 Sift flour with baking powder, and resift over creamed mixture. Fold in lightly with a spatula. (C)

6 Divide batter evenly between prepared pans and level off tops.

7 Bake layers (on the same shelf if possible) in a preheated for 25 minutes, or until they are a rich golden color on top, have shrunk slightly from sides of tins and spring back when pressed lightly. (D)

8 Turn layers out on to a folded cloth and peel off base papers. Turn right side up again and cool on wire rack.

9 When layers are quite cold, sandwich with good red jam, warmed to make it spread more easily, and dust with confectioners' sugar.

Makes 6 portions

Ingredients

Butter
1 cup all-purpose flour
1 teaspoon baking powder
½ cup sugar
Few drops vanilla extract or finely grated lemon rind
2 eggs
Red jam
Confectioners' sugar

The lightness of a cake has much to do with its handling. Some cooks seem to have the knack, while others have to practice before their creations are a success. (Recipe for Orange Layer Cake, page 169)

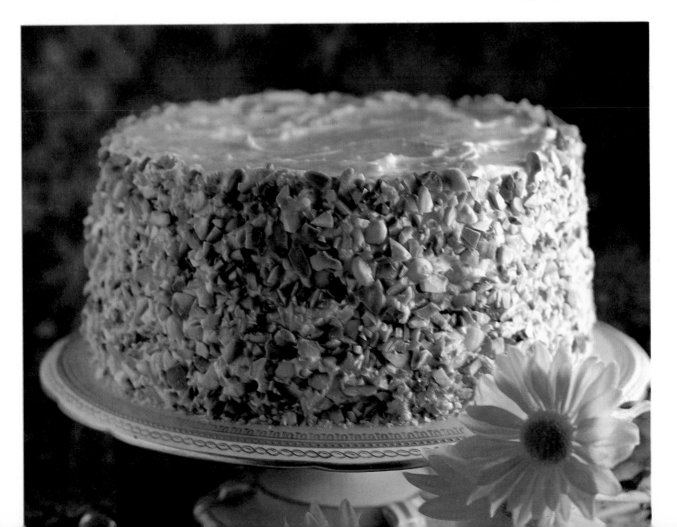

Genoese Sponge

Ingredients

¾ cup all-purpose flour
3 tablespoons cornstarch
Unsalted butter
4 eggs
½ cup sugar
1 teaspoon vanilla extract or finely grated rind of ½ lemon

Excellent for layer cakes, iced cakes and *petits fours*.

1 Preheat oven to moderate (350°F).

2 Sift flour with cornstarch three times.

3 Take the bowl in which you intend to beat the cake and select a large saucepan over which it will fit firmly. Pour 2 inches water into the pan and bring to the boil.

4 Place about ¾ cup unsalted butter in another, smaller pan; lower it into the heating water so that the butter melts without sizzling or bubbling. Remove pan from water.

5 Brush two 7½- or 8-inch cake pans with a little melted butter. Line bases with waxed paper and brush with butter as well.

6 Combine eggs, sugar and vanilla extract or grated lemon rind in the bowl. Set it over barely simmering water and beat vigorously until very thick, light and lukewarm.

7 Remove bowl from heat. Stand bowl on a cool surface and continue to beat until mixture leaves a distinct trail on the surface when beaters are lifted (3–5 minutes if beating with an electric mixer at high speed).

8 Gradually resift flour mixture over surface, at the same time folding it in lightly but thoroughly with a large metal spoon or spatula.

9 Add 8 tablespoons melted butter and continue with the folding motion until it has been completely absorbed. This may take slightly longer than you expect, so work as lightly as you can to avoid deflating the mixture.

10 Divide batter evenly between prepared pans.

11 Bake in preheated oven for 15–20 minutes, or until cakes are well risen, golden brown on top and springy to the touch.

12 Turn out on to wire racks. Peel off lining paper and allow cakes to cool completely before using.

Makes two 7½- to 8-inch layers

Italian Cream Torte

Ingredients

3 oz. semisweet chocolate
1–2 tablespoons cognac
1 baked sponge cake layer (see page 163)
4 tablespoons *maraschino* liqueur
5 cups heavy cream
½ cup sugar
¼–½ teaspoon vanilla extract
6 teaspoons chopped glacé fruits
Swirls of whipped cream (optional) and chopped glacé fruits for decoration

1 Melt chocolate with ⅔ cup water in the top of a double boiler. Remove from heat and stir in cognac. Cool.

2 Cut sponge layer in half to make 2 thin layers; then cut each half into thin strips as high as the soufflé dish that you are going to use to mold the torte.

3 Dip each sponge strip into *maraschino* liqueur diluted with 4 tablespoons water. Line sides of soufflé dish with them.

4 Whip heavy cream until stiff. Divide into 2 portions. Sweeten the first portion with sugar and flavor with vanilla extract, to taste. Fold in chopped glacé fruits and spoon the mixture into the sponge-lined mold to form the bottom layer of torte.

5 Fold the chocolate sauce into the remaining whipped cream and mix well. Spoon chocolate cream over the glacé fruit filling. If mixture does not come to top of sponge strips, trim them level with a sharp knife. Place torte in the freezer to freeze until firm.

6 When ready to serve: unmold torte on a chilled platter and decorate top with swirls of whipped cream, if desired, and a ring of chopped glacé fruits; cut *torte* into wedges and serve immediately.

Serves 6–8

Almond and Hazelnut Cake

1 Roast almonds and hazelnuts separately in 2 trays; remove husks by rubbing in metal strainer. Combine nuts in an electric blender or a mortar, and crush very finely. Add granulated sugar and mix well.

2 Beat egg whites until they form peaks and mix with nut mixture without letting eggs fall. Spoon mixture into 4 well-buttered, shallow, rectangular cake pans and bake in a preheated moderate oven (350°F). Allow to cool.

3 To make chocolate cream: cream cold butter well with sugar, then blend this thoroughly and slowly with cold *crème pâtissière*, added little by little. Stir in melted and cooled unsweetened baking chocolate, to taste.

4 To make Prâline Cream: mix equal quantities of blanched almonds and sugar, and heat mixture in a thick-bottomed frying pan until well caramelized, stirring to brown it evenly. Add a few drops vanilla extract. Cool on a baking tray until it hardens. Crush to a powder by chopping and pounding with a heavy rolling pin. Cream cold butter well with 1 tablespoon sugar, then blend this thoroughly and slowly with cold *crème pâtissière* added little by little. Stir in powdered prâline, to taste.

5 To assemble cake: put one layer on a flat serving dish; spread with chocolate cream; top with another layer; spread thickly with prâline cream; top with another layer; spread with chocolate cream; top with final layer. Smooth sides, sprinkle top of cake with sugar and sides with chocolate shavings. Keep for 24 hours before serving.

Ingredients

½ lb. almonds
1 cup hazelnuts
1 cup granulated sugar
8 egg whites
Butter
Sugar
Chocolate shavings

CHOCOLATE CREAM

¾ cup cold butter
2 tablespoons sugar
⅔ cup cold crème pâtissière (see page 160)
Unsweetened baking chocolate, melted and cooled

PRÂLINE CREAM

Blanched almonds
Sugar
Vanilla extract
¾ cup cold butter
⅔ cup cold crème pâtissière (see page 160)
Powdered prâline

Chocolate Almond Cake *(Illustration, page 166)*

1 Grind the almonds in electric blender or food processor. They should be as fine as possible.

2 Preheat oven to moderate (375°F).

3 Butter the sides of an 8-inch round cake pan. Line the bottom with waxed paper.

4 Melt the chocolate in the top of a double boiler over hot but not boiling water. Work ½ cup diced butter with an electric beater until soft and light-colored. Gradually beat in the sugar. Then add the eggs one at a time, beating with electric beater until each egg is thoroughly assimilated into the mixture. Mixture might look curdled at this point. Don't worry.

5 Stir in the melted chocolate, ground almonds, orange rind and breadcrumbs.

Pour mixture into the prepared cake pan and bake in preheated oven for 25 minutes.

6 Remove cake from oven; invert pan and allow cake to cool on a cake rack for 30 minutes. Then remove cake from pan; strip off waxed paper and cook cake. Leave cake overnight.

7 The following day, slice cake carefully into 2 or 3 layers. The center of the cake should still be a little moist and soft.

8 To make chocolate icing: melt chocolate in cream with butter over hot water in a double boiler. When smooth, add sieved confectioners' sugar. Mix well.

9 Cool slightly before using to spread between cake layers and over top and sides of the cake.

Ingredients

5 oz. almonds, skin on
Butter
¼ lb. semisweet chocolate
⅔ cup sugar
3 eggs
Grated rind of 1 large orange
4 tablespoons fine dry breadcrumbs

CHOCOLATE ICING

6 oz. unsweetened or semisweet chocolate
½ cup heavy cream
¼ cup butter
3 cups confectioners' sugar, sieved

Chocolate Almond Cake. (Recipe, page 165)
Savarin aux Fruits.

Savarin aux Marrons

1 If using fresh yeast, dissolve it in 4 tablespoons lukewarm water in a bowl. If using dried yeast, sprinkle granules over 4 tablespoons lukewarm water in a bowl; beat well with a fork and leave for 10 minutes, or until liquid is frothy and granules have dissolved.

2 Gradually sift 5 tablespoons of the flour into dissolved yeast, mixing with a spoon to make a stiff batter. Cover bowl and leave to rise until frothy and doubled in bulk, about 20 minutes.

3 Sift remaining flour with sugar and salt into a large bowl. Make a well in the center; add yeast mixture and lightly beaten eggs, and incorporate into flour gradually, beating vigorously with your hand or a wooden spoon.

4 When dough is smooth, beat in softened butter. Continue to beat or work the dough by hand until butter is thoroughly incorporated. The dough should be soft and shiny.

5 Cover bowl with a cloth or plastic wrap and leave dough in a warm place to rise until doubled in bulk, about 1½ hours.

6 Grease a 5-cup ring mold with oil or melted butter. Gather dough up out of bowl and place on a floured surface; with floured hands knead lightly until smooth, then break off a 2–3 inch piece of the dough and press lightly into the bottom of the prepared mold. Continue rapidly with the rest of the dough until mold is a third to half full. Do not bother to smooth surface of dough as it will smooth out as it rises. Cover loosely with a cloth and leave to rise in a warm place (80–100°F), or until the dough has risen to fill the mold.

7 Preheat oven to moderate (375°F).

8 Brush *savarin* lightly with egg yolk, beaten with a little water, to glaze. Place mold in the middle of preheated oven and bake for about 30 minutes. If top browns too much during baking, cover lightly with aluminum foil. The *savarin* is done when it is a rich golden color and has begun to shrink a bit from the sides of the mold. Remove from oven and let cool for 5 minutes then turn out of mold and leave to cool.

9 When *savarin* is lukewarm, prick the rounded sides with a skewer or roasting fork. Place *savarin,* rounded side up, in a deep dish just large enough to hold it. Pour lukewarm syrup (1½ cups sugar, cooked to syrup stage in 2 cups water with a strip of orange peel and a vanilla bean, to which you have added 6 tablespoons dark rum or kirsch) over *savarin* and allow to stand for at least ½ hour.

10 When ready to serve: pour off excess syrup and save for another use. (You'll find it very good with a fresh fruit salad.) Transfer *savarin* to a clean serving dish. Sprinkle with 2 tablespoons dark rum or kirsch. Paint with a light apricot glaze and fill center with whipped cream or *crème pâtissière* and top cream with chestnuts in syrup.

Serves 6

Ingredients

BASIC SAVARIN

1 oz. fresh yeast or ¼ oz. dried yeast (1½ teaspoons)
2¼ cups all-purpose flour
2 tablespoons sugar
½ teaspoon salt
4 eggs, lightly beaten
½ cup softened butter
Flavorless oil or melted butter, for mold
1 egg yolk beaten with a little water, to glaze

SYRUP

1 cup sugar
Strip of orange peel
Vanilla bean
6 tablespoons dark rum or kirsch

FILLING

2 tablespoons dark rum or kirsch
Apricot glaze (see page 160)
Whipped cream or crème pâtissière (see page 160)
1 can chestnuts in rum-flavored syrup

Savarin aux Fruits

1 Make Basic *savarin,* Steps 1–8, using a 5-cup cake pan instead of a ring mold.

2 Make syrup and pour over *savarin,* Step 9, and allow to stand for at least ½ hour.

3 When ready to serve: pour off excess syrup and save for another use. Transfer *savarin* to a clean serving dish. Sprinkle with 2 tablespoons dark rum or kirsch. Decorate with "flowers" made of diced canned pineapple and glacé cherries with "leaves" of angelica. Paint with a light apricot glaze.

Serves 6

Ingredients

1 recipe basic savarin (see above)
Syrup (see above)
Dark rum or kirsch
Diced canned pineapple, glacé cherries and angelica
Apricot glaze (see page 160)

Little Summer Fruit Towers

Ingredients

SPONGE

Butter
3 eggs
½ cup sugar
¾ cup all-purpose flour, sifted

STRAWBERRY BAVAROISE FILLING

24–30 strawberries, mashed
Finely grated rind of 1 orange
⅔ cup milk
1 egg yolk
2 tablespoons sugar
1 teaspoon gelatin
⅔ cup heavy cream
2 tablespoons Grand Marnier or Cointreau
Red food coloring
2 egg whites

RASPBERRY CREAM

1¼ cups heavy cream
¼ teaspoon vanilla extract
1 pint raspberries
Confectioners' sugar
Lemon juice or framboise liqueur

DECORATION

Whipped cream and ripe raspberries or strawberries

1 Preheat oven to moderate (350°F).

2 Grease a 12 × 8-inch jelly roll pan and line with buttered waxed paper.

3 To make sponge: beat eggs and sugar over hot water until mixture leaves a trail on the surface. Remove from heat and fold in flour with a metal spoon. Pour into prepared tin. Bake in preheated oven for 15–20 minutes, or until sponge is golden and springy. Turn out onto a wire rack; peel off lining paper. Cool.

4 To make strawberry *bavaroise* filling: combine orange rind and milk and bring to the boil, stirring constantly. Remove from heat. Beat egg yolk with half the sugar; then gradually beat in hot milk. Sprinkle gelatin over 2 tablespoons cold water in a cup and leave for 10 minutes. Place cup in a bowl of hot water and stir until gelatin has completely dissolved. Blend thoroughly with milk and egg mixture. Whip cream lightly; fold into strawberry mixture. Add Grand Marnier or Cointreau, and a little red food coloring to tint mixture a rich pink. Fold in mashed strawberries. Beat egg whites until stiff; add remaining sugar and continue to beat until stiff and glossy. Fold into strawberry mixture.

5 To line six ¼-pint turret molds with sponge: carefully slice sponge cake into 2 thin layers ¼ inch thick, using a serrated knife. Cut a circle of sponge to fit the bottom of each mold. Then cut a strip to fit completely round inside of each mold, trimming ends so that there is no overlap.

6 Fill sponge-lined molds with strawberry mixture and chill until firmly set.

7 To make raspberry cream: whip cream until stiff. Beat in vanilla extract. Purée raspberries with a little confectioners' sugar and lemon juice, or *framboise* liqueur, to taste. Add to whipped cream and beat until thoroughly blended.

8 When ready to serve: turn strawberry towers out onto a wire rack over a flat dish. Mask each tower completely with raspberry cream and transfer to individual serving dishes. Top each tower with a swirl of whipped cream and garnish with a ripe raspberry or strawberry.

Serves 6

Brandy Snaps with Cream

Ingredients

½ cup butter
¼ brown sugar
4 tablespoons corn syrup
4 tablespoons flour
1 teaspoon ground ginger
¼ teaspoon grated nutmeg
Grated rind of ½ lemon
1 tablespoon cognac
Whipped cream flavored with cognac

1 Melt butter, brown sugar and corn syrup; remove from heat and stir in flour, ground ginger, nutmeg and lemon rind; finally, stir in cognac.

2 Stir mixture vigorously, off the heat, until well blended.

3 Drop mixture, 1 teaspoonful at a time, on to a greased baking sheet (the mixture will spread out during baking to about 4 inches across, so make sure they are at least 4 inches apart).

4 Bake in a moderate oven (350°F) until golden brown; leave for just a few seconds to cool, then roll each brandy snap up over the handle of a wooden spoon.

5 When cool, fill with whipped cream flavored with a little cognac. The brandy snaps should be toffee-colored, full of air-holes, and crisp when cold.

Makes about 24

Orange Layer Cake *(Illustration, page 163)*

1 To make cake: beat egg yolks, sugar, 2 tablespoons water, orange rind and salt until light and fluffy (5 minutes in mixer at high speed). Sift flour and cornstarch, and gradually blend in egg yolk mixture. Beat egg whites until stiff but not dry, and fold gently into yolk mixture. Place equal quantities of batter into three 8-inch cake pans which have been buttered and lightly dusted with flour. Bake in a preheated moderate oven (350°F) for 45 minutes, or until golden brown. Invert layers on wire racks. When cool, loosen edges and remove from pans.

2 To make topping: beat eggs, sugar and orange rind together until foamy; add sifted flour and orange juice, and cook in the top of a double boiler, stirring all the time, until smooth and thick. Cool.

3 Fold in whipped cream, reserving some for decoration.

4 Spread two cake layers with orange topping and put cake together.

5 Cover sides of cake with topping and pat chopped toasted almonds firmly round; cover top and decorate with chocolate curls.

Makes 8–12 portions

Ingredients

CAKE

6 eggs, separated
¾ cup sugar
Grated rind of 1 orange
Generous pinch of salt
¾ cup flour
1 tablespoon sifted cornstarch
Butter and flour for cake pan

ORANGE TOPPING

1 egg
½ cup sugar
Grated rind and juice of 1 orange made up to ⅔ cup with water
¼ cup sifted all-purpose flour
1¼ cups heavy cream, whipped
¾ cup chopped toasted almonds
Chocolate curls

Caprice Saint Sylvestre

This delicious dessert cake uses canned glacéed chestnuts as a glamorous garnish. It is a French classic.

1 Preheat oven to moderately hot (400°F).

2 Beat sugar and eggs until light and fluffy (12 to 15 minutes in mixer at high speed). Sift flour and cocoa together in a bowl and fold into egg mixture. Fold in cooled melted butter.

3 Pour mixture into a well-buttered 8-inch ring mold which you have sprinkled with coarsely chopped toasted almonds. Bake in preheated oven for 25 to 30 minutes, or until cake detaches itself slightly from edges of mold. Remove from oven; turn out onto a wire rack and allow to cool.

4 Make *crème chantilly* as in recipe below. Split cake in two; moisten the 2 cut sides with equal quantities of rum and syrup from chestnuts, and spread with *crème chantilly.*

5 Ice cake with melted chocolate and decorate with whole glacéed chestnuts.

Serves 6 to 8

Ingredients

CAKE MIXTURE

½ cup sugar
4 eggs
1 cup flour
4 tablespoons powdered cocoa, unsweetened
½ cup melted butter, cooled
2 tablespoons coarsely chopped toasted almonds

CRÈME CHANTILLY (see below)

SYRUP

4 tablespoons Jamaica rum
4 tablespoons syrup from chestnuts

GARNISH

¼ lb. melted chocolate
6–8 glacéed chestnuts, drained, reserving syrup

Crème Chantilly

1 In a bowl whip heavy cream with sugar until stiff; add iced water and vanilla extract, and whip again until cream is soft and fluffy.

2 Fold in coarsely chopped glacèed chestnuts. Chill.

Ingredients

1¼ cups heavy cream
2 tablespoons sugar
2 tablespoons iced water
Few drops of vanilla extract
4 glacéed chestnuts, coarsely chopped

Desserts

A very good dinner deserves a happy ending. Something just that much more exciting than a salad of fresh fruits (even when doused with champagne) or a fresh fruit sorbet topped with puréed raspberries (*à la Cardinale*) or blackcurrants (*au cassis*). Yet, to be memorable a dessert need not be elaborate or difficult to make. I often serve a large open tart of thinly sliced fresh fruit—apples, pears, peaches or pineapple—brushed with dark rum and melted butter and served piping hot with mounds of chilled whipped cream, or diminutive little chocolate "pots" topped with a float of orange-flavored curaçao or Grand Marnier.

For more festive occasions, I like to make the edible tulip-shaped pastry cups taught to me many years ago by René Lasserre, whose elegant restaurant *Chez Lasserre* is located just off the Champs Elysées in Paris. *"Tulipe glacée Lasserre"* combines 1¼ cups each flour and confectioners' sugar with 3 egg whites and 2 egg yolks. This creamy batter is spread thinly in a saucer-sized circle on a baking sheet, baked for 5–6 minutes only in a preheated moderate oven (350°F) and pressed while still hot over an orange to form a round-bottomed tulip-shaped cup. *Chez Lasserre* fills the cup with vanilla ice cream, fresh fruits and a liqueur-flavored syrup and caps the whole confection with a gossamer-light froth of spun sugar. My version is simpler: no spun sugar, just a decorative swirl of whipped cream to finish it off (see page 175).

I find that top French restaurants often make a speciality of delicious desserts and puddings that look and, indeed, sound far more complicated than they actually are. I have chosen a series of favorite desserts that are perfect for a special dinner party, for most of the preparatory work can be completed the day before the event, leaving just the finishing touches for the last minute.

Summer apple charlotte, a French baked pudding served with wine-glazed apples and chilled whipped cream, is one of the few exceptions. The pudding (see page 171) can indeed be prepared the day before the party, but it must be baked for 45 minutes before guests arrive and then kept warm in the lowest of ovens until time to serve. Another exception is French steamed pudding with a topping of chilled whipped cream melting down the sides (see page 173). This too can be prepared the day before the party, but must be steamed for 1½ hours just prior to serving.

Peaches in Brouilly *(Illustration, page 155)*

1 Put peaches in a saucepan with the sugar, $\frac{2}{3}$ cup water, orange peel, cinnamon and cloves. Simmer them, covered, for about 15 minutes. Add $1\frac{1}{4}$ cups Brouilly and continue to cook, uncovered, over a low heat for 15 minutes, or until peaches are tender but have not lost their shape.

2 Holding peaches in a clean towel to keep you from burning your fingers, remove skins gently with the point of a sharp knife. Return peaches to cool in syrup.

3 When cool, transfer peaches to a deep glass serving dish and chill in the refrigerator.

4 In the meantime cook the liquid until it is reduced to the consistency of a light syrup. Add 4 tablespoons Brouilly and cool.

5 Pour syrup over the peaches and put in the refrigerator to chill. Serve very cold with whipped cream.

Serves 4

Ingredients
$2\frac{1}{2}$ lb. small peaches
1 cup sugar
Peel of 1 orange
1 stick cinnamon
2 cloves
Brouilly
Whipped cream

Summer Apple Charlotte

1 Peel and core apples and chop coarsely. Add chopped bananas and pineapple. Cook chopped fruit in $\frac{1}{4}$ cup butter with grated orange rind and lemon juice, covered, for about 10 minutes, or until the fruit is soft. Remove cover and cook, stirring continuously to prevent scorching, until mixture is quite dry. Sweeten to taste with sugar and apricot jam.

2 Butter bottom and sides of a 8–9 cup charlotte or soufflé mold and dust with sugar.

3 Trim crusts from sliced bread; cut enough triangles to cover bottom of mould.

4 Clarify remaining butter and dip triangles one by one in butter and line bottom of mold, overlapping the triangles to make an attractive pattern. Line the sides of the mold with strips of bread dipped in clarified butter, also overlapping. Fill the mold with the fruit mixture, and cover with overlapping triangles of bread dipped in clarified butter; cover with a buttered paper and bake in a preheated moderate oven (375°F) for 45 minutes, or until the bread is golden. Let the mold stand for 5–10 minutes after removing from oven.

5 To serve: invert the charlotte on a heated serving dish. Surround with peeled, cored and halved apples which you have poached in red or white wine (see Peaches in Brouilly, above). Serve with chilled whipped cream.

Serves 6

Ingredients
8 eating apples
2 bananas, chopped
4 pineapple slices, chopped
$\frac{3}{4}$ cup butter
1 teaspoon grated orange rind
Juice of $\frac{1}{2}$ lemon
Sugar
2 tablespoons apricot jam
1 loaf sliced bread
Poached apple halves
Chilled whipped cream

Compote of Berries in Red Wine

1 Combine $\frac{2}{3}$ cup water, sugar, cinnamon stick and peel of $\frac{1}{2}$ orange in a saucepan. Bring to the boil and cook until the sugar dissolves, stirring constantly. Add the red Burgundy and continue to cook until sauce comes to the boil again. Remove from heat. Cool.

2 Wash and hull or stem red currants, strawberries, raspberries and blueberries, discarding any that are not perfect.

3 Combine prepared fruits in a glass serving bowl. Pour the cooled Burgundy syrup over fruit and chill for several hours before serving.

4 Just before serving, add *julienne* of remaining $\frac{1}{2}$ orange and serve with whipped cream.

Serves 4–6

Ingredients
6 tablespoons sugar
1 stick cinnamon
Peel of 1 orange
$\frac{2}{3}$ cup red Burgundy
1 pint red currants
1 pint strawberries
1 pint raspberries
1 pint blueberries
Whipped cream

Ananas Givrée

Ingredients

2–3 well-ripened small
    pineapples
2–3 tablespoons dark rum
2–3 tablespoons
    confectioners' sugar
1 pint pineapple water-ice,
    or sherbet
Small fresh flowers

1 Cut the pineapples in half vertically, slicing straight through the leaves, to make 4–6 "boats."

2 With a small sharp knife cut out the flesh of the pineapple, being careful not to pierce the skin. Slice flesh of each pineapple; discard core and dice flesh into a bowl; add dark rum and confectioners' sugar. Chill diced pineapple and pineapple shells for 2 hours.

3 When ready to serve, drain the diced pineapple and spoon it into the shells. Top each pineapple shell with a scoop of pineapple water ice (or sherbet). Decorate leaves of pineapple with 3 or 4 fresh flowers and serve at once.

Serves 4–6

Mrs. Moxon's Lemon Posset

Ingredients

Grated rind and juice of 2
    lemons
2½ cups heavy cream
½ cup dry white wine
Sugar
Whites of 3 eggs

1 Add the grated lemon rind to 2½ cups of heavy cream and beat until stiff.

2 Stir in lemon juice and dry white wine. Add sugar, to taste.

3 Beat egg whites until they form peaks and fold into whipped cream mixture. Serve in a glass serving dish or in individual glasses.

Serves 4–6

Crème Caramel à l'Orange

Ingredients

1¼ cups milk
⅔ cup light cream
Strip of orange peel
A piece of vanilla bean,
    split
¼ cup sugar
3 eggs, beaten
1 egg yolk, beaten
4 tablespoons orange juice
½ teaspoon vanilla extract

CARAMEL

½ cup sugar
1–2 tablespoons water

1 Preheat oven to moderate (350°F).

2 Combine milk and cream in a pan with strip of orange peel, vanilla bean and sugar, and bring to the boil. Remove pan from heat; cover and leave to infuse for 5–10 minutes.

3 Remove orange peel and vanilla bean from milk (bean can be wiped dry and stored in a stoppered jar for future use). Stir milk mixture into beaten eggs—do *not* beat it in; (this, together with a too-hot oven, is what usually causes the air bubbles). Flavor with orange juice and vanilla extract.

4 To prepare caramel: select a straight-sided, 4-cup metal mold. Add sugar and 1–2 tablespoons water, and swirl pan over a low heat until dissolved. Raise heat and boil rapidly, without stirring, until syrup turns into a rich, dark caramel. Watch it like a hawk, drawing the caramel away from the

heat before it is quite ready, as it carries on cooking from the heat of the mold and will burn at the slightest provocation.

5 Holding handle of mold in a thick cloth, swirl caramel around with great care so that bottom and sides of mold are well coated. Cool slightly.

6 Pour in egg mixture; cover mold with a piece of foil and stand it in a baking pan. Pour in hot water to come halfway up sides of mold.

7 Transfer to the oven and immediately reduce temperature to 325°F. Bake custard for 35–40 minutes, or until set.

8 Cool mold, then turn out carefully on to a deepish serving dish to catch the caramel syrup.

Serves 4–6

French Steamed Pudding

1 Cream butter.

2 Soak bread, trimmed of crusts, in 1¼ cups heavy cream.

3 Shred soaked bread and add (along with cream) to butter; mix well. Add ground blanched almonds, sugar and chocolate, which you have melted over hot water and cooled.

4 Beat with electric mixer until smooth; then beat in eggs and yolks.

5 Pour the mixture into a tall mold. Cover or seal the mold and place in a large saucepan of boiling water (the water should come halfway up the mold). Cover the saucepan and steam the pudding for 1½ hours, adding more boiling water from time to time.

6 Whip remaining cream; sweeten with confectioners' sugar and serve hot pudding accompanied by whipped cream.

Serves 6

Ingredients

¾ cup butter
8 slices white bread
3 cups heavy cream
½ cup blanched almonds, ground
1 cup sugar
6 oz. unsweetened chocolate
4 eggs
2 egg yolks
Confectioners' sugar

Petits Pots au Chocolat

1 Break chocolate into the top of a double boiler.

2 Finely grate the rind of 1 large orange; squeeze its juice and add both to the chocolate, together with butter.

3 Heat over simmering water, stirring occasionally, until chocolate has melted. Then remove pan from heat; add 1 tablespoon Grand Marnier or curacao, and beat until smooth.

4 In a bowl, beat egg yolks thoroughly. Strain in chocolate mixture through a fine sieve, beating constantly. Allow to cool.

5 In another bowl, beat egg whites un-til stiff but not dry. Fold into chocolate mixture gently but thoroughly with a spatula.

6 Pour mixture into individual 1-cup pots or soufflé dishes. (Do not use metal pots, as chocolate may discolor.) Chill until set.

7 Just before serving, cut 2 thin slices from the center of the remaining orange. Quarter each slice and lay 2 quarters, point to point, on top of each pot. Pour over a teaspoonful of Grand Marnier or Curacao; swirl around very gently so that entire surface is moistened.

Serves 4

Ingredients

¼ lb. unsweetened chocolate
2 oranges (1 large, 1 medium-sized)
2 tablespoons butter
Grand Marnier or curacao
2 eggs, separated

Cold Chocolate Soufflé

1 Soak gelatin in a little cold water until soft.

2 Heat milk to boiling point and beat into the egg yolks, sugar, instant coffee and melted chocolate until well blended.

3 Place chocolate mixture in the top of a double boiler and cook over water, stirring constantly, until mixture coats the back of a spoon. Strain if necessary; beat in gelatin; pour into a bowl and allow to cool. Then stir over ice until the mixture begins to set.

4 Fold in whipped cream and then the stiffly beaten egg whites. Pour into a prepared 8–10 cup soufflé dish, edged with a standing collar of waxed paper 2 to 3 inches above the rim of the dish. Refrigerate to set.

5 Remove band of paper, coat sides of soufflé with grated chocolate or powdered coffee and decorate top with piped cream and chocolate *bâtons*.

Serves 4–6

Ingredients

1 oz. gelatin
1¼ cups milk
4 egg yolks
½ cup sugar
1–2 tablespoons instant coffee
¼ lb. semisweet chocolate, melted
1¼ cups heavy cream, whipped
4 egg whites, stiffly beaten

DECORATION

Grated chocolate or instant coffee
Whipped cream
Chocolate bâtons

Cold Vanilla Soufflé with Chopped Glacé Chestnuts

Ingredients

1¼ cups milk
1-inch vanilla bean
3 egg yolks
3 tablespoons sugar
1 tablespoon gelatin
⅔ cup cream, whipped
4 marrons glacés, chopped coarsely
4 egg whites
4 marrons glacés and swirls of whipped cream, to decorate

1 Heat milk with vanilla bean. Remove bean and keep milk hot.

2 Beat egg yolks and sugar until thick and lemon-colored. Add hot milk and cook over hot water without allowing mixture to boil.

3 Dissolve gelatin in 3 tablespoons of warm water and add to custard; strain and cool.

4 Stir custard mixture over ice, and when it begins to set fold in whipped cream and chopped *marrons glacés* followed by egg whites, beaten until stiff but not dry.

5 Tie a band of double waxed paper around the outside of a 6-cup soufflé dish to stand 3 inches above the rim of the dish. Pour in mixture and allow to set in refrigerator. Remove paper carefully and decorate soufflé with *marrons glacés* and swirls of whipped cream.

Serves 4

Individual Amaretti Soufflés Glacés

Ingredients

½ teaspoon gelatin
4 egg yolks
½ cup sugar
1¼ cups milk
3–4 tablespoons amaretti liqueur
Few drops of vanilla extract
1¼ cups heavy cream
5 egg whites
Salt
6 small Italian macaroons (amaretti), crushed

1 Turn refrigerator down to lowest temperature, i.e. highest setting.

2 Select 6 individual soufflé dishes about 2½ inches wide across the base and tie double-thickness collars of waxed paper around them to come 1 inch above the top.

3 In a small cup, sprinkle gelatin over 1 tablespoon cold water and leave to soften.

4 In a bowl, beat egg yolks with sugar until thick and light.

5 Pour milk into the top of a double boiler and bring to the boil over direct heat. Then beat into egg mixture in a thin stream.

6 Return mixture to double boiler and stir over gently simmering water until it coats back of spoon, taking care not to let custard boil, or egg yolks will curdle. Cool slightly.

7 Dissolve softened gelatin by standing cup in hot water and stirring until liquid is clear. Blend into cooling custard, together with *amaretti* liqueur and a few drops of vanilla extract, to taste.

8 Beat heavy cream until soft peaks form. Fold into custard.

9 Place egg whites in a large spotlessly clean and dry bowl. Add a pinch of salt and whisk until stiff but not dry. Fold into custard.

10 Divide mixture among prepared soufflé dishes. It should come well above the rim of each dish.

11 Freeze for about 5 hours, or until very firm. Then transfer to the main compartment of the refrigerator for about 1 hour before serving.

12 To serve: sprinkle top of each iced soufflé with finely crushed macaroons, patting the crumbs in lightly to make them stick; then carefully peel off paper collars. Serve immediately.

Serves 6

This soufflé glacé is a trompe l'oeil soufflé. Its high-rise lightness is achieved with a "collar" made of waxed paper, which keeps the airy structure floating lightly above the dish.

Tulipes Glacées

1 Sift flour and confectioners' sugar into a mixing bowl; add egg yolks and whites and mix well.

2 Grease a cold baking sheet and mark 4 circles on it with a saucer. Spread 1 tablespoon of mixture over each circle, using back of teaspoon. Bake in a preheated moderate oven (350°F) for 5–6 minutes, or until just turning brown at edges.

3 Remove each round from baking sheet; turn over and, working quickly, place each circle over the top of a greased orange. Place dish towel over pastry to prevent burning hands and mold pastry to fit orange. Remove and continue as above, baking 2–4 circles each time and shaping them over oranges as you go. These will keep for days in a biscuit tin. This recipe makes 12–16 *tulipes*.

4 To serve: fill 8 pastry *tulipes* with diced fresh pineapple, which you have marinated in kirsch; add a scoop of vanilla ice cream and decorate each *tulipe* with a few strawberries and raspberries and a swirl of whipped cream.

Serves 8

Ingredients

1¼ cups flour
1 cup confectioners' sugar
2 egg yolks
3 egg whites
1 large orange, greased, to form pastry shapes
1 fresh pineapple, peeled, cored and diced
Kirsch
Vanilla ice cream (see page 176)
Fresh strawberries and raspberries
Heavy cream, whipped

Frozen Almond Creams bring a light Italian touch to summer menus.

Frozen Almond Creams

Ingredients

1¼ cups heavy cream
2 egg whites
Sugar
Salt
¾ cup chopped toasted almonds
Sherry, marsala or cognac

1 Whip cream.

2 Beat egg whites; add sugar and salt to taste, and continue beating until mixture is stiff and glossy.

3 Fold chopped almonds (reserving 2 tablespoons for garnish) into egg mixture with whipped cream. Stir in sherry, Marsala or cognac, to taste, and spoon mixture into 6 or 8 individual soufflé dishes or custard cups. Sprinkle with reserved almonds and freeze for 4 hours.

Serves 6–8

Vanilla Ice Cream

Ingredients

4 egg yolks
4 tablespoons sugar
Salt
2 cups heavy cream
1 vanilla bean

1 Turn refrigerator to its lowest temperature (i.e., highest setting).

2 Combine egg yolks and sugar and a pinch of salt in a bowl, and beat until light, fluffy and lemon-colored.

3 Bring cream to the boil with a vanilla bean. Remove vanilla bean and pour vanilla-flavored cream over egg yolk mixture in a thin stream, beating vigorously. Add a pinch of salt and beat again.

4 Pour mixture into the top of a double boiler and stir over lightly simmering water until it thickens into a custard which coats the back of a spoon. Take great care not to let it boil, or egg yolks will curdle.

5 Strain custard through a fine sieve and leave to cool.

6 Pour cooled custard into a freezing tray and freeze, stirring the mixture up vigorously with a fork every ½ hour, or until half-frozen, then leaving it for a further 2 or 3 hours until frozen hard.

7 Transfer ice cream to main cabinet of refrigerator about 1 hour before serving.

Serves 4

Claret Granita Michel Guérard

1 Make a syrup by boiling water and sugar together for 1 minute in a medium-sized saucepan. Pour the syrup obtained into a bowl and allow to cool.

2 To make *granita:* when the syrup is cold, add wine and orange and lemon juice and mix together with a small whisk. Pour the mixture into a large flat dish or container and put it in the freezer or freezing compartment of the refrigerator. The shallow depth of the liquid allows it to set more rapidly. During the course of the day, fork over the solidifying liquid regularly, scraping the crystals from the edges of the dish into the still-liquid central part. Continue until the whole is set into a mass of small light crystals.

3 Fill 6 claret glasses with the *granita,* shaping it into a dome-shape with a spoon.

4 Arrange poached fruit and a few mint leaves prettily on top of each sorbet.

Serves 6

Ingredients

Bottle of red wine, preferably St. Emilion
Juice of 1 orange
Juice of 1 lemon
6 fresh mint leaves (optional)
Poached fruits for decoration

SYRUP

¾ cup water
1 cup sugar

Michel Guérard does wonders with wine-flavored granitas *topped with poached fruits.*

Index